✓

DATE DUE

FEB 2 5 1962			
MAR 2 5 1962			

IN HIM WE LIVE

In Him We Live

THE
GOOD WORD FOR
TODAY

By ALBERT P. McGRANN, O.M.I.

THE BRUCE PUBLISHING COMPANY
MILWAUKEE

IMPRIMI POTEST:
RAYMOND J. HUNT, O.M.I.
Provincial, Eastern Province

NIHIL OBSTAT:
JOHN A. SCHULIEN, S.T.D.
Censor librorum

IMPRIMATUR:
✠ ALBERT G. MEYER
Archiepiscopus Milwauchiensis

October 5, 1955

The New Testament quotations are from *The New Testament,* rendered from the original Greek by James A. Kleist, S.J., and Joseph L. Lilly, C.M. (The Bruce Publishing Co., Milwaukee).

The Old Testament quotations are from the Douay Bible, except those from the Psalms which are taken from *The Psalms, in Rhythmic Prose* by James A. Kleist, S.J., and Thomas J. Lynam, S.J. (The Bruce Publishing Co., Milwaukee).

Spiritual writers of the Church are from various sources and *The Imitation of Christ,* by Thomas à Kempis: Croft-Bolton translation (The Bruce Publishing Co., Milwaukee).

To MARY
OUR LADY OF HOPE

Prologue

The idea for these thoughts for each day was prompted by a small incident. One rainy morning, I happened into the corner drugstore.

The pharmacist, with whom I was quite friendly, greeted me.

"Hello, Father. What's the good word for today?"

His seriousness caused me to hesitate. "Just what do you mean?" I asked.

"Oh, you know, Father," he answered, "Some good word to help us over the dark spots!"

On my way home, I pondered over this request. There must be countless people everywhere looking for a "good word for each day" — some inspiration to give them a motive to continue steadfast in the everyday duties of life.

Immediately, my mind turned to Scripture. Christ, true Man as well as true God, realized that we, His children, need something over and above the tangible things around us to keep us going; something to quiet our worries and to calm our fears; something to comfort us with the knowledge that "here we have no permanent city," but that there is for all who follow His teaching a definite, deathless and delightful Home where, as St. Paul has told us, "Eye has not seen nor ear heard, nor has it entered into the heart of man, what things God has prepared for those who love him."

God not only promises us this Home, but He likewise gives us the necessary means to obtain it. These means are the Church and Scripture. Out of Scripture, I have selected a GOOD WORD for each day. Closely allied to these passages cited from the Bible, are the inspiring instructions which I have quoted from the works of the spiritual writers of the

Church. May these holy truths bring faith, consolation, and hope to the reader who can profitably recall the announcement of Christ's birth by the Angel to the Shepherds, "Do not be afraid, for behold, I bring you good news of great joy which shall be to all the people."

The subject matter for these daily meditations is not treated exhaustively. These observations are simply offered as verbal pegs upon which, it is hoped, the reader will each day hang his own spiritual thoughts. "Blessed be the Lord day by day: the God of our salvation will make our journey prosperous to us."

IN HIM WE LIVE

Now

Behold in this small hour
  Great gain or loss!
Past and Future sleep.
  Grasp thou the Cross
That guides thy destiny
  Ere time has flown
For God has given thee
  "Now" for thine own
Herein may lie the key
  (Thy grace, O Christ!)
To Immortality
  So dearly priced.
Yet, grow not faint with fear
  For God is kind.
He does not ask the deed
  That passes mind
And body to perform.
  But humbly pray
To know, and do His will,
  With joy today.
    *"For in him we live and move and
    have our being"* (Acts 17:28).

"But if you want to enter eternal life, keep the commandments" (Mt. 19:17).

Television is a modern "miracle." To sit down in a comfortable chair in the pleasant surroundings of one's home and to watch the actual playing of a football or baseball game, an entertaining drama, or to listen to and see an inspiring concert, hundreds of miles away, is indeed a remarkable accomplishment.

On a small screen the whole picture is smoothly presented in all its completeness. Yet, that picture is made up of millions of tiny dots in a definite and precise formation. If through some mechanical defect any of the dots is forced out of alignment, the picture is thrown into disjointed and shaky confusion. Instead of presenting an inviting and enjoyable representation, the distorted image forces the viewer to turn away his eyes.

The picture of one's life as a whole is made up of small events. Taken one by one they do not seem important, but together they form the picture that makes up the individual. If the daily acts of one's life are not in conformity with the beneficent will of his Creator, the picture that such a personality presents to God is most displeasing.

It is only when the sinner seeks forgiveness for his transgressions against God's laws, and strives to adjust his ways to God's commandments, that he exhibits a pleasing and acceptable image to his Creator and final Judge. "O teach me judgment, teach me sense, because in your commands I trust" (Ps. 118:66).

> *"My Child, walk before Me in truth and seek Me always in the simplicity of your heart"*
> (*Imit.*, Bk. 3, C. 4).

[2] Man's Need of God

"Jesus . . . said: 'The sick have need of a physician, not the healthy'" (Mt. 9:12).

"One-a-Day" vitamin tablets are very popular today and, according to many learned medical men, very helpful. The purpose of these vitamins is to satisfy the "hidden hunger" of the recipient. Even though a person may eat the normal amount of food, many doctors believe that there is a deficiency in the supply of the necessary vitamins. Thus, it is essential for man's physical well-being to supply this added nourishment and to appease the hidden hunger.

There are countless souls in the world today suffering from spiritual malnutrition. These unhappy people are unable to diagnose their condition correctly but they do know that there is something wrong with themselves. They are restless, discontented, upset, disturbed, and in general have no peace of mind. In most of these cases, the cause of the disturbance is hidden spiritual hunger. These discontented souls seek out any and every remedy but the correct one. Man must realize that he is composed of body and soul. His soul needs spiritual food just as his body requires material nourishment.

To appease this "hidden" spiritual hunger, Christ offers this invitation to all His children, "O come to me, all you who are weary and overburdened, and I will refresh you. Take my yoke upon you, and master my lesson . . . . Thus you will find refreshment for your souls. For my yoke is easy, and my burden light" (Mt. 11:28–30).

The wise, prudent, and humble soul hastens to the Divine Physician in order to regain or to preserve his spiritual health.

"Immediately consoled and comforted he resigned himself to the divine will, and the anxious uncertainty ceased" (Imit., Bk. 1, C. 25).

*"I love you, Lord, my strength, O Lord, my rock,
my fortress, my deliverer"* (Ps. 17:2, 3).

"Amo — amas — amat." Every high school student who has
studied Latin will recall these three words from his first days
in class. Translated, they read, "I love — you love — he loves."
In a sense, these words sum up man's life, for love of God
and love of neighbor are the foundation stones of Christianity.

"I love, you love, he loves." In other words, everybody loves
and desires to be loved. The song with greatest appeal to the
public has love as its theme. A novel needs a love plot to be
successful. The play that is "box office" must center around
a hero and heroine very much enamored of each other.

The great love stories of history, real or imagined, awaken
the interest of all generations. These epics of sacrifice and
devotion and fidelity never die.

The creature's heart craves for love. Men, women, and
children are ever on the search for someone to fill that void
in their hearts that can be filled only with a worthy object
of their affections. Human love, however, can never completely fill this vacuum. Sweethearts soon discover that even
their life partners possess imperfections. That greatest of all
love, between mother and child, is not entirely satisfying.
Where, then, can this craving be satiated? Only with and by
the love of God. Those searching for an Object that will
completely gratify this uneasy longing should hasten to the
company of Christ. "Keep yourselves in the love of God, while
you await the mercy of our Lord Jesus Christ, which will
bring you to eternal life" (Jude 21).

> *"Cling, therefore, to Jesus in life and death: trust
> yourself to the faithfulness of Him who alone can
> help you when all others fail"* (Imit., Bk. 2, C. 7).

"For I have set you an example, so that what I have done to you, you, too, should do" (Jn. 13:15).

The first requirement of a successful painter is a suitable model; some person to pose for him, in order that he may place on canvas that which he sees before him. The great artist, however, is not content simply to portray the physical aspects of the model, but he looks deep into the very soul of the individual and endeavors to depict with paint and brush the personality that lies behind that framework of flesh and blood. The skillful and successful painter studies, analyzes, and meditates upon his subject until he is able by his graceful touch to delineate on canvas those innate qualities which distinguish and characterize the person whom he has chosen as his inspiration.

The true Christian models himself upon Christ. He endeavors to follow in the footsteps of the Master. In order to accomplish this great task, however, he must first *know* Christ. He gains this knowledge of his Model by meditating upon His life, by studying His history, by putting into practice His teaching, by praying to Him for light and guidance.

The more closely the faithful strive to imitate Christ, the more Christ reveals Himself to them. Thus it is that saints are made. "The hearing ear, and the seeing eye, the Lord hath made them both" (Prov. 20:12).

"Charity deserves to be increased, that when increased it may deserve to be made perfect"
(St. Augustine).

*"And I in turn, say to you: You are Peter, and upon
this rock I will build my Church, and the gates of
hell shall not prevail against it"* (Mt. 16:18, 19).

" 'Then you are a king after all!' Pilate said to him. 'You
are right, replied Jesus; 'I am a king. For this purpose I was
born, and for this purpose I came into the world, to give
testimony to the truth. Only he who is open to the truth gives
ear to my voice.' 'What is truth?' Pilate said to him" (Jn.
18:37, 38).

"What is truth?" Pilate's question reeked with sarcasm.
Pilate, the pragmatist, denied the reality of objective truth.

Yet long before this trial, Christ had proclaimed to all men
the essence of truth: "If you make my teaching your rule of
life, you are truly my disciples; then you will know the truth,
and the truth will make you freemen" (Jn. 8:31, 32).

The same skepticism which Pilate displayed 2000 years ago,
however, is rampant in the world today. Proud, arrogant
men who do not know Jesus, nor His doctrine, and are
determined not to know them still emulate the scoffing
Pontius Pilate.

On the contrary, the stalwart disciples of the God-Man,
Jesus Christ, and His Church, rejoicing in the truth, free
of harassing doubts and ignoble fears, live and die secure in
the knowledge that their faith in Christ's teaching has not
been misplaced.

"I am the way, and the truth, and the life" (Jn. 14:6). And
again, "I am the light of the world. He who follows me will
not walk in the dark, but have the light of life" (Jn. 8:12, 13).

*"You will find, apart from Him, that nearly all
the trust you place in men is a total loss"*
(*Imit.*, Bk. 2, C. 7).

> *"Why, open your eyes, the kingdom of God is already in your midst"* (Lk. 17:21).

Man is made to the image and likeness of God. Each one is an individual with an intellect and a free will. Each one is a personality different from all others, really understood only by Him who created him. If each person were offered the opportunity to become someone else, in the final moment he would refuse. No, each one wants to be himself. This little story of ancient times brings this thought home.

A certain man constantly cried out against his cross. One day he fell asleep by the wayside and an angel appeared to him and told him he could have any cross he wished, to replace his own. He promptly selected one of gold and hurried off. Ah, but in a few hours, the weight bore him down and the sun's rays heated the gold and seared his back. He fell exhausted by the roadside. The angel appeared and offered him another cross. He selected the light one of roses; but soon the thorns tore his flesh, and the branches interfered with his walking. Wretched, he slept. The angel appeared to him and offered to him his final choice. He eagerly grasped his old cross and went merrily on his way, happy again to be himself. "How many are the things you do, O Lord! With wisdom you accomplish everything! And with your creatures teems the earth" (Ps. 103:24).

> *"When you have Christ you are rich and He is sufficient for you. He will provide for you. He will supply your every want so that you need not trust in frail, changeable men"* (Imit., Bk. 2, C. 1).

"Really it is God who of his good pleasure accomplishes in you both the will and the attainment"
(Phil. 2:13).

St. Augustine was reared a pagan by his pagan father, despite the protestations and prayers of his Christian mother, St. Monica. Augustine indulged himself in every whim and every passion. He reveled in all the so-called joys that the world had to offer. Finally, through the grace of God, his saintly mother's prayers conquered. He was baptized a Christian and eventually became Bishop of Hippo in Africa. His *Confessions* is a literary classic and a complete revelation of his soul. In the *Confessions,* St. Augustine, who found only turmoil in worldly pursuits and peace only in Christ, writes these beautiful, consoling words, "Thou hast made us for Thyself, O Lord, and we are restless unless we rest in Thee."

Yes, God has made man for Himself. All the trials and tribulations and temptations that men must endure here are but a spiritual refining process, as it were, by means of which souls are purified. The devoted follower of Christ uses these means to draw closer to his heavenly Father, both here and hereafter.

No soul can find happiness without God. The object of the creature's soul is the Creator. He alone can satisfy the soul of man. Therefore, it behooves the sincere seeker after happiness to turn to God with love and confidence. He will not be disappointed. "I will never abandon or forsake you" (Hebr. 13:5).

> *"Free me from evil passions and cleanse my heart of all disorderly affection so that, healed and purified within, I may be fit to love, strong to suffer, and firm to persevere"* (*Imit.*, Bk. 3, C. 4).

> *"The Lord loves those who hate the wrong;*
> *he guards his dear devoted friends; from godless*
> *hands he rescues them"* (Ps. 96:10).

There is an old saying to the effect that "nothing succeeds like success!" Perhaps this is one of the reasons why people are so anxious to read the biographies and autobiographies of successful men. Men, being *naturally* proud, seek to find in the lives of these conquerors the recipe for their so-called success in the hope that they too may one day be "world conquerors."

There is another group of leaders, however, whose lives are far more worthy of emulation. These are God's saints. The Caesars, the Attilas, the Napoleons have sought to conquer men, and nations, and even the whole world, but the saints of God have conquered far more difficult obstacles and far greater enemies. They have conquered *themselves!* Great numbers of people, both Catholic and non-Catholic, do read and meditate upon and profit by the lives of these holy souls. But all who sincerely desire to be numbered among God's heroes should familiarize themselves with the trials, struggles, and victories of these saints.

"For this reason on bended knees I beseech the Father ... that he may grant you ... to be strengthened with power through the Spirit for the development of your inner selves, and to have Christ dwelling through faith in your hearts, and to be rooted and grounded in love. Thus will you have the power to grasp fully, together with all the saints, what is the breadth and length and height and depth of this mystery, and to know Christ's love which surpasses knowing ... " (Eph. 3:14-19).

"Of all those who are dear to you, let Jesus be
your special love" (Imit., Bk. 2, C. 8).

*"My heart and my soul exult in longing for the
living God"* (Ps. 83:3).

A summer storm was in the making. At the first clap of
thunder, Mother dashed across the lawn from a friendly
chat with her next-door neighbor. The happy shouting of
children at play abruptly ceased and the little ones scurried
for home. The family dog sped around the corner seeking
shelter. The summer swallows hurried to the safety of the barn
loft. The little chicks darted into the downy protection of
the mother hen's wings. When the storm broke, all creatures
were safely ensconced in the familiar shelter of their homes.

It is natural, in time of danger or distress to want to be at
home. In the presence of loved ones, all feel more secure.
The same is true when sickness strikes. Many who, in the
exuberance of robust health, have never given a thought to
the family fireside quickly turn their thoughts toward their
loved ones when ill-health overtakes them.

Thus, deep down in everyone is the desire for a safe anchor-
age, a port of security and protection and love, where they will
be shielded and defended against the things without.

This fundamental longing for sanctuary extends far beyond
the protective goodness of relatives and friends, and ascends
to the Presence of the all-protecting Father in heaven. Whether
many diagnose this longing correctly or not, it is always
present in the human heart. The creature constantly yearns
for the company and love and protection of the Creator.
"One thing I ask of the Lord, one I request: to live in the
house of the Lord all my life" (Ps. 26:4).

> *"Above all things and in all things O my soul,
> rest always in God, for He is the everlasting rest
> of the saints"* (Imit., Bk. 3, C. 21).

> *"The prayer out of the mouth of the poor shall*
> *reach the ears of God"* (Ecclus. 21:6).

There was no bread in the "Home" for breakfast. The Little Sisters had given out the last loaf to their old people for supper Sunday night. That evening, the prayers of all were intensified as they petitioned their never failing patron, St. Joseph. "We must have bread!" was their insistent supplication.

Early Monday morning, a nearby baker drove up to the door of the Home with a truckload of freshly baked bread.

He explained his arrival at such an unusual hour. "My first baking last night somehow got burned, not badly, but my customers won't buy it. It's all yours, Sister. Haven't got room for it at the shop." "Thank God — and good St. Joseph!" exclaimed the good Mother as she explained to the exasperated baker their prayers for bread.

"Well, I don't mind helping out St. Joseph once in a while," declared the good man, "but just tell him not to make a habit of this!"

Christ admonishes His disciples "that they must persevere in prayer and not lose heart" (Lk. 18:1). The sincere soul who prays with confidence will always be heard. The petitioner must pray, however, with faith, perseverance, and determination. "The fervent prayer of a holy person is very powerful" (James 5:16).

It may be days, or it may be years, before his prayer is granted, but if the request is for the best interest of the supplicant, God will grant his petition. "Be patient in tribulation, persevering in prayer" (Rom. 12:12).

"For You, O sweetest Lord, deal with me above
all my merits and above all that I dare to hope
or ask" (Imit., Bk. 3, C. 8).

*"Be pleased, O Lord, to rescue me; make haste to
help me, Lord"* (Ps. 39:14).

During the shipping season, enormous boats, loaded with
grain and iron ore and oil, hurry day in and day out, from
the headwaters of the Great Lakes to the great industrial ports
of the United States, Canada, and even Europe.

The wheat is necessary to feed countless millions. The ore
makes the steel that erects buildings and bridges and produces automobiles, telephones, and refrigerators. The oil
keeps the wheels of industry and transportation turning.

The delivery of this necessary raw material by boat is
made possible by one thing only, the man-made canals and
their locks. In order that the lake craft may reach the
source of this supply, it is necessary to raise the boats to the
level of the higher waters ahead. Man does this by putting
the ship in a lock and then pouring enough water into this
enclosed pit to raise the vessel to the necessary height to make
it possible for the boat to continue on its journey.

God has given His children the waterways. He has also
given them strength and intelligence. He expects His creatures
to utilize these gifts to feed and improve themselves.

God has created man, however, for a higher destiny than
eating and comfort. He has destined him for eternal happiness.
He expects and demands that the creature use all His gifts
toward that high end. If the faithful worker by the sweat
of his brow builds the spiritual "canal and locks," God will
pour therein the grace necessary to raise him to the heights
of heaven.

*"Love will tend upward; it will not be held
down by anything low"* (*Imit.*, Bk. 3, C. 5).

> *"And whoever hears these words of mine and does not act accordingly is like a foolish man who built his house upon sand"* (Mt. 7:26).

Perhaps the greatest attraction to the tourist in New York City is the enormous skyscrapers. These mighty buildings are well named, for not infrequently the tops of the structures are hidden in low-hanging clouds. This is particularly true of the Empire State Building which raises its mighty head over one hundred stories above street level. So gigantic are these towering edifices that they are a never ending source of wonder for all visitors to the Big City.

Why is it that of all the great metropolitan cities in the world, New York alone has such tall buildings? The main reason is that Manhattan Island is a solid rock and thus has the necessary foundation for supporting such lofty structures. Without this firm stone base, the skyscraper could never rear itself into the heavens. The enormous weight of concrete and steel would sink in softer material, and unless firmly anchored, the heavy gales would bring the big buildings clattering to the ground.

Just as these towering buildings must have a firm foundation on a material basis, so too the individual soul that would rise above the things of earth and withstand the vicissitudes of everyday life, must have a solid spiritual foundation. The faithful soul places his faith in the solid words of David: "My help is from the Lord, the maker of heaven and earth" (Ps. 120:2).

"Faith is the beginning of man's salvation, the foundation and root of all justification, without which it is impossible to please God ..."
(Council of Trent, Sess. 6, c. 8).

*" . . . thou shalt not harden thy heart, nor close
thy hand, but shalt open it to the poor man,
thou shalt lend him, that which thou perceiveth
he hath need of"* (Deut. 15:7, 8).

A Jewish lady approached the priest in the library and asked
him if he would recommend some good books for her to
read. Although the lady spoke English quite well, she wished
to acquire a facility in the language of her adopted land.

On being asked her native city, she replied quickly, "Berlin,
and I spent the whole war there!"

She went on, "I feel free to address a Catholic Priest
because a Catholic family in Berlin hid me in their home
during the war. For four years I did not see the sun. I
was secreted in the cellar. This family had five small children and hardly enough to eat, but they shared what they
had with me. They did so at the risk of their own lives. I
shall never, never forget their charity. Whatever my husband
and I can do for them, we are doing now. But, my case is
not an exception, Father," she hurried on. "During that
awful, terrible time for the Jewish people, many, many
Catholic families gave shelter to my persecuted people."

A friend in need is a friend indeed. These humble people
in Berlin left themselves open to be slaughtered rather than
to offer up a human sacrifice to the gods of destruction. Herein
is a perfect example of Christian charity. "Beloved, let us love
one another, because love takes its origin in God" (1 Jn. 4:7).

*"Without charity external work is of no value;
but anything done in charity, be it ever so small
and trivial, is entirely fruitful"*

(*Imit.*, Bk. 1, C. 15).

> *"The Lord will guard your going out and coming in, both now and evermore"* (Ps. 120:8).

A taxi stopped before the austere vine-clad building. A teen-aged boy stepped from the cab into the driving rain. Darkness had settled and only pale light emanated from the uncurtained windows of the seminary.

As the youngster tendered the driver a bill, tears welled up in his eyes and ran down to mingle with the rain on his cheeks. After all, this was his first trip away from the family fireside. The observing taximan took in the situation at a glance. As he counted out the change, the wise man spoke, "Cheer up, lad. Remember you are not doing this alone!"

Today, that young boy is a very successful priest. In all the labors, sufferings, and joys that have followed since that night before the seminary gate, he has never once forgotten the kindly advice of the taxi driver.

All honest souls who are working out their "salvation with fear and trembling" (Phil. 2:12) may profit from the admonition, "Remember, you are not doing this alone!"

God is always at hand to render aid to each one who calls upon Him for assistance, for guidance, for courage, and for strength. All humble, prudent, and faithful souls lean on God's arm at all times. The Psalmist declares, "Have trust in God . . . my God, my savior, and my comforter" (Ps. 41:12).

"Keep me from all sin and I will fear neither death nor hell. Do not cast me out forever . . . and whatever tribulation befalls will not harm me" (Imit., Bk. 3, C. 17).

*"And he said: 'Let us make man to our image
and likeness!'"* (Gen. 1:26).

Frequently someone says, "I like to go to the top of a tall
building and look down on the people streaming by. One
really gets a bird's-eye view of man's smallness and unimpor-
tance from such a height."

It is true that man looks small and insignificant *physically*
from a lofty position, but man is more than just physical.
He is also spiritual! His spiritual soul is not small. It can
transcend the greatest heights and travel over the farthest
distances; it can master the greatest problems; it can and
should ascend to the throne of God. Man may seem insignificant physically, but spiritually there is no limit to his
size. "God is my help, the Lord sustains my life" (Ps. 53:6).

An external example of man's spiritual faculties at work is
evidenced in the animal trainer in the circus. Surrounded
by ferocious lions and tigers, he is dwarfed by their physical
prowess, yet through his keen intellect and indomitable will,
he can force these jungle beasts to do his bidding.

So important is man that Christ, the second Person of
the Blessed Trinity, died on the cross that his soul might be
redeemed and live eternally with God in heaven. Despite his
comparatively small physical stature, the complete man is a
being whose spiritual faculties are limitless. "You know well
that . . . not with perishable things, such as silver or gold,
were you redeemed . . . but with the precious blood of Christ,
that unblemished and spotless lamb" (1 Pet. 1: 18).

*"Left to myself, I am nothing but total weakness.
But if You look upon me for an instant, I am
at once made strong and filled with new joy!"*
(*Imit.*, Bk. 3, C. 8).

> *"Rejoice in the Lord always; I repeat, rejoice"*
> (Phil. 4:4).

The following story proves how difficult it is to capture with brush or chisel or pen the superhuman and supernatural love the true mother possesses.

An Oblate missionary to the Arctic told this incident. One spring, an Indian mother and her two young sons went North by canoe to pick berries and to seek peace and quiet in their native habitat.

Before they realized it, the cold Arctic winter began to move down on them. The rivers began to freeze. One morning, the mother called the boys and told them they must leave at once for civilization. "You must hurry. The rivers will freeze quickly and you will be stranded.

Realizing the seriousness of what their mother said, they protested. "But, Mother, you must come with us!"

"No," she replied firmly. "I would only hamper you. The boat would be too heavy and you could not travel fast enough to avoid the 'big freeze.' God will take care of me."

She finally won out. The boys departed with her only request deep in their hearts, to return in the spring and give her bones a Christian funeral.

They returned in the spring. To their great surprise and joy, their mother was still alive. She had managed to survive that awful winter. God had rewarded her trust in Him.

Mother love had conquered life and death! "This is my commandment; love one another as I love you" (Jn. 15:12).

"Maternal love is born of love itself: it is as the flower and the fruit. But love itself is the root and trunk of this beautiful tree which embellishes the earthly paradise" (Imit. of Mary).

*"O be to me a rock of refuge and a citadel, and
thus save me"* (Ps. 70:3).

A terrifying winter storm was lashing the North Atlantic
while the mighty ocean liner plowed its tortuous way on
toward New York. The captain had been on the bridge
continuously for thirty-six hours. As the fifty-foot waves
tumbled down upon the battered ship the Master and his
officers kept a careful watch, seeking to penetrate the cavernous darkness just ahead of the boat. The howling wind and
lashing seas, as perilous as they were, were not the chief
concern of the Captain and his crew. The ocean liner had
been built to withstand such an onslaught from the sea.

The unwavering eyes on the bridge were trying to seek
out in the black night any stray piece of debris or a possible
derelict abandoned to the tumultuous ocean. For such a
deserted craft or a floating mass of timber was quite capable of
staving in the bulkheads or fouling the propellers and rudder.

While the violence of the storm was sufficient to cause a
certain uneasiness to the ship's officers, what these experienced
men feared the most was that something they could not see.

It is true in all walks of life that those things which cause
man the most worry are the unknown and the events over
which he has no control. Thus, it is imperative for all men
to put their trust and faith in One greater than themselves
— God. God, who is all-knowing, all-wise, and all-seeing, will
guide, direct, and protect His faithful children who place their
confidence in Him. "Know ye that no one hath hoped in
the Lord and hath been confounded" (Ecclus. 2:11).

> *"Vain and brief is all human consolation. But
> that which is received inwardly from truth is
> blessed and true"* (Imit., Bk. 3, C. 16).

[18]   *The Mercy of God*

> *"Yea I have loved thee with an everlasting love,*
> *therefore have I drawn thee taking pity on thee"*
> (Jer. 31:3).

As the transatlantic airplane pilot plots his course across this 2000-mile stretch of water, he is most exacting in his calculations. At one place on his chart, he draws a red line and marks it "P.N.R." In the language of the air service, this is the abbreviation for the phrase "Point of No Return." Once the plane has crossed this line, the pilot knows that he must strive to continue on to his destination. From this point on, he may not turn back no matter what happens.

Some souls become so involved in sin that they try to convince themselves that they have crossed the "point of no return." In this thought they are energetically abetted by their archenemy, Satan. How mistaken these unfortunate souls are! In the spiritual life there is no "P.N.R." No matter how low a person has sunk in the morass of sin, or how contemptuously he has treated God, there is always hope for him. God's mercy is beyond all human understanding. With the Psalmist, let the sinner cry out, "I wander like a straying sheep: Come, seek your worshiper, for your commands I will never forget" (Ps. 118:176). And God will hear his every plea and glorify him as he did the Prodigal Son.

It is never too late to turn to God. He stands waiting and ready for every sinner, and when that soul comes back to Him, He receives him with open arms. "I tell you there is joy in heaven over one repentant sinner . . . (Lk. 15:7).

> *"Convert us to you, that we may be thankful,*
> *humble, and devout, for you are our salvation,*
> *our courage and our strength" (Imit.,* Bk. 3, C. 8).

"Now he who plants and he who waters the seed work in harmony, yet each will receive his own salary befitting his efforts" (1 Cor. 3:8).

It may come as a shock to the reader to know that the mighty New York police force has one great fear. Yes, there is one thing that every member of this efficient organization dreads. It is not the gunman or the jewel thief or the safecracker; all of these enemies of society can be taken care of nicely by "New York's Finest." What all policemen fear is a great mob out of control.

There is not a police officer on duty, from the Commissioner down to the rookie, who does not breathe an audible sigh of relief, when the tremendous crowds that gather in Times Square for New Year's Eve or election night or some similar event, disperse and go home. For the experienced officer knows that "mob psychology" is a reality. Once panic breaks out in a crowd of people, no one can tell where it will end.

The smartly dressed officer astride his well-trained and meticulously groomed horse who pushes through the crowd is not there for show. Both horse and rider have a definite job to do; to avert an incipient stampede.

Man is tremendously affected by the actions of his fellow men. The bad example of his neighbor pulls him down; the good example raises him up. Therefore, it behooves each one to realize that all his actions have an effect on someone, for good or evil. The man who walks in the footsteps of Christ preaches a sermon wherever he goes. "Open my lips, O Lord: my tongue will hymn your praise" (Ps. 50:17).

> *"Make the best of every opportunity, so that if you see or hear good example you may be moved to imitate it"* (Imit., Bk. 1, C. 25).

> *"The Lord is near to the crushed of heart; and broken spirits he restores"* (Ps. 33:19).

The new method of learning a foreign language by means of recordings has proved most efficacious to the student. The advantage of adding the sense of hearing to that of sight in attaining proficiency in language is evident. The teacher gives the correct pronunciation, the proper intonation, and the perfect articulation so essential to a beginner. Experience proves that by means of this system of teaching, the serious student becomes adept at expressing himself in a new language within a reasonably short time. In his accomplishment, the speaker acquires new enjoyment, and not infrequently, he wins monetary rewards.

In gaining these worth-while ends, however, the pupil must apply himself, setting aside a brief period each day to put into practice the instructions he has received.

To make progress in obtaining knowledge, understanding, and love of Christ, it is necessary for each one to listen to Him, to imitate Him, to put into practice His admonitions. "If anyone wishes to come after me, let him deny himself, and take up his cross, and follow me" (Mk. 8:34). The faithful should resolve to set aside a few minutes each day in silence and solitude to listen to Christ. He has many things to say to each one. Then by putting into practice His teachings, and by sincerely seeking to imitate His life, the Christian will become a joyful follower of Christ. "Now will I listen to the Lord God's words; assuredly, his words are words of peace, meant for his people and his saints . . . " (Ps. 84:9).

"A spiritual man quickly recollects himself, because he has never wasted his attention upon externals" (Imit., Bk. 2, C. 1).

" . . . we wear ourselves out with manual labor"
(1 Cor 4:12).

St. Paul's advice to the Corinthians was carefully followed out by himself. He gave example as well as admonition. There is no satisfaction like a job well done. Paul admonishes his followers, "Whether, then, you eat or drink, or do anything else, do everything for God's glory" (1 Cor. 10:31, 32).

A full day's work for a full day's pay is the basis of justice. Our fathers and forefathers were proud of their jobs, and took great pride in their work. They have set a worthy example. The story is told of an ancient guild artist laboring on one of the beautiful Cathedrals of the Middle Ages. High up on the scaffold, he scrupulously carved the figures of the Angels which were to support the roof. A visitor admiring his work, criticized the good man's zeal in trying to make his art perfect, and said to him, "you should not exercise such exactitude way up here where no one will see your work." The artist simply answered, "God will see it."

Any work worth doing is worth doing well. Great grace and merit can be gained by the doer in offering up every undertaking to God. The artisan, or artist, in doing this not only gains God's blessing but also His help. The most exacting and perfect work of all should be the salvation of one's soul. "Restore to me the joy which your salvation brings, and by a generous spirit make me strong" (Ps. 50:14).

> *"Who perseveres in praising God the whole day? I will show you how you can praise Him the entire day, if you wish to do so: do well whatever you do and you have praised God. In the innocence of your works prepare to praise God all the day"* (St. Augustine.)

> *"The eyes of the Lord in every place behold the good and the evil"* (Prov. 15:3).

The commercial air liner, loaded with passengers, raised itself aloft from the runway on a routine flight. To the consternation of the onlookers, the plane fought vainly to gain the necessary altitude. Suddenly there was a tremendous explosion and a flash of devastating flame as the mighty ship crashed into a row of apartment houses just beyond the airfield.

What had happened? Who was responsible for the great loss of life? What was the cause of this tragic accident? After a thorough investigation of the pieces of the wrecked plane, the inspectors declared the airship was overloaded. The high-powered engines were simply unable to lift this excessive weight into the air. Someone unwisely had defied the law of gravity, and this inexorable law of nature had exacted its terrible retribution — death and destruction in a raging fire.

Man knows from bitter experience that his every offense against nature's laws is severely punished whether in the physical or material order.

The Ten Commandments are God's laws in the spiritual order of things. While nature demands a penalty for every offense against her laws, God in His infinite mercy generally withholds His avenging hand in the hope that His wayward children will repent of their evil ways, and return to Him. "Have mercy on me, God, for you are merciful; blot out my sin, for you are richly merciful" (Ps. 50:3).

"Leave vanity to the vain. Set yourself to the things which God has commanded you to do"
(*Imit.*, Bk. 1, C. 20).

"Christ has put an end to the Law and has opened the way to sanctification for everyone who believes" (Rom. 10:4).

The infinitesimal atom which is causing so much consternation in the world today is often described by scientists as a miniature universe. Like all things created by God the atom in itself is controlled by definite laws. The electrons and protons and neutrons that make up this smallest item of God's handiwork perform their allotted task in strict conformity with the will of their Creator.

Man has finally discovered that by splitting this component part of all nature, he can set up a chain reaction so powerful that it may even destroy himself. He can accomplish this terrible disorder by following the well-ordered laws that govern the existence of the atom. In other words, he can take something good and turn it to evil.

This process of using a good thing to an evil end is not new in the world.

Man is the most beautiful handiwork of God. He can walk; he can talk; he can think; he can will. He is autonomous. But he belongs to God who created him and he has the obligation to fulfill the end for which he was created; namely, to honor God, and, by co-operating with God's will, to save his own immortal soul. "Eternal is the justice of your law, your law will never change" (Ps. 118:142).

Man himself can change the world for good or evil, depending upon whether he fights for or against God.

> *"Behold, heaven and earth, which You created for the service of man, stand ready, and each day they do whatever You command"*
> *(Imit.,* Bk. 3, C. 10).

> " . . . *Christ, our paschal victim, has been sacri-*
> *ficed*" (1 Cor. 5:8).

The daughter taught school in the city. Her brother lived in the old homestead, a farm house, ten miles distant from the nearest church. Each week end the daughter came home to be with her mother, and especially to drive the devout soul to Holy Mass; for either to miss assisting at the Holy Sacrifice on Sundays was a tremendous loss.

The winters were severe at times in the Midwest. Not infrequently the country roads, piled high with snow, were impassable. This obstacle, however, did not deter these good people from going to Mass. On such occasions, the daughter would hitch a small trailer to the big-wheeled tractor. The mother would seat herself in the trailer, swathed in blankets and furs, and the daughter, facing the bitter winter wind, would drive across the snow-covered fields to the village church. When the pastor saw these good souls arrive under such trying conditions, he realized more and more what the Holy Sacrifice of the Mass means to the faithful.

The Sacrifice of the Mass is the center around which the Universal Church revolves. All who are not prevented by a grave inconvenience should let nothing stand in the way of their assisting at the Holy Sacrifice, which pours into the hearts and souls of the faithful infinite grace. The prophecy of Malachias has been fulfilled. "For from the rising of the sun even to the going down . . . in every place there is sacrifice and there is offered to my name a clean oblation" (Mal. 1:11).

"Behold, I offered my self wholly to the Father
for you; I even gave my whole Body and Blood
for food that I might be all yours, and you mine
forever" (Imit., Bk. 4, C. 8).

*"He that feareth the Lord shall tremble at noth-
ing, and shall not be afraid; for he is his hope"*
(Ecclus. 34:16).

Very few people have ever had the terrifying experience
of being present during an earthquake. However, many, if
not most people, have suffered this experience by proxy from
witnessing the realistic portrayal of such a fearful phenomenon
in the "movies."

When the very earth beneath one gives way, when deep
caverns open up in the solid ground, when mighty buildings
quiver and fall, frightened man realizes, at last, that the
things of earth are indeed transitory.

Many suffer a similar experience when their accustomed
ways are interrupted by the loss of a dear one, or loss of
their bread-winning employment, or grievous failure in some
chosen undertaking.

All these events prove to man that he must have something
more solid than earth or material things on which to depend.

He must be wholly dependent upon God who never
changes. He must put his confidence and faith and hope in
Him who consoled Peter when He grasped the Apostle's
hand as he feared he was falling into the sea. "How little
faith you have! What made you doubt?" (Mt. 14:31.) "O be
to me a rock of refuge and a citadel, and thus save me: in
truth, my rock, my citadel are you!" (Ps. 70:3.)

"Times change, but not faith" (St. Augustine).

"Children, yield obedience in the Lord to your
parents, for that is right" (Eph. 6:1).

There were sweet odors emanating from the kitchen.
Mother had put on a crisp clean starched dress, tied on her
apron, and was busily engaged with pots and pans. The sun's
rays were bending decidedly toward the west. A feeling of
contentment was creeping along the shady avenue. A look of
joyous expectancy was on the faces of the quiet children,
waiting patiently at the nearby corner; "Daddy was coming
home." The whole complexion of the fun-filled and happy
day seemed to change as suppertime drew near; the paper
boy tossed the evening edition upon the porch from his
flashing bike; the neighboring children drew close to their
own fireside; the office and shop workers began their homeward trek. There was peace and security as evening gently
dropped its gorgeous curtain lower and lower over the surrounding hillsides. Soon the father of the household would
appear, smiling, around the corner. With joined hands, Daddy
and the children would wend their way along the street and
into the palace of palaces — home.

This scene is repeated a million times around the world
each evening, as the day draws to a close, and twilight
descends. The family circle is not complete until "Daddy
comes home."

The love of a hard-working father for his family is great,
but it pales into insignificance compared with the love of
God for His children. The joys and happiness and peace of
the family circle are but a foretaste of the everlasting joys
of heaven.

"If you hear Me and follow My voice you will be
able to enjoy much peace" (Imit., Bk. 3, C. 25).

*"Do not let your heart be troubled! You have
faith in God: have faith in me also"* (Jn. 14:1).

In one of the most desperate prisons in the country, a
condemned prisoner, rebellious against God and man, through
the grace of God, was converted by the Catholic chaplain
shortly before his execution.

God's grace had wrought such a change in the man that
the attendants were amazed at his docility and humility. In
consequence, they sought in every way they could to grant
his few last requests. These were very simple. He asked only
for a large piece of canvas, paints, and a few small brushes.
During the remaining days of his life on earth, he labored
long and tirelessly in his cell. Although the officers were
curious to know what he was doing, they respected his
privacy. Shortly after his execution they visited his cell.
There against a sun-lighted wall hung the not quite finished
canvas, and, on it, a most touching picture of the Crucifixion
—the last gesture of a grateful penitent. " . . . you will weep
and lament, while the world rejoices. You will be plunged
in sorrow, but your sorrow will be turned into joy" (Jn.
16:20, 21).

*"Fear God, and you will not be afraid of the
terrors of men"* (Imit., Bk. 3, C. 36).

"Let no one lead you astray with empty arguments, since on account of these sins the wrath of God comes upon the unbelievers" (Eph. 5:6).

Everyone has heard of the Trojan Horse. The part it played in legend is related in Vergil's *Aeneid*.

In the Greek-Trojan war, the Greeks built a large, hollow, wooden horse and placed it outside the walls of Troy, which they were besieging. The Trojans' curiosity was aroused and they finally dragged the horse into their city. During the night, the Greeks, who were hidden inside the horse, stealthily slipped from their hiding place and opened the gates to their comrades. The Greeks, once inside Troy, destroyed the city.

Satan is a past master in the art of deception. He will use any and every means he can to worm his way into the hearts of man. Curiosity is one of his most efficient weapons. Scripture warns man, "Be prudent, then, like serpents" (Mt. 10:16). The prudent man prays constantly to God for enlightenment to protect himself from evil. "If, however, any of you lacks wisdom, he should ask it of God, who gives to all simply and with never a word of reproach, and wisdom will be given to him" (James 1:5, 6).

"My Child, walk before Me in truth, and seek Me always in the simplicity of your heart. He who walks before Me in truth shall be defended from the attacks of evil . . . "

(Imit., Bk. 3, C. 4).

*"God, do not stand aloof from me; my God,
make haste to bring me help"* (Ps. 70:12).

The Medal of Honor is the highest tribute awarded by the
United States to members of the services for individual acts
of heroism in battle. In order to win this great distinction,
the warrior must perform some outstanding act of bravery
far beyond the call of duty. The recipient of this award
must display extraordinary courage and fortitude. This coveted
medal is given only after searching investigation and ir-
refutable testimony as to the worthiness of him who receives it.

The word "courage" comes from the Latin *cor,* meaning
"heart," and is defined as "that quality of will which meets
danger or opposition with intrepidity, calmness, and firm-
ness." Courage is a virtue admired by all and, it might be
added, desired by all.

Courage based on faith in God is the Christian's strongest
weapon; while, on the other hand, *dis*couragement is Satan's
most powerful instrument for destruction.

To the sinner, the devil constantly proclaims the task of
overcoming sin as too great to undertake. To the proud, he
points out the long road that leads to humility. To the weak
of faith, he asserts that greater faith requires too much effort.

The one who lets himself be discouraged by these tricks
is preparing himself for the loss of the greatest of prizes,
eternal glory. Everyone can profit by Paul's words to the
Thessalonians: "But the Lord keeps faith and he will make
you steadfast and will guard you from the wicked one"
(2 Thess. 3:3).

> *"Your life is our way and in your holy patience
> we come nearer to you who are our crown"*
> *(Imit.,* Bk. 3, C. 18).

" . . . we exult in tribulations also aware that tribulation produces endurance, and endurance proven virtue, and proven virtue hope"

(Rom 5:3, 4).

Human suffering is one of the great mysteries of mankind. Why the innocent have to suffer with and for the guilty is a problem, but those who love God know that whatever trial He sends them is for their ultimate benefit.

In order that man may get an insight into the reason why he must undergo sorrow for the wrongdoing of another, Christ has given him the Parable of the Weeds.

"The kingdom of heaven reminds me of a man who has sown good seed in his field. But, while everybody is asleep, his enemy comes and sows weeds among the wheat, and goes away. Eventually the blades spring up and put forth heads, but by that time the weeds also crop out. So the help of the landowner approach him and say: 'Sir, was it not good seed that you sowed in your field? How, then, is it overrun with weeds?' 'That is the work of an enemy!' he replies. 'Well!' say the help to him, 'do you want us to go and gather them up?' 'Not at all'; he answers: *'Otherwise, in gathering the weeds, you might pull up the wheat along with them.* Let both grow until the harvest, and when harvest time has come, I will say to the reapers: "Gather up, first of all, the weeds and bind them in bundles to be burnt; after that, store the wheat into my barn"'" (Mt. 13:24–30).

The humble man offers up his suffering in union with the suffering of Christ, realizing that his reward will be great.

"Take courage, brethren, let us go forward together and Jesus will be with us"

(Imit., Bk. 3, C. 56).

*"He gave his angels charge of you to keep you
safe in all your ways"* (Ps. 90:11).

It has been discovered by those who made a study of such
things that the bat has been given by nature a sort of "radar"
equipment that protects the little animal in its rapid flight,
from dashing itself to death against some inflexible obstacle.
The bat in flight constantly utters calls too high-pitched for
human ears to detect, and these sounds are reflected as echoes
when the bat approaches any object.

Man has been given a conscience by God to warn him
against impending evils dangerous to his eternal salvation.
The good man whose heart is delicately attuned to the things
of God instinctively hears this "still, small voice" echoing
back the warning of spiritual perils that lie ahead. These
prudent, wise, and generous Christians quickly and truly
turn aside from such evils and avoid a catastrophe that might
mortally wound their immortal souls. "My son, attend to my
wisdom: and incline thy ear to my prudence" (Prov. 5:1).

In order that one may avoid temptation, or overcome it,
it is necessary that he keep open the channel of grace that
flows from God into his soul. By constantly appealing to
God for guidance and help, he will escape the fatal crash
that might ruin his soul. "Because the Lord giveth wisdom:
and out of his mouth cometh prudence and knowledge. He
will keep the salvation of the righteous, and protect them
that walk in simplicity" (Prov. 2:6, 7).

> *"Protect and preserve the soul of Your poor
> servant among the many dangers of this corrupt-
> ible life, and direct him by Your accompanying
> grace, through the ways of peace, to the land
> of everlasting light"* (Imit., Bk. 3, C. 59).

"O how I love your law, O Lord! The livelong day I ponder it" (Ps. 118:97).

Julius Caesar, Roman emperor, established a calendar called, after him, the Julian Calendar. An error in Caesar's calculations, however, during the course of the years, caused a discrepancy of several days between his chronological system and astronomical time. Pope Gregory XIII corrected this mistake in 1582 by declaring that October 15 should follow October 4; thus adjusting the calendar to A.D. 325 the year of the Church Council of Nicea. The Gregorian Calendar is used by practically all nations today and is close to mathematical accuracy.

The Church in her love for her children has wisely divided the ecclesiastical year into seasons of repentence and rejoicing. She has dedicated almost every day of the year to God or Mary or one of her saints. "He who has a mind to observe the day, does so for the Lord's sake" (Rom. 14:6).

The practical Christian should keep close at hand a Church calendar and should strive to unite himself to the spirit of the Church by observing the feast or commemoration to be honored on that particular day. In this manner, the faithful will be united daily to the spirit of the Church and will consequently draw down upon themselves countless blessings from God and His saints. "Moreover, grow in grace and in the knowledge of our Lord and Savior, Jesus Christ. To him belongs glory both now and unto the day of eternity" (2 Pet. 3:18).

"O sweet and joyful service of God, which makes man truly free and holy!" (*Imit.*, Bk. 3, C. 10).

"God is not unjust, he will not forget what you have done and the love you have shown for his sake in the services you have rendered and continue to render to the saints" (Hebr. 6:10, 11).

A little boy overheard a new maid tell his mother what she expected in the way of salary.

The next day, Johnny left on his plate at breakfast an itemized list of his daily chores with a price attached for each: fifty cents for cutting the grass, ten cents for going to the store, fifteen cents for cleaning up his room.

The following morning he discovered a note on his breakfast plate from his mother:

"For bringing Johnny into the world, nothing.

"For getting up at night to watch over him, nothing.

"For buying him clothes and food, nothing.

"For love and affection, nothing."

With tears in his eyes, Johnny rushed to his mother, and apologized for his thoughtlessness.

Love is priceless. No one realizes this better than those who know and love each other best. Those who really love, never count the cost. Christ willingly suffered — the shameful death of the cross for love of His children — the supreme act of love. "A contrite spirit is my sacrifice, O God; a crushed and humbled heart, O God, you will not loathe."

"The cause of our love of God is God Himself" (St. Bernard).

> *"Look up to him! Be cheered! Let not your faces blush with shame!"* (Ps. 33:6).

Many people have heard the humorous story of the man who at the insistence of his family finally visited the oculist to have his eyes examined.

"I'm sure I don't need glasses, Doctor," he declared, "but for the sake of peace at home, I want my eyes tested."

"Well, we can soon find out the truth," said the doctor. "Read the *first line* on the chart in front of you."

The nearsighted gentleman looked searchingly in the direction indicated; then asked, "What chart?"

There are countless self-satisfied souls who have convinced themselves that they do not need any assistance in seeing God and the things of God. They never ask His help. They never pray. They never enter a church. They never read a spiritual book. They never listen to a sermon. Yet if these spiritually nearsighted souls would turn to God for aid and help and grace, they would see the really important things in life. The man who thought he did not need glasses was happily surprised to behold, through his improved vision, all the beauty in life he had missed before because of unknowingly impaired eyesight. The sincere soul who turns to God for light will likewise rejoice in the glories of his Creator that through his own fault have previously been hidden from him. "For you, Lord, make my lamp to shine; my God, you turn my darkness into light (Ps. 17:129).

> *"Enlighten me, good Jesus, with the brightness of internal light, and take away all darkness from the habitation of my heart"* (Imit., Bk. 3, C. 23).

"O may my cry reach out to you, O Lord; according to your promise lesson me" (Ps. 118:169).

The newspaper recounted this wild-life episode. In the course of constructing a dam in the mountains, the workmen laid a foundation of cement and then covered the fresh cement with straw. In the morning when the men returned to the job, they were startled to see a young deer standing motionless in the concrete foundation.

The explanation was soon evident. The hungry animal during the course of its nightly meandering through the forest had come upon the fresh straw. Here was a godsend. All this luscious food just waiting to be eaten! The doe promptly undertook the enjoyable task of devouring as much as she could. Unknown to herself, however, the animal was gradually sinking into the soft cement. Too late the unsuspecting deer discovered her mistake. Her four feet were imbedded in the hardening cement. She was trapped!

Vigilance is of the utmost importance to the faithful Christian. Evil never rests. The deceits of the wicked are infinite. How many unfortunate souls there are who have found themselves caught in a position similar to that of the doe — lured on by false promises or tinseled sins.

In this life, there are many snares set for the unwary. "If thou be wise, thou shalt be so to thyself: and if a scorner, thou alone shalt bear the evil" (Prov. 9:12).

Each one should plead daily with God for direction and light. All should sing with the Psalmist, "My shelter and my shield are you: and in your word I trust" (Ps. 118:114).

"My child, hear My words . . . surpassing all the knowledge of the philosophers and wise men of earth" (Imit., Bk. 3, C. 3).

> " . . . *rejoice in the fact that your names are
> engraved in heaven*" (Lk. 10:20).

The Romans were a masterful race. They were great law-makers as well as students of human nature. Their punishments were exacting, yet tempered with a keen understanding of man's weaknesses.

One of the greatest punishments the Romans meted out to culprits — those who committed crimes against the State — was to erase the individual's name from all public records. His and his family's names were to pass into oblivion. Even the pagans understood that no man likes to be forgotten. All wish to leave some trace of their passing on the sands of time. If this be true of a pagan, how much more true is it of a Christian, who knows that his immortal soul will live on forever? The true Christian desires above all else that his name and his soul be listed among the elect of God. "I will give them an everlasting name which shall never perish" (Isa. 56:5).

*"What God prepares for those who love Him,
is not understood by faith, is not tasted by hope,
nor taken hold of by charity; it surpasses all
desires"* (St. Augustine).

*"In God we gloried all the time; we never ceased
to praise your name"* (Ps. 43:9).

Do you know what causes the seasons of the year? Winter
and summer, spring and fall are brought about by a slight tilt
in the earth's axis. As the sun moves across the equator
toward the tropic of Capricorn, its northern rays become more
and more slanted, and thus the North Temperate Zone becomes colder, and gradually winter takes over. As the sun
moves north again toward the tropic of Cancer, its warm
rays become more and more direct, melting the wintry snows
and giving warmth and vitality to the frozen earth.

This slight tilt to the axis of the earth, with its manifold
blessings to mankind, is but one example of divine favor
which God has given to His children.

The mechanism of the human body, too, is so intricate
and delicately adjusted that the surgeon and the doctor daily
marvel over the Creator's wisdom.

If God is so glorified in His creation of the material, how
much more is He exalted by His handiwork in the creation
of man's soul which is made to His own image and likeness
and which has as its ultimate reward eternal happiness?
Every human being should employ that free will with which
he has been endowed to glorify and exalt his Creator at all
times and in all places. "And more than this, we exult also
in God through our Lord Jesus Christ, through whom we
have now received this reconciliation" (Rom. 5:11).

> *"All things come from You; therefore You are
> to be praised in all"* (Imit., Bk. 3, C. 22).

> *"He who is bent on saving his life must part*
> *with it anyway; but he who freely parts with*
> *his life for my sake will save it in the end"*
> (Lk. 9:24–25).

St. Thomas Aquinas was perhaps the most brilliant scholar in the Church, and withal, he was a most humble and holy man.

One day, his sister came to him and asked him how to become a saint. It may be, that realizing his tremendous learning and knowledge, she thought her gifted brother could suggest a short cut to this much desired end.

St. Thomas' answer was brief and to the point. It offered no panacea. It simply gave the sound, solid reasoning of a brilliant and holy man. "If you wish to be a saint, *will* to be one."

There is no other answer. "Thus to pray is good and acceptable in the sight of God our Savior, who wills that all men be saved and come to the knowledge of the truth" (1 Tim. 2:3, 5).

> *"Reflect seriously on that one thing, because it is*
> *the one thing necessary, and it is infinitely more*
> *important than all others"* (St. Augustine).

"Of patience, indeed, you have need, that, having done the will of God, you may receive the promised reward" (Hebr. 10:36).

There is an ancient story in *Aesop's Fables* that tells how one day, the Sun and the Wind made a wager. Each claimed that he would be the first to force a certain traveler to remove his overcoat.

Confidently, the Wind set about his task. He swooped down upon the man with all his force and strove to tear the coat from the man's back. Despite his most violent efforts, however, the man clung tightly to his garment. The more the Wind increased, the greater effort the man made to retain his coat. In disgust, the Wind gave up.

The Sun then sought to win the wager. He smiled gently down upon the man. Gradually, the traveler opened his coat to get cool. As the Sun increased its warmth, the man finally took off his coat.

The patient warmth of the Sun had become victorious. " . . . every child of God has enough strength to become a victor over the world. And this is the victory that has conquered the world, our faith" (1 Jn. 5:4, 5).

> *"O desirable weakness, which is compensated by the strength of Christ! Who will grant me not only to become weak, but cease altogether to be myself, that I may become strong with the strength of the Lord?"* (St. Bernard.)

"And just as we have borne the likeness of the man of dust, so shall we bear the likeness of the heavenly One" (1 Cor. 15:49).

Michelangelo was one of the greatest artists of all times. He was a sculptor as well as painter. So anxious was he to make his masterpieces perfect, that he studied anatomy for years in order that he might have every muscle and organ in its proper place.

The greatest of all his works of sculpture is the statue of Moses in the Church of St. Peter-in-Chains in Rome.

After the artist had put the finishing touches to this mammoth block of marble, he was so well satisfied with his handiwork that according to legend, he gently struck the statue, and cried out, "Now speak."

But the statue remained silent. The spark of life, the immortal soul, was absent.

With God's help and by dint of prayer, penance, and perseverance, the faithful can mold their immortal souls into such shape that they will bespeak the glory of God. Everyone should strive toward this end. "A kindly look grant to your worshiper, and teach me thy decrees" (Ps. 118:135).

"If the mind is directed by a firm intention, it considers sweet whatever is bitter in this life, and considers as repose everything that afflicts"
(St. Gregory).

*"Look at the birds of the air: they do not sow,
or reap, or store up provisions in barns, and yet
your heavenly Father feeds them!"* (Mt. 6:26.)

This scene took place in a nationally known orphan's home. A shabbily dressed mother was there with her two little boys, one about eight and the other about ten. She had traveled over a thousand miles, from the deep South, to place her fatherless children in a good Catholic home.

However, when it came time to say good-by to them, she was unable to stand the separation.

She said to the priest in charge, "I will leave only one. I cannot bear to part with both."

The good priest kindly told her to do whatever she wished.

When the decision was reached, the little lad who was to remain promptly started to cry and refused to stay alone. Again a conference was held between the children and the mother. The outcome was that the mother decided to take the two boys back home with her. As she thanked the priest and started on her long return journey, the bystander felt confident that God's bounty would supply all needful things for such a devoted family. " . . . if we love one another, God abides in us and our love for him reaches perfection" (1 Jn. 4:12).

"He who is poor with Christ is rich enough"
(St. Jerome).

> *"A rock of refuge be to me, a castle, fortified to rescue me"* (Ps. 30:3).

Hidden treasure is always intriguing, and especially so, when there is a map to designate its location. John Smith's heart was beating rapidly as he held such a map in his hand. Upon solving the enigmatic letters and numbers scratched on the ragged, soiled parchment, he knew he would find at last the solution to all his secret longings.

For some time John's family life had been disintegrating. He was gradually losing interest in his wife, his family, and his home. He was restless. He wanted to be free to roam the world. The old rambling house felt empty now that his wife and children were away for the summer vacation. Yet, the solitude gave him an opportunity to work out a plan of action.

Mike, the ancient gardener, had been a sailor in his youth. John liked to spend the long evenings talking with him about strange lands and faraway places. In the course of these visits, Mike occasionally hinted that he had a treasure map, picked up in his ramblings about the world. When the old man died suddenly, John found among Mike's few belongings an envelope addressed to himself. In it was the map he now grasped with his shaky fingers.

Hours later the task of decoding the map was completed. John's restlessness had vanished. A contented smile spread over his face. Faithful Mike had drawn his map wisely. The decoded numbers showed the alluring X to mark the longitude and latitude of John's own home. "By wisdom the house shall be built; and by prudence it shall be strengthened" (Prov. 24:3).

"Forsake yourself, renounce yourself and you shall enjoy great inward peace (Imit., Bk. 3, C. 37).

*"Oh, the depth of the riches and of the wisdom
and of the knowledge of God!"* (Rom. 11:33.)

Fables, being basically true, frequently can be helpful to
all of us. One tells of the hunter who was out gunning with
his favorite hawk.

After several hours of traveling in the hot sun, the hunter
came to a waterfall where he knelt down to scoop up a
refreshing drink. As he raised the cup to his lips, the hawk
swooped down and knocked it from his hand. Startled at
this unusual action upon the part of his favorite, he raised
the cup again; and again, the hawk knocked the receptacle
from his hand. Thoroughly angered by this time, the hunter
drew his sword and raised the cup a third time. Again the
hawk swooped down; quick as a flash he severed the bird
in twain. Remorseful of his rash act, the hunter dropped the
cup into his sack, and stumbled away from the scene of his
"crime." As he ascended a steep hill, he came upon a little
pond, the source of the waterfall. There rotting in the water
was the body of a poisonous snake.

Everyone should remember that God sees all things, past,
present, and future. He knows what is best for each one.
Whatever trial He sends has a purpose. The faithful soul
accepts all crosses with the knowledge that, borne patiently,
these trials will react to his spiritual welfare. "To me this
knowledge is a passing wonder; it is sublime beyond my
grasp" (Ps. 138:6).

> *"The just man is distinguished from the sinner
> in this that the just man in adversity confesses
> the glory of the all-powerful God, that he is not
> crushed by his condition, that he does not fall
> with the fall of his exterior glory"* (St. Gregory).

> *"It is a proverb: A young man according to his way. Even when he is old he will not depart from it"* (Prov. 22:6).

During the depression years of the 1930's, a business executive was in a large Eastern city to arrange a long-term lease for storage space for his company's products. Several offers had been made to this man, who will be known as John, by real-estate agencies, but none proved satisfactory.

Then he met an agent who was sure that he had just the proposition. His company would give John $125,000 for his own use if he would sign their high-priced lease.

The real-estate representative, convinced that "money talks," held out his pen confidently.

"Just a minute," interrupted John. "Let me tell you a little story. When I was a young lad, I went with some chums, into an ice-cream parlor. Each of us had a nickel. After finishing our ice cream, someone suggested we skip out without paying. We did. On reaching home, I told my mother what we had done, quite proud of my achievement. 'Young man,' said my mother sternly, 'you march right downtown and give that man HIS money.' I did. It was a very embarrassing, but a very, very effective, lesson."

The agent looked long and thoughtfully at John, put away his pen, gathered up his papers, and quietly departed.

The loving parents who see in their children the image and likeness of God will, by example and precept, lay a solid spiritual foundation upon which these future men and women will rear a living monument to them and to God.

> *"Let this be your wish: That whether in life or in death God may be glorified in you"*
> (*Imit.,* Bk. 3, C. 49).

*"Make glad your servant's soul, O Lord, because
to you I lift my soul"* (Ps. 85:4).

"Ten seconds for station identification." How often does
this statement come over the radio when the listener is en-
grossed in some particularly interesting program?

The interruption may be disconcerting to those who resent
interference with the continuity of a football or baseball game,
the opera, or the drama. However, the local announcer does
not hold up the progress of the program just to hear his
own voice. Each radio station is required by law to identify
itself at regular intervals.

The wisdom of this ordinance is quite evident. If an
unidentified radio station were allowed to broadcast at ran-
dom, confusion on the airways would be rampant and
propaganda of the worst type would flood the home. The
call letters of the radio station must be announced so that
the auditors may know the source of the program to which
they are listening.

It is true that man must labor hard to gain the material
things he needs for himself and his family. But, in his daily
toil he should frequently interrupt his work for "Station
Identification." He should forget for a few moments the
things of earth and listen to the voice of God, the Source of
all his help and joy and merit. For as St. James writes, "None
but a good gift and none but a perfect donation comes from
above. . . . from the Creator of the heavenly luminaries . . .
(James 1:17, 18).

> *"Consider these things, my soul, and close the
> doors of your senses so that you can hear what
> the Lord our God speaks within you"*
> (*Imit.*, Bk. 3, C. 1).

> *"They that trust in him shall understand the
> truth, and they that are faithful in love shall
> rest in him: for grace and peace is to his elect"*
> (Wisd. 3:9).

A prominent attorney liked to relate the story told him
by his grandfather. The grandfather worked in the Pennsylvania coal mines. Deep down in the bowels of the earth
the good man shared his lunch with a mine rat. One night
as he sat on a ledge eating his lonely meal, friend rat appeared as usual. Ignoring the delicious tidbits that were tossed
to him, the rat insisted instead on tugging at the toe of the
miner's boot. Mystified at the animal's actions, the miner
arose to investigate. As he left the ledge, the ceiling above
where he had been sitting crashed to the floor.

This story may not be true but its moral is clear. Even
the despised rat reacts to kindness. Volumes are written on
the loyalty and gratitude of animals as a result of kindness
shown to them by man. If God's lowest creatures respond so
generously to man's charity, how much more does man
himself? St. Paul declares, "Love, therefore, is the complete
fulfillment of the Law" (Rom. 13:10). The true Christian,
the true follower of Christ, finds that the exercise of the
virtue of charity is his best investment; both here, and hereafter. "Above all things practice constant love among yourselves; it wins forgiveness for many sins" (1 Pet. 4:8).

> " . . . *God weighs the love with which a man
> acts, rather than the deed itself"*
> (*Imit.*, Bk. 1, C. 15).

*"The Lord is near. Have no anxiety, but in every
concern by prayer and supplication with thanksgiving let your petitions be made known in your
communing with God"* (Phil. 4:6).

It is most interesting and instructive to visit a telephone switchboard. This is especially true if the board handles transatlantic calls.

A few seconds or minutes suffice for the operators to connect parties halfway around the globe. What joy this instrument brings to loved ones whose familiar voices span the countless miles! In sickness and in health, the very opportunity of talking with a dear one brings consolation and joy.

This opportunity of communicating with relatives and friends is as near as the closest phone — at a price.

People marvel at this great invention.

Yet, man can communicate with the Source of all happiness, all joy, and all consolation, simply by lifting up his heart and mind to God in prayer, any time, anywhere — and there is no charge. "I loved the Lord, because he heard my pleading voice" (Ps. 114:1).

> *"The man who knows how to pray well, knows
> how to live well"* (St. Augustine).

"Strange that you see the splinter in your brother's eye, and do not notice the log in your own!"
                                                    (Lk. 6:41).

"And the Lord sent Nathan to David: And when he was come to him, he said to him: There were two men in one city, the one rich, and the other poor.

"The rich man had exceeding many sheep and oxen.

"But the poor man had nothing at all but one little ewe lamb, which he had bought and nourished up, and which had grown up in his house together with his children, eating of his bread and drinking of his cup, and sleeping in his bosom: and it was unto him as a daughter.

"And when a certain stranger was come to the rich man, he spared to take of his own sheep and oxen, to make a feast for that stranger, who was come to him: but took the poor man's ewe, and dressed it for the man that was come to him.

"And David's anger being exceedingly kindled against that man, he said to Nathan: As the Lord liveth, the man that hath done this is a child of death.

"He shall restore the ewe fourfold: because he did this thing and had no pity.

"And Nathan said to David: Thou art the man" (2 Kings 12:1–7).

Then Nathan proceeds to point out to David all the blessings the Lord had given to him, and yet how unjustly David had acted toward God's creatures.

In reading over these words of Scripture, it will be well for each one to ask himself, "Am I like unto David?"

"But because my love is as yet weak and my virtue imperfect, I must be strengthened and comforted by You" (Imit., Bk. 3, C. 5).

*"A hard heart shall fear evil at the last: and he
that loveth danger shall perish in it"*
                              (Ecclus. 3:27).

A colossal movie was in the making. The director was
instructing the male star how to conduct himself in the
"sooper-dooper" climax, "You dash to this point and stop
right on this mark. The lion will chase you exactly as far
as this point. Now," demanded the director, "you are sure
you know where to stop?" "I know where to stop all right,"
declared the uneasy actor casting an anxious eye at his fellow
performer, "but does that lion know where to stop?"

There is a constant struggle between the honest man and
his lower instincts. St. Paul warns, "Therefore put to death
the passions . . . immorality, uncleanness, lust, evil desires and
avarice, which is a form of idol-worship" (Col. 3:5). The
spiritual man must constantly mortify himself and seek to
restrain the evil passions which lie dormant within him.

If the individual temporizes with these ugly and demanding
passions, he shall be devoured by them. He may think that
he is able to put them down as he wishes but he will find
to his sorrow, that not unlike the lion in the foregoing story,
his aroused sensual appetites respect no limitations. To remain
in the friendship of God, man's prayers and God's grace are
essential. All should cry out with the Psalmist, "A heart
all pure create in me, O God; a spirit new and firm breathe
into me" (Ps. 5:12).

> *"The man who only shuns temptations out-
> wardly and does not uproot them will make
> little progress . . . "* (Imit., Bk. 1, C. 13).

"In the sweat of thy face shalt thou eat bread till thou return to the earth, out of which thou wast taken" (Gen. 3:19).

Sometimes people wonder whether success in life comes from hard work or plain luck. This is a hard question to answer, but the old adage is still true, "God helps those who help themselves."

Go through the countryside and view the plentiful crops ready for the harvest. God gave the soil; He gave the seed; He gave the weather; but, the farmer had to work from dawn to dusk to cultivate the crops. And the farmer soon discovers he has the best luck with the row he hoes the most.

God has told man that he must earn his bread by the sweat of his brow. Whatever his state in life, ordinarily speaking, man succeeds in proportion to the effort he puts into his work. In the spiritual life, as well as the material, everyone must work to gain his objective. One of the saints has laid down a sound principle, "Work as if everything depended on you; pray as if everything depended on God."

"Just as a field, though neither sown nor planted, produces grass, so also man, if not occupied with necessary work will, since he is, as it were, under the necessity of doing something, give himself up to bad actions" (St. Chrysostom).

*"Now he who plants and he who waters the seed
work in harmony, yet each will receive his own
salary befitting his efforts"* (1 Cor. 3:8).

There was great need for a hospital in the small, not too prosperous, community. A meeting was called to consider ways and means of raising sufficient funds for the undertaking.

A hundred and one suggestions were offered by the assembled gathering. All were hackneyed and worn-out ideas. Finally, the chairman called upon one man who had made a financial success of himself by years of arduous labor.

"From long experience, I have found out," said this gentleman, "that God has buried gold in the earth and the only way to get it out is to dig for it."

The chairman closed the meeting promptly with the admonition to his audience to heed the advice. Within a comparatively short time, the community was blessed with a new hospital.

For a man to succeed in any aspect of life, he must "dig for it." Ordinarily speaking, the individual gets out of his work what he puts into it and nothing more. And in the very digging, he derives a satisfaction that repays him for his efforts.

That person who is determined to gain heaven has to labor at his task. He does not work alone, however, for God is always beside him, to assist him and aid him, but he must do his part. "The goodness of the Lord our God descend on us; and speed the work of our hands for us. O speed the work of our poor hands" (Ps. 89:17).

> *"Grant that I may always will and desire that
> which is most acceptable and pleasing to you"*
> *(Imit., Bk. 3, C. 15).*

*"For by your deeds, O Lord, you gladden me;
your handiwork is my delight"* (Ps. 91:5).

"Now Israel loved Joseph above all his sons, because he had him in his old age: and he made him a coat of divers colours. And his brethren seeing that he was loved by his father, more than all his sons, hated him, and could not speak peaceably to him" (Gen. 37:3, 4).

The biblical story of Joseph is a classic example of the malevolence wrought by the vice of jealousy. Joseph's brothers, fearing to kill him, sold him as a slave into Egypt. God was with Joseph, however, and in time it was Joseph who saved his brethren from death through starvation.

The evilness occasioned by the malignant malady of jealousy is impossible to calculate. Once this malicious and devastating passion invades the heart, like a ferocious beast let loose, it destroys and devours all the goodness the individual formerly possessed. Jealousy agitates the soul; it darkens the mind; it eats up the energy of the body of the offender, while it wreaks untold sorrow and suffering on the object of its venomous spite. St. John declares, "But he who hates his brother is in darkness and walks in it. He has no idea where he is going, because the darkness has blinded his eyes" (Jn. 2:11). The only antidote for this destructive poison is the realization and acknowledgment of one's own manifold gifts from God and a true Christian spirit of gladness in a neighbor's achievements. "See what kind of love the Father has bestowed on us, that we should be children not merely in name but in reality" (1 Jn. 3:1).

*"Nature likes to receive honor and reverence, but
grace faithfully attributes all honor and glory to
God"* (*Imit.*, Bk. 3, C. 54).

"Well for the race whose God is the Lord"
(Ps. 143:15).

There was nothing particularly noteworthy about the man. One passing him on the street would take him to be a laborer dressed in his Sunday clothes. Yet, this individual had spent forty of his sixty-five years behind prison bars.

He had called at the rectory seeking financial assistance.

His record showed no really vicious acts. His great failing was his inability to leave other people's property alone.

"You know, Father," he said, "I wish they had let me stay. I'm lost outside."

Here was a man who had spent the greater part of his life behind gray prison bars. He had become used to the routine. He and his fellow inmates had things in common to talk about. The State looked after his material welfare. Outside the walls, he missed these familiar things; he was a derelict.

How true it is that every man's particular way of life grows on him unconsciously, even behind prison walls.

Many people are never content where they are. In their imagination distant places, persons, and things appeal to them. "Faraway fields look greenest." Once he has left behind the old familiar faces and streets and homes, it gradually dawns on the wayfarer that he has given up more than he has gained. Not in distant, vague, intangible places, but ordinarily speaking, *where he is now,* can everyone do his best work for God. "And I will show mercies to you and will take pity on you and will cause you to dwell in your own land" (Jer. 42:12).

> *"Desires often inflame you, and drive you madly on, but consider whether you act for My honor, or for your own advantage"* (Imit., Bk. 3, C. 11).

"Has not God chosen those who are the poor in the eyes of the world to be rich in faith and heirs of the kingdom which he promised to those that love him?" (James 2:5.)

Three of the most beautiful shrines in the world dedicated to the Blessed Virgin have had miraculous beginnings. Mary came down upon earth and revealed herself to her children and instructed these messengers to tell the proper authorities that she wished these shrines erected to her honor.

One of the most interesting things about these visits of Mary is the kind of messenger she chose.

Those who received this grace were not the learned, the powerful, or the wealthy. Mary revealed herself in each case to the poorest of the poor, the unlettered, and the pure of heart.

At Fatima she selected three children — children of very poor parents; at Guadalupe a poor, illiterate Indian.

At Lourdes, Mary selected Bernadette, a little girl whose parents were so poverty stricken they sought refuge in the cellar of the village jail.

It is quite evident from these observations that Mary, the Mother of God, has a special predilection for the poor of spirit, the humble of heart, and especially for childlike faith and purity. To be a close friend of Mary, one *must* strive to acquire these virtues. " . . . he heeds the poor men's prayer, and does not disregard their prayer" (Ps. 101:18).

"If God's works were such as to be easily understood by human reason, they could not be called unspeakable. Neither has faith any merit if its object can be proved by reason and experience"
(St. Augustine).

"We see now by means of a mirror in a vague way, but then we shall see face to face. Now my knowledge is incomplete, but then I shall have complete knowledge, even as God has complete knowledge of me" (1 Cor. 13:12, 13).

The college professor was greatly admired by his students, not only because of his sound ideas on education, but also because of his practical common sense. He was a man who loved God, understood his students, and still believed in the three R's as the foundation stones of true education.

"One day two high school pupils came to me," he related, "and presented their problems. Both were anxious to enter West Point but feared they could not pass the entrance exams, especially mathematics. They asked me to tutor them. I agreed to coach them if they would follow my system. It was comparatively easy. Simply this: review their subjects each day. Review four or five pages of past material every day, and keep repeating this process during the school term. Both boys," he continued, "passed their entrance exams to West Point with flying colors and stood very close to the top of their graduating class."

"Repetition is the mother of studies" is the foundation of academic life. This principle should be applied to every branch of life, and especially to the reading of Scripture. A working knowledge of the Bible, the world's "Best Seller" brings everyone closer to God. "Your word—it is a lamp to guide my feet, a light to show my path" (Ps. 118:105).

"A little of the time that is being wasted is the price of eternity" (St. Jerome).

"Jesus, remember me when you return in your royal glory" (Lk. 23:42).

Everyone likes to be remembered. If further proof is demanded for this statement, one need merely turn to the greeting-card industry to learn that five billion cards were purchased last year. This almost inconceivable number of friendly gestures brings home the fact very forcefully of man's desire not to be forgotten.

How pleased one feels when a chance acquaintance remarks, "Oh, I remember you. We met on such and such an occasion." The longer ago the occurrence, the more flattered the recipient of this remark feels.

Political parties, as every newspaper reader knows, have been built on the solid foundation of leaders who did not forget their constituents.

Every person is an individual and the fact that he has been singled out for remembrance stirs up within himself the thought that he is really important after all. Since so much happiness and gratitude can be brought about by exercising one's memory a bit, it is surprising how many people ignore its possibilities.

But if man desires to be remembered and recognized by his fellow men, how infinite will be his joy when he is recognized by God as one of His own when he appears before Him to give an account of his stewardship. "You search me and you know me, Lord: you know me when I sit or rise" (Ps. 138:1, 2).

"Great thought! The heart of him who thinks of these eternal years will be filled with peace"
(St. Augustine).

"And let patience accomplish a perfect work, that you may be perfect, flawless and without short-coming" (James 1:4).

This man could hardly read or write and yet he was paid $25,000 a year. He was superintendent of a large paper mill.

It was his job to produce paper and the mill's production report justified his unusually large salary. He knew how to handle men, for he had come up from the ranks. Above all, he knew how to make paper. When the high-salaried chemists with their costly equipment were unable to locate the cause of poor-grade paper, this man would take up a sample of the stock in his sensitive fingers, and tell immediately whether there was too much or too little of the necessary ingredients. He was successful because he *knew* his business. He strove to be perfect in his undertaking.

Man has the obligation, first of all, to be perfect in his spiritual life. He also has the obligation of striving to do his daily work to the best of his ability, according as God has given him the intellectual and physical power to perform this work. Strive to be perfect as your heavenly Father is perfect. "Whatever you do or say let it always be in the name of the Lord Jesus, while you give thanks to God the Father through him" (Col. 3:17).

> *"There is no greater loss to us than the loss of time wasted"* (St. Bonaventure).

> *"Unless the Lord erects the house, in vain is the toil of the builders"* (Ps. 126:1).

St. Augustine declares that *Faith* lays the foundation for the House of God, *Hope* erects the building, but it is *Love* that completes it.

The Holy Family should be an exemplar of every Christian home. St. Joseph, the foster father of Jesus, together with Mary His mother, strove in every way to make the family circle an ideal place to rear the Child Jesus. Love of God dominated the household and this love was reflected among the members so that real, honest family happiness reigned supreme. *Faith* in God, *Hope* in His protection and reward, and *Love* for Him and each other is the cornerstone of a truly happy family life. We obtain these blessings by prayer.

And concerning this Holy House, St. Luke writes:

"And when they had fulfilled all things as prescribed in the Law of the Lord, they returned into Galilee, to their own town of Nazareth. And the child grew and became strong. He was full of wisdom and the grace of God was upon him" (Lk. 2:39, 40).

The home should be the happiest place on earth. Here, father, mother, and children should enjoy the greatest joy this side of heaven. If the members of the household are devoted to God, and strive daily to put His teachings into practice, their home is sure to be what every home should be, the antechamber to heaven. "O well for you who fear the Lord and walk the ways he has enjoined!" (Ps. 127:1.)

> *"My Child, he who attempts to escape obeying withdraws himself from grace. Likewise he who seeks private benefits for himself loses those which are common to all"* (Imit., Bk. 3, C. 13).

"O train me to observe your law, and I will cherish it with all my heart" (Ps. 118:34).

A very wealthy old man once became engaged in conversation with a young boy. During the course of the talk, the millionaire, prompted no doubt by the thought that lay hidden in his mind, said to the lad:

"Where do you expect to go when you die?"

Without the least hesitation and with the utmost conviction, the boy answered, "To heaven!"

"My, my," said the old man, with a sigh, "I'd give a million dollars if I knew how to get to heaven."

"Well," replied the little lad magnanimously, "I'll tell you for nothing! If you want to go to heaven, keep the Commandments."

Out of the mouths of children comes much wisdom. This young boy was simply repeating Christ's answer to the rich young man in the Gospel, when he asked our Lord what he must do to save his soul. The answer of Christ is the same today as it was when He answered the youth, "If you want to enter eternal life, keep the commandments" (Mt. 19:18).

> *"Lord, give strength to do what Thou commandest, and command what Thou pleasest"*
> (St. Augustine).

"Refrain your tongue from ill, your lips from treacherous words" (Ps. 33:14).

Frequently, the comedian for the purpose of sharing in the originator's glory will quote a humorous passage with the added phrase, "Wish I had said that."

There comes a time, and perhaps many times, in the lives of most people when they sincerely declare, "I wish I had *not* said that." "That" might be an unkind word, a choice bit of scandal, or an angry outburst. Once the speaker of these words realizes the harm he has done to others or to himself, he would give much to have remained silent at that particular time. "Silence is golden" is an oft-repeated maxim. No one realizes this more than the individual who has spoken "out of turn." The Psalmist sings, "I said: I shall be watchful of my ways, lest I should trespass with my tongue" (38:2).

What a wonderful gift is that of speech! This faculty is given to man to praise God and to communicate with his fellow men. Isaias declares: "The Lord hath given me a learned tongue, that I should know how to uphold by word him that is weary" (50:4).

In Ecclesiasticus it is written, "Who will set a guard before my mouth, and a sure seal upon my lips, that I fall not by them, and that my tongue destroy me not?" (22:33.)

It is very clear from these quotations from the Bible that man must ever be on his guard lest he speak unwisely. That glorious instrument of speech, the tongue, should be used only to express God's language — that is love — love of God and love of one's neighbor.

"It is easier to be silent altogether, than not to speak too much" (Imit., Bk. 1, C. 20).

"Beware thou never join in friendship with the inhabitants of that land, which may be thy ruin"
(Exod. 34:12).

A little humor frequently carries home a point more accurately than a lengthy discourse.

A young lady confident of her ability to face the world and overcome any evil that might beset her path, assured a well-wisher with the shop-worn phrase, "Oh, I can take care of myself!"

Her friend, somewhat of a philosopher, reminded the young lady, "That's what the canary said when he went to the animal hospital to sing for the cats!"

This silly little story is not half as silly as some young people may think. Many hearts have been broken because young girls and boys, and older people too, have placed themselves in predicaments which they thought held no dangers for them.

By following the advice of a loved one, the younger generation can avoid most of the pitfalls of life. By following the teachings of God, all can spare themselves much sorrow, temporal and eternal. "Teach me judgment, teach me sense, because in your commands I trust." (Ps. 118:66).

> *"Have for your advisers and the witnesses of your life and honor, persons who are wise in council, obedient to authority, and faithful to their friends and companions"* (St. Bernard).

> *"Or what price can a man pay down to purchase life forever?"* (Mt. 16:27).

Sir Thomas More was a celebrated English lawyer and a favorite of King Henry VIII. More than this, he was a devout Christian who practiced his religion to a high degree.

Because of his refusal to place the commands of his earthly king above those of Christ, he fell from Henry's good graces. He was condemned to be executed.

At the place of executions, the steps leading to the block were worn and shaky.

More, being a true servant and friend of God, could see the humorous side of earthly life. As he started up the steps, he said to the attendant, "Give me a hand up — as for coming down, I will shift for myself."

The "Sir" has been changed to "Saint."

To the true servant of God, the so-called important things in this life fade into insignificance. Thomas More had power, prestige, and position, yet he gaily surrendered these worldly honors, rather than sacrifice the only truly worth-while dignity; a humble position in the Court of the King of Kings. "Your precepts are my everlasting heritage, because they are my heart's delight" (Ps. 118:111).

"As we do not easily forget anything that we hold in our hands, so we should never forget the question of our souls; and that care of our souls should always fill our hearts" (St. Bernard).

*" . . . but glory, honor, and peace will be the lot
of every man intent on doing good"* (Rom. 2:10).

"Let's ask Fred." A serious financial problem had arisen
in the family and the young people were stalemated until
they thought of their loyal friend. After conferring with
Fred, their difficulties were soon ironed out and a satisfactory
solution reached.

Unfortunately there are too few "Freds" in this life; high-
principled men whose wisdom, kindness, and generosity are
a never ending source of consolation and help to others.

These few individuals, respected and admired by all, go
about their daily tasks quietly and efficiently, seeking not
their own glory but striving at all times to bring consolation,
peace, and contentment to others. These "faithful Freds" are
guided by the high principles of Christ. Some unworthy
people, looking for an "easy mark," sometimes seek to impose
upon these Christian gentlemen, mistaking their guilelessness
for gullibility, but such counterfeit characters soon discover
these "Freds" possess an uncanny ability to penetrate the
hearts of all. Back of their kind and generous personalities
they maintain a firm, resolute, steel framework of noble principles that the true follower of Christ always possesses.

All men should strive to put into daily practice the example
that Christ has given to men. In this striving, the faithful
will find great happiness themselves and will bring immeasurable joy and consolation to others. " . . . for I have set
you an example, so that what I have done to you, you, too,
should do" (Jn. 13:15).

> *"Where heavenly grace and true charity enter in,
> there neither envy nor narrowness of heart nor
> self-love will have place"* (Imit., Bk. 3, C. 9).

> *"God is light. . . . If we should say that we are united with him while we continue to shape our conduct in an atmosphere of darkness, we are liars"* (1 Jn. 1:5, 6).

An expedition traveled far into the bleak regions of the Arctic Circle. As they advanced, they set up caches of food and supplies every few miles. Secure in the thought that they had taken every precaution against disaster, the hardy explorers pressed on to their objective. Rejoicing over their achievements, they started the return trip in the darkness of the six months' cycle. Before long a terrific storm arose, and the stinging ice and penetrating cold forced them off their trail. Gradually, the wrath of the elements conquered and all were frozen to death. In the spring a rescue party discovered the explorers' bodies — all within a short distance of the caches. In the darkness and storm, they had perished within a few feet of food and warmth.

Many souls have wandered far from their Father's House and go through this life burdened down by sin, which has darkened their hearts with the shadow of death. They walk around in circles, knowing no objective, their souls withering from lack of spiritual nourishment; and finally they die, with not a thought of what awaits them beyond the grave. Yet but a short distance away, almost on any corner, Christ waits in His tabernacle home for them to come to Him, and partake of Himself, the Spiritual Food that would assure them a happy, purposeful life here, and a crown of glory hereafter.

"For the honor and glory of Your name receive me, You who have prepared Your Body and Blood as food and drink for me"
                                        (*Imit.*, Bk. 4, C. 4).

*"The Lord is near to all who call on him, to all
who call on him sincerely"* (Ps. 144:18).

"He also told them a parable to show that they must
persevere in prayer and not lose heart. 'Once upon a time,'
he said, 'there was a judge in a town somewhere who did not
fear God and had no regard for man. In the same town there
lived a widow who used to come to him and say: "See that
justice is done me! Rid me of my persecutor!" For a long
time he refused: but later he said to himself, "I do not fear
God, and have no regard for man; but at any rate, since this
widow is pestering me, I will see that justice is done her. I
am afraid she may finally come and beat me black and
blue!"'" Lk. 18:1–5).

Christ employs this parable to encourage all to persevere
in prayer. It is clear from the parable that the timid, the
easily discouraged, and the weak of heart must change if
they expect to gain the object of their petitions. If one desires
a special grace, he should be willing and ready to appeal to
God with all his strength and determination, always, of
course, with the understanding that his request be granted
in accordance with God's will. Christ assures His children,
"the kingdom of heaven is to be taken by storm, and only
by storm do men lay hold of it" (Mt. 11:12, 13).

> *"Refer all things principally to Me, therefore,
> for it is I who have given them all"*
> *(Imit.,* Bk. 3, C. 9).

> *"From the day when John the Baptist appeared, down to this day, the kingdom of heaven is to be taken by storm — and only by storm do men lay hold of it"* (Mt. 11:12, 13).

This scriptural quotation lays before man the fact that he must make a great effort to achieve salvation. Christ has told man that if anyone would come after Him, he must *take up* his cross and follow Him. Each one has *his own cross to carry*. "To *carry*" — not to drag after him, nor *push* before him, nor to inveigle someone else into carrying for him! And in *carrying* it, he will suffer hardship, disappointment, discouragement, and perhaps even ridicule. But he must force himself; he must conquer himself; always with confidence in God's grace; "Come to me, all you who are weary and over-burdened, and I will refresh you" (Mt. 11:28–29).

The ambitious man seeking success in worldly affairs wears himself out physically striving to accomplish his end. He thinks nothing of laboring long hours, sacrificing his social life, even the company of his family and friends, acquiring ulcers, enduring rebuffs, suffering humiliations; all to gain fleeting honors. Should the sincere seeker after eternal salvation be less zealous than he? In order to gain the great reward of heaven, everyone should be willing and ready to spend himself for Christ. "My elect shall not labor in vain, nor bring forth in trouble; for they are the seed of the blessed of the Lord, and their posterity with them" (Isa. 65:23).

> *"The passions wage war, do you wage war with them; they attack, do you attack; they assault, do you assault; see to this one thing, that they do not conquer"* (St. Augustine).

"He that walketh sincerely, walketh confidently"
(Prov. 10:9).

Sincerity is a quality that is lacking in many and yet it is the mark of the true gentleman as well as the honest Christian.

The origin of the word carries with it a lesson.

In ancient times, there was to be an exhibit of the greatest sculptors in Rome. One of the artists, particularly, labored long and hard on what was to be his masterpiece. He succeeded in producing the greatest creation of his career. He was overjoyed at the comments of his fellow artists.

In transporting the statue to the exhibition hall, a minute piece of marble was unfortunately chipped from the nose. Horrified at this accident, the artist decided to remedy the fault by placing a bit of wax in the crevice. He was about to receive the first prize when one of the judges discovered the subterfuge.

After that, all contestants in such exhibits were warned to portray their subjects *"sine cera"*: two Latin words, meaning "without wax" or "sincerely."

Sincerity is a virtue admired by all. He who sincerely strives to follow the teachings of Christ will be richly rewarded. "A perverse heart is abominable to the Lord: and his will is in them that walk sincerely" (Prov. 11:20).

"We should cultivate virtue itself, not the appearance of virtue" (Lactantius).

"The Lord is good to all, to all his creatures merciful. The Lord is near to all who call on him . . . sincerely" (Ps. 144:9, 18).

A priest on duty in a large city parish received a call from the local hospital that a patient was dying and had called for a priest.

The priest answered the call promptly. He was assisting temporarily in the parish, and not being familiar with the layout of the hospital, he asked the nurse at the desk where the patient's room was.

The supervisor was definite in her instructions; the sick person was in the second room on the right, straight down the hall. After the priest had administered the Last Sacraments to the grateful patient, the young lady who had but a short time to live asked him, "Who called you, Father?"

"Why," he responded, "you did."

"No, *I* didn't," she replied. "I have been praying to see a priest for days but I lacked the necessary courage to call one."

Mystified, the priest returned to the desk and asked the supervisor if she had directed him to the right room.

Very apologetically she said, "O Father, I made a mistake. I should have told you the room was on the *left-hand* side of the corridor." The supervisor had not made a mistake. She was simply an unwitting instrument in the hands of God. The prayers of the dying patient were answered. "O blest be God, who did not spurn my prayer, nor turned away from me his tenderness" (Ps. 65:20).

"If God did not love sinners, He would not come down from Heaven to earth" (St. Augustine).

*"Love the Lord, your God with your whole
heart, and with your whole soul, and with your
whole mind"* (Mt. 22:37).

"Neither snow nor rain nor heat nor gloom of night stays
these couriers from the swift completion of their appointed
rounds." This quotation expresses the spirit of the mail carrier
whose cheery greeting brings much joy to all.

The mail carrier is welcome because he is the instrument
through whom dear ones are kept informed of each other's
activities: their health, their sorrows, and their joys.

It is a matter of experience that friendships have been
retained for years through correspondence. As long as the
interested parties keep in contact with one another, the friendship thrives; but as soon as the correspondence weakens, and
finally stops, friendship dies.

This condition is also true in the spiritual relationship
between man and God. As long as man keeps in contact
with his heavenly Father through prayer, the Sacraments,
and the Mass, he is a friend of God; but when he deliberately
shuts off the relationship between himself and his Creator
by failing in his obligations toward Him, he suffers the loss
of the friendship of his dearest Friend. However, God does
not desert him, but persistently seeks to win back his love, and
with extreme patience eagerly awaits his return. All former
friends of Christ should hasten to renew their friendship.

The mail carrier, by the faithful "completion of his
appointed rounds," sets a good example for the Christian
in his obligations toward Christ. "My eye will search the
land for honest souls, that they may dwell with me: and only
men above reproach shall be my servants" (Ps. 100:6).

*"The measure of our love for God is to love
Him without measure"* (St. Bernard).

> *"And just as we have borne the likeness of the*
> *man of dust, so shall we bear the likeness of the*
> *Heavenly One"* (1 Cor. 15:49).

The seesaw has served to while away the golden hours of childhood for most everyone. This method of entertainment for children has its counterpart in practically every land. In order to secure the most pleasure out of this plaything, it is necessary that the players be evenly matched in weight. A chubby youngster on one end of the plank and a frail lad on the other spoils the fun — the seesaw is thrown off balance.

Man is composed of a body and a soul. In order that he may achieve the end for which he was created, there must be the proper equation between his spiritual and physical self. That individual who concentrates upon catering solely to the flesh and ignores the needs of the spirit is off balance.

History is replete with stories of so-called brilliant men who completely ignored God, their Creator and Last End, and turned the world into confusion. Not being properly balanced themselves, they permitted their pride, lust, selfishness, and atheism to upset the world, caused their own downfall and, unfortunately, the physical suffering and spiritual ruin of countless others. The old maxim "A healthy mind in a healthy body" may also be rendered, "A healthy *soul* in a healthy body." It should be the watchword of all the children of God. "May God Himself, the Author of peace make you perfect in holiness. May every part of your being, spirit, soul and body be preserved blameless for the day when our Lord Jesus Christ shall come" (1 Thess. 5:23, 24).

> *" . . . consolations and spiritual joy . . . exceed all*
> *earthly delights and pleasures of the body"*
> (*Imit.*, Bk. 2, C. 10).

" 'Capital!' he [the noble] said, 'You are a first-rate official. You have been faithful in managing a very small amount; Therefore you shall have the governorship over ten cities!' " (Lk. 19:17).

How frequently do the insignificant things of life exercise a tremendous influence upon man's well-being. Very few people ever consider the important role that paper plays in modern civilization. This essential element in our modern-day life is so plentiful that most people just take it for granted. Yet, there was no paper in Europe until the twelfth century. It was only after the invention of papermaking machinery in the early nineteenth century that this very important product became an everyday necessity.

Someone has said that the pen is mightier than the sword; but it is well to remember that without paper the pen would be powerless! But the plentiful supply of paper causes many today to look with disdain on this most important product. Yet men and machines have labored unceasingly to transfer from far places the mighty trees of the forest, to guide the logs down deep and treacherous rivers, to carry them over snow packed trails to the mighty mills, where millions of dollars are invested. Countless minds have labored to devise these machines which eventually produce that bit of paper.

The book the reader is even now perusing is made possible through the ingenuity of man and the goodness of God. God gave the trees; man's intelligence worked out the method of using them. Do not despise little things; everything is important in the sight of God. "See how great a forest is set ablaze by a very small fire" (James 3:5).

" . . . the peaceful man, being good himself, turns all things to good" (Imit., Bk. 2, C. 3).

*"The Lord is true in all his words; and holy
in all his deeds"* (Ps. 144:13).

St. Augustine describes graphically the occasion of his conversion to Christianity. "So was I speaking and weeping in the most bitter contrition of my heart, when, lo! I heard from a neighboring house a voice, as of boy or girl, I know not, chanting, and oft repeating, 'Take up and read; Take up and read' . . . so checking the torrent of my tears, I arose: interpreting it to be no other than a command from God to open the book, and read the first chapter I should find. . . . I seized, opened, and in silence read that section on which my eyes first fell: 'Let us walk becomingly as in the day, not in revelry and drunkenness, not in debauchery and wantonness, not in strife and jealousy. But put on the Lord Jesus Christ, and as for the flesh, take no thought for its lusts.' . . . No further would I read; nor needed I: for instantly at the end of this sentence, by a light as it were of serenity infused into my heart, all the darkness of doubt vanished away" (*Confessions*, Eighth Book).

In his hour of mental turmoil, Augustine turned to the inspired Word of God Himself. He took up the New Testament and found in its sacred message the very words which, through the grace of God, changed him from a debased sinner into a stanch champion of Christ and His Church.

The true seeker after serenity of soul, spiritual satisfaction, and, above all, sanctity finds the path to all these by following the Word of God. "Your precepts make me wise; hence I abhor whatever is iniquitous" (Ps. 118:104).

*"Teach me, Lord, to do Your Will. Teach me to
live worthily and humbly in Your sight . . ."*
                                        (*Imit.*, Bk. 3, C. 3)

"Thanks be to God for his unutterable gift"
(2 Cor. 9:15).

"Poems are made by fools like me, but only God can make a tree." Joyce Kilmer's beautiful sonnet on trees charms the hearts of all nature lovers.

A tree is a wonderful example of God's handiwork. The majesty and stateliness of the elm, the maple, and the oak delight the eye. In summertime the shade cast by the leafy boughs refreshes hot and weary humanity. Its wood builds homes to shelter a good share of mankind and gives warmth to countless millions. From the tree come fruits without number, sugar, and medicines. It furnishes the fibers that make paper and clothes. The forest holds back the snow and rain to protect the land from floods. The ever gracious apple tree in the back yard willingly holds the ropes which swing the children into a fairyland that only they can enter.

The tree, however, and all the other inanimate and animate creatures less than man, exist in this world for one purpose only — to minister to the needs and delights of man.

God has given into the hands of men the mastery of His lesser creatures. These things, however, must be wisely used, and never abused. The wanton destruction of His material gifts or the cruel and inhuman treatment of His animate creatures will bring down a penalty upon the offender. All men should express daily to God their thanks for His multitudinous gifts and should use these benefactions for the greater glory of God, and as a means toward their own sanctification. "All those who fear the Lord trust in the Lord; their helper and their shield is he" (Ps. 113:11).

> *"All things come from You; therefore, You are to be praised in all"* (*Imit.*, Bk. 3, C. 22).

"None but a good gift, none but a perfect dona-
tion comes from above. It comes down from the
Creator of the heavenly luminaries. With him
there is no shadow or variation . . ." (James 1:17).

During World War II, one phase of the conflict was paramount — control of the air. So successful had the Nazis been
in this form of warfare that they took many opposing nations
within a few days. Before the ground invasion, the enemy
demolished all strategic elements from the air and left the
country defenseless.

The Battle of Britain in which the Royal Air Force defeated
the Luftwaffe was the turning point of the war. For once
the Nazis realized they could not control the air over England,
they knew that their hope of invading the British Isles was
doomed.

It is man's relationship with God that protects him from
evil. As long as man's thoughts are intimately linked with
God, he has no fear of being overcome by earthly enemies.

Before Satan can overcome the soul, he must first win
control of the mind. He must sever the spiritual relationship
which binds man to God before he can invade man's heart.
Prayer is the golden chain that keeps the soul in contact with
God. As long as each one keeps that chain intact, he has
"control of the air" as it were, and can safely repel any
invader. "Hear, Lord, my cry! List to my prayer!" (Ps. 60:2.)

"Love tends upward; it will not be held down
by anything low" (*Imit.*, Bk. 3, C. 5).

*"A pilgrim am I here on earth: do not conceal
from me what you demand"* (Ps. 118:19).

When Christopher Columbus started out on his momentous
journey, his heart and the hearts of the crew were filled with
high hopes, yet mingled with fear, at the prospects of traveling an uncharted course over a dark, unknown sea.

In this hour, Columbus turned to the Mother of God for
protection and guidance and placed himself and his crew
under her banner. Each evening as the sun dropped from
sight behind the limitless waters, and the dark night settled
down, these dauntless sailors chanted the beautiful hymn,
"Salve Regina."

How wise Columbus and his crew were in placing their
confidence in the Mother of God, history testifies. All travelers through this vale of tears should recite this prayer to
Mary every day:

*Hail, Holy Queen, Mother of Mercy, our life, our sweet-
ness, and our hope. To Thee do we cry, poor banished
children of Eve. To Thee do we send up our sighs, mourn-
ing and weeping in this valley of tears. Turn, then, most
gracious advocate, thine eyes of mercy toward us. And after
this, our exile, show unto us the blessed fruit of Thy
womb, Jesus. O clement, O loving, O sweet Virgin Mary.*

Pray for us, O Holy Mother of God.

That we may be made worthy of the promises of Christ.

*" . . . it is a divine prerogative to help men and
free them from all distress"* (Imit., Bk. 2, C. 2).

" . . . the people . . . bask, Lord, in your beam-
ing smile. Your name is their unbroken happi-
ness" (Ps. 88:16, 17).

No traveler has ever seen the International Date Line for
the simple reason that it is imaginary. For the sake of solving
a problem, it has been declared that a line approximately 180
degrees longitude west of Greenwich shall be the point
where the difference between sun time and Greenwich time
is rectified. Thus, the westbound voyager adds an extra day
and the eastbound mariner subtracts a day in computing his
time schedule. While, in reality, the sailor is not deprived of a
day's existence, his diary would show no record of the missing
twenty-four hours.

Looking back on his voyage, the tourist can quickly
account for this missing day by recalling his passage across
this invisible line in the mid-Pacific.

How many people there are, however, who would be hard
put to explain away the "missing days" in their own lives!
For those days or months or years in which man fails to
honor his God and to gain some grace for himself are indeed
wasted. "For my days are vanished like smoke: and my
bones are grown dry like fuel for the fire" (Ps. 101:4).

The faithful Christian is determined not to have any "missing days" in his life; not to let pass a single day without
praising God; and by his charitable labors for Christ's sake
to strive tirelessly to win heaven. "Teach us to number o'er
our days, so that we may attain to wisdom of the heart"
(Ps. 89:12).

" . . . he who has true and perfect charity seeks
self in nothing, but searches all things for the
glory of God" (Imit., Bk. 1, C. 15).

" . . . and I, once I have been lifted up from the earth, will draw all men to myself" (Jn. 12:32).

Emperor Constantine was the first of the Roman rulers to permit Christianity to be practiced publicly. In the year 312, he was attacked by Maxentius. His enemy, with vastly superior forces, threatened the very existence of Constantine's empire.

In this crisis, he thought of the crucified Christian God whom his mother, Helena, worshiped, and, kneeling down, prayed God to reveal Himself and to give him victory.

Suddenly, at noonday, a cross of fire was seen by the Army in the calm and cloudless sky and, beneath it, the words, *"In hoc signo vinces"* — "Through this Sign thou shalt conquer." Inspired by this vision from heaven, Constantine obtained a complete victory over his enemy. "Whereas the message that the cross proclaims is nonsense to those who are on the road to destruction, to us who are on the road to salvation, it is the power of God" (1 Cor. 1:18, 19).

> *"There is no vice for which we do not find a remedy in meditating on the passion of Christ. His body, torn by scourges is a remedy against impurity; His great poverty, against avarice; His meekness, against anger; His spirit of forgiveness, against revenge. In a word 'This medicine, given to man is so great that nothing greater can be thought of'"* (St. Augustine).

> *"Here is my resting place forevermore; here will
> I dwell, for I have chosen it"* (Ps. 131:14).

A young G.I. returned from the Pacific area with the determination to enter the Trappist Community, the strictest order in the Catholic Church. A friend of his tried to dissuade him from such a drastic step.

"I have made up my mind," said the ex-soldier. "This is not a hasty decision. I gave this matter a lot of thought in the foxholes of those fever-infested jungles where we were afraid to fall asleep lest the enemy slit our throats.

"I figured out if I could give four years of my life in those awful places for my country, I surely can make a few sacrifices for my God."

St. Helena thought it the glory of her life to find the cross of Christ and to raise a temple at the site of the Crucifixion in thanksgiving. To those happy souls who find their vocation in following Christ, the temple they rear to His honor is most acceptable to Him — the temple of themselves. "O Lord, I love the house in which you dwell, the place in which your glory is enshrined" (Ps. 25:8).

*"Truly beyond the power of words is the sweet-
ness of contemplation You give to those who love
You"* (Imit., Bk. 3, C. 10).

*" 'Rabbi, is there something good that I can do
so as to earn eternal life?'
" ' . . . If you want to enter eternal life keep the
commandments' "* (Mt. 19:16, 18).

It is interesting to look down from a tall building at a
busy intersection and watch the automobiles controlled by
the traffic lights. Cars rush from all directions. Obedient to
the red lights, they stop. A few seconds later the green light
beckons them on. As long as the traffic obeys the silent signals
all goes well; but, if even one car disregards the lights, there
is an immediate jam, if not a serious accident. Time is lost,
tempers boil, frequently the ambulance dashes up to remove
the injured.

God's laws may be considered the traffic lights on man's
journey through life.

If man obeys the Ten Commandments, he brings down
upon himself God's blessings; he avoids untold trouble for
himself and others; he fulfills his obligations toward God
and man. "I crave salvation at your hands, O Lord; your
law is my delight" (Ps. 118:174).

> *"Your works are exceedingly good, Your judg-
> ments true, and Your providence rules the whole
> universe"* (Imit., Bk 3, C. 21).

> *"Like a good soldier of Christ Jesus, join the ranks of those who bear hardship"* (2 Tim. 2:3, 4).

The ostrich is a most unusual bird. It is claimed that the ostrich will eat anything: wood, iron, stones, and all those things which a more discerning animal would hesitate to devour. The reason advanced for these unorthodox eating habits of this extraordinary creature is that the ostrich has no sense of taste or smell. Without these senses that all other birds and animals possess, it is understandable why this inhabitant of Africa is unable to distinguish between a choice tidbit and an indigestible rock.

Man's experimental knowledge comes to him through his five senses of sight, hearing, smell, taste, and touch. God has given to His intellectual creatures these gifts in order that His children may use them wisely and well. All men should pray daily to God for guidance and direction in the proper employment of their senses. The Book of Wisdom writes of wisdom, "For she is an infinite treasure to men: which they that use, become the friends of God, being commended for the gift of discipline" (7:14).

The ostrich eats contrary to other beings because it is incapable of doing otherwise. The man, however, who debases his God-given senses for whatever purpose, is held accountable to God for his evil acts. "Now they who live under the control of their lower instincts set their minds on the carnal, but they who live under the control of spiritual ideals set their minds on the spiritual" (Rom. 8:5, 6).

> *"Behold, all things are Yours, even those which I have and by which I serve You"*
>
> **(Imit., Bk. 3, C. 10).**

"Where pride is, there also shall be reproach: but
where humility is, there also is wisdom"
(Prov. 11:2).

An old priest tells this story about himself, when he was
young, to prove that "Pride goes before a fall."

A mission was being given in St. Mary's Church. The older
priest was experienced in the ways of God and the world.
His sermons were solid, unemotional, and salted with the
years of experience.

The younger missionary was determined to set the world
on fire. He was bursting with enthusiasm. Down deep in
his heart he thought the seasoned missionary had lost his
zeal — he did not quite understand people.

This particular evening the young priest was outside the
church, dressed in his mission cape, running over in his
mind the exact sermon he thought the people needed.

An old lady came along and asked him if he would assist
her up the many steps to the church door. She was very
heavy and the evening was unusually warm. Father was glad
when they reached the top.

"Oh, by the way, Father," the parishioner said, "which missionary is preachin' tonight?"

"Why, I am," answered the young missionary, proudly.

"Pardon me, Father," said the good soul, "but would you
mind helping me down again?" "The Lord guards simple
souls: I was in misery, and he delivered me" (Ps. 114:6).

> *"God became humble; man should blush to be*
> *proud"* (St. Augustine).

"When man fails God still avails" (Lk. 18:27).

The weasel is not a pleasant animal to have around. The vicious little carnivore is a near relative of the rat. Its speed, strength, and pugnaciousness classify it as a great fighter. Even its appearance is repugnant.

In the warm weather, the weasel is hairless, but as the cold weather comes on, a beautiful coat of white fur covers his nakedness. This fur is called ermine. Thus from one of the most vicious and repugnant of animals come the gorgeous trimmings that grace the robes of royalty. Nature's law has decreed that one of the lowliest of creatures should furnish the garments of kings.

The Author of the natural law is even more generous in the supernatural law. Through His grace, the basest sinner can be transformed into the greatest saint. Grace is a free gift of God that He sends where He wills. The robber, a vicious criminal, hanging on the cross beside the dying Christ, asked for mercy. Christ promised him a place in His eternal Kingdom!

"This gift surpasses all others; namely, that God should call man son, and man should call God, Father" (St. Leo).

"The steps of man are guided by the Lord"
(Prov. 20:24).

A blacksmith shop was a place of great curiosity to a child. To watch the sparks fly from the sputtering horseshoe as the mighty smith brought down his hammer on the resounding anvil was a never ending delight. The purpose of this labor was quite evident to all the children who gathered about their hero. The horseshoes had to be tempered in the roaring fire in order that they might be properly molded to fit the feet of the laboring horses.

Even a child knew that the smith had a purpose in his action. He tempered the horseshoe in the fire to *form* it, not just to watch it burn.

Is God less considerate of us than the blacksmith is of a horseshoe?

God has a purpose in mind in permitting or sending trials and sufferings to His children. Not infrequently, it happens that the creature becomes quite independent of the Creator. He feels that he is sufficient unto himself. Then God steps in and by some reminder brings the proud man to a realization that he has not here a "lasting city" (Hebr. 13:14). By humbly accepting these sufferings from the hand of God, the soul is molded into a likeness of Christ. "For I myself will show him how much he must suffer for my name" (Acts 9:16).

> *"You were always mercifully severe, sprinkling my illicit pleasures with the most bitter vexations"*
> (St. Augustine).

"The good men shall possess the land, and shall forever dwell upon its soil" (Ps. 36:29).

"Happiness is not geographical," contended the young man in a friendly argument regarding the relative merits of change. This assertion is strictly American.

For the most part, Europeans remain settled on the same farm, in the same village, and in the same cities for generations. They dislike surrendering those familiar and well-established places for the uncertain and doubtful fortunes which lie far afield.

Even in this country, the great majority of people desire to sink their roots deeply into that spot where they were born, reared, and spent the happiest years of their lives.

When circumstances of one nature or another induce him to change his abode, the traveler leaves some part of his heart behind him. "Trust in the Lord; do what is good: long will you live on earth, lapped in security!" (Ps. 36:3.)

This longing for stability is natural to man for his ultimate goal is eternal life with God. The young couple striving to save enough money to buy a home for themselves and their children is expressing man's innate longing for a firm and stable sanctuary, safe and secure from the vexations of change. Man's soul is drawn toward God as steel to the magnet. In His Kingdom, at last, the soul shall find eternal rest and security. "O well for those who dwell within your house, O Lord, unceasing is their praise of you" (Ps. 83:5).

"Your life is our way, and in Your holy patience we come nearer to You, Who are our crown"
                    (Imit., Bk. 3, C. 18).

"Let everyone heed what he has heard"
                    (Mt. 11:15).

The intercontinental telephone system has devised a clever method to insure privacy. The message that is hurled across thousands of miles of open water by radio cannot be understood by anyone except the intended receiver. The conversation leaving the radiophone station is "scrambled." Instead of being sent in the regular order, the words are mixed up by an ingenious machine. When the message reaches its proper destination, another device unscrambles the words and the listener hears clearly and distinctly the voice of the caller.

Should the receiving set become defective, the message would be meaningless to the auditor.

Christ, after His resurrection, admonished His Apostles, "Go into the whole world and preach the gospel to all creation. He that believes and is baptized will be saved; he that does not believe will be condemned" (Mk. 16:15, 16).

The sweet tidings of the Gospel as preached by the Apostles and the Church ring out clear and strong. Frequently, however, there are defects in the hearer. He will not believe. The allurements of the world, the seductions of the flesh, the deceits of the devil — all these evils combine to distort the hearts and minds of those who should welcome the loving and salutary message of Christ. The sincere seeker after eternal happiness must strive to eradicate from his soul all these vices which interefere with the proper reception of the Gospel of Jesus Christ. "My mother and my brothers are they who hear God's word and live up to it" (Lk. 8:21).

> *"I will hear what the Lord God will speak in me"* (*Imit.*, Bk 3, C. 1).

> *"I am the good shepherd; and I know mine and mine know me"* (Jn. 10:14).

When St. Paul was preaching in Athens, he stood up in the midst of the people in the city square and declared, "Men of Athens, I see that in every respect you are remarkably religious. For as I was going about and observing objects of your worship, I found an altar with this inscription: 'To the Unknown God.' What, therefore, you worship unknowingly, I make known to you" (Acts 17:22, 23).

St. Paul then proceeded to render a discourse on the true God to these wary people.

How many today worship an unknown God — some intangible, distant, vague, impersonal Thing that they neither understand nor love? They are unwilling to take time to ask for divine guidance and to seek out the teachings of Christ. If they did, they would find the True God of whom St. Paul writes so zealously, "For in him we live and move and have our being, as indeed some of your own poets have said, 'For we are also his offspring'" (Acts 17:28).

"Invincible ignorance will not be imputed to you as a fault; but ignorance ceases to be invincible and will be imputed as a fault, when you can acquire the necessary knowledge and neglect to do so" (St. Augustine).

*"The eye serves your person as a lamp; so long,
then, as your eye is sound, your whole person will
have light"* (Mt. 6:22–23).

Man's soul has been compared to a camera in that it
retains the picture placed there by the eye. This figure holds
true particularly in the case of temptation against the holy
virtue of purity.

The eyelids are the camera's shutters. When the shutter
is opened upon an indelicate scene, the image (temptation)
of the picture reflects itself on the film (the soul). In this
moment of temptation, the victim can do one of two things.
He can take that image into the darkroom, and there develop
the picture and succumb to the temptation; or he can immediately open the camera and eradicate the objectionable
picture by exposing the film to the sunlight of God's grace.
St. John declares, "The light shines in darkness, and the
darkness did not lay hold of it" (1 Jn. 1:5, 6).

In the latter case, man has triumphed over temptation, he
has strengthened his will; he has retained the priceless friendship of Christ. "Blessed are the singlehearted, for they will
see God" (Mt. 5:8).

> *"When any impure thought disturbs me, I fly to
> the wounds of Christ"* (St. Augustine).

*"I say: O Lord, have mercy on me; I sinned
against you: heal me, then"* (Ps. 40:5).

"Doctor of Motors" is a slogan used frequently for advertising purposes by the automobile mechanic. The ability of these ingenious workmen to diagnose and correct car trouble is amazing. Many of these men have spent months of labor and study in the manufacturing plants learning how a modern automobile motor is made. The garage mechanic is able to restore the motor to perfect condition because the automobile is made by man.

The medical doctor, however, deals with an entirely different situation. It is his duty to diagnose and to cure the diseases of the human body. He must exercise his skill, learning, and perception, not in behalf of a man-made article, but for the benefit of a person created by God and endowed with an immortal soul.

The physician cannot reproduce the worn-out organs of the body. At times he finds it difficult if not impossible to readjust the delicate functions of nature. The soul of man, which has such an important relationship to the health of the individual, is not subject to his science. Man is the marvelous creation of God Himself.

It is true that man is obliged to take advantage of the helps of medical science to aid his ailing body, but above all else he has the obligation of pleading with the Divine Physician to safeguard his soul. In finding peace of soul with God, all men can do much to keep their bodies, the temples of the Holy Ghost, in health. "Are you not aware that your bodies are members of Christ's body?" (1 Cor. 6:15.)

*"The flesh will murmur against you but it will be
bridled by fervor of spirit"* (Imit., Bk. 3, C. 12).

*"Young men and maidens too, old men, and little
boys also. Let them praise the name of the Lord"*
(Ps. 148:12, 13).

Baby shoes! What happy memories these little symbols of
babyhood bring to loving parents! So anxious are many devoted fathers and mothers to retain the pleasant recollections
of their children's first years that they have their babies'
shoes cast in bronze.

It is indeed a loving and thoughtful act to have the little
ones' first footwear molded into imperishable metal. Far
more important than casting the baby's shoes in bronze,
however, is the fashioning by the fond parents of those little
feet so that they will follow in the footsteps of God. "The
just that walketh in his simplicity, shall leave behind him
blessed children" (Prov. 20:7).

From example first, and then by teaching, the small child
quickly absorbs knowledge. It is most important in their
formative years, that the little ones are so instructed in the
ways of God that they will not deviate from His path in
later life.

Childhood is short; manhood is long. It is these few brief
years, when the child is completely dependent on father and
mother, that will decide to a great extent which road the
adult will follow, away from God or toward God. "But Jesus
called for the infants and said, 'Let the little children come
to me, and do not stop them. The kingdom of heaven belongs to such as these'" (Lk. 18:16, 17).

*"My Child, I must be your supreme and last
end, if you truly desire to be blessed"*
(Imit., Bk. 3, C. 9).

> " . . . *each individual's work will be made mani-*
> *fest. The day will make it known because fire*
> *will lay it bare . . . "* (1 Cor. 3:12).

Some men seem to believe that religion is for women only. While members of the so-called weaker sex always have taken an enviable place in devoting themselves to God, men must understand that they too have souls to be saved.

No one can read the lives of the saints and truthfully say that religion is solely a feminine pursuit. To overcome oneself is the greatest of all conflicts. To conquer the flesh and "to bring it into subjection" (1 Cor. 9:27) as St. Paul writes, takes great strength. To stand with God, when the world turns from Him is not a task for the weak. To kneel down for one's beliefs, no less than to stand up for them, is not the work of the fainthearted. To believe in God, and to practice that belief today, calls for grace and courage.

Listen to the great Apostle and ask yourself if you think Paul was weak-kneed. "Three times I was scourged, once I was stoned, three times I suffered shipwreck; a night and a day I was adrift on the high sea; in frequent journeys on foot, in perils from floods, in perils from robbers, in perils from my own nation, in perils from the Gentiles, in perils in the city, in perils in the wilderness, in perils on the sea, in perils from false brothers; in fatigue and hardship, in many sleepless nights, in hunger and thirst, in fastings, often in cold and nakedness" (2 Cor. 11:25–28). Be a man: be a follower of Christ!

"If the sun, and moon, and stars serve God, why
do I not serve Him? The heavens serve Him and
the earth does not serve Him, and unhappy man
does not serve Him!" (St. Jerome.)

*"After all, it is the mission of the Son of Man to
seek and to save what is lost"* (Lk. 19:10).

PERSONAL

JOHN — WHEREVER YOU ARE, GET IN TOUCH WITH
ME. YOUR MOTHER IS HEARTBROKEN. ALL IS FORGIVEN.
COME HOME AT ONCE. YOUR LOVING FATHER.

Not infrequently, such a classified advertisement appears in
the daily newspaper. The reader can well imagine the sorrow
and tragedy behind this appeal.

May not this entreaty, however, be directed to countless
souls who have left their Father's house and shut themselves
off from contact with Him through serious sin? The Blessed
Virgin, Mother of men, is sad indeed at this separation from
her beloved children. The sinners' Father in heaven laments
the loss of these souls as Christ did those who turned from
Him when He walked the pleasant hillside country around
Jerusalem. Gazing over the beautiful city from a neighboring
hilltop, Christ wept, "How often have I been willing to
gather your children, as a mother bird gathers her brood
under her wings! But you refused it!" (Mt. 23:37.)

Let the sinner return to his Father's house, as the Prodigal
Son did of old, and free himself of the awful burden of sin.
His joy in being reunited to his Father and his Mother,
Mary, will surpass his greatest expectations! And there will
be great rejoicing in heaven at his return. "Keep yourselves
in the love of God, while you await the mercy of our Lord
Jesus Christ, which will bring you to eternal life" (Jude 21).

> *"The mercy of God is so great that it cannot be
> explained in any words, understood by any
> created intelligence, or conceived by any mind. It
> is above human reason"* (St. Chrysostom).

> *"But the things that were an advantage to me,
> these for the sake of Christ I have counted loss"*
> (Phil. 3:7, 8).

"You can't take it with you" is a slogan that has been repeated so often, and frequently so lightly, that few realize the depth of meaning that is hidden in these few words. Man comes into this world without any material personal effects and he is to depart in the same manner. The material goods that he may acquire here are to be used for a definite end, namely, to the honor and glory of God and for the salvation of his own soul.

If the possessor of wealth uses that which has been lent to him by a beneficent God, wisely and well, he can gain tremendous "interest" in the kingdom of heaven. Scripture says, "lay up treasures for yourselves in heaven, where neither moth devours nor rust consumes, nor thieves break in and steal" (Mt. 6:20, 21).

The prudent and charitable soul who understands thoroughly the nature of this loan *"can* take it with him." After all, there is only a difference in quantity between the owner of wealth and the possessor of little. Each has the same obligation of using whatever he has received for the same end. "Has not God turned to nonsense the 'wisdom' of this world?" (1 Cor. 1:20.) The truly wise man follows Christ's admonition, " . . . let your first consideration be of God and what he requires of you; then you will have all these things thrown in for good measure" (Mt. 6:33, 34).

> *"I have given all things. I will that all be returned
> to me again, and I exact most strictly a return of
> thanks"* (Imit., Bk. 3, C. 9).

*"I tell you the plain truth, inasmuch as you did
this to one of these least brethren of mine, you
did it to me"* (Mt. 25:40).

The two small brothers were alive with anticipation at
the prospects of caddying. Their family had moved near
the country golf club and the boys immediately sought "employment." Their chance came one day after all the regular
caddies had "gone out." Grasping the golf bags of their
employers, they started out happily on this momentous safari.

It was soon quite evident to the employers that their employees were novices. The young lads knew nothing about
caddying — and their willingness to learn only added to the
confusion.

The anger of one of the men, noted for his irascibility, was
immediately and vocally apparent. However, the other player
was a *gentleman*. He interceded for the confused boys; he
surreptitiously pointed out the proper procedure; he en-
couraged them; he stanchly refused to "send them in" — a
degradation that, no doubt, would have prevented the caddies
from enjoying the long, happy, glorious years that followed
on the links. After many, many years, the kindness, consideration, and thoughtfulness of that man still holds a special
place in the hearts of those two enthusiastic, bewildered novices. "A good man is remembered forevermore" (Ps. 111:6).

God has said, "Love, therefore, is the complete fulfillment of
the Law" (Rom. 13:10). Those who love Christ and their
fellow men will offend neither. " . . . he that showeth mercy
to the poor, shall be blessed" (Prov. 14:21).

> *"Each man is a neighbor to every other man;
> long descent must not be thought of where
> nature is common"* (St. Augustine).

"When you so sin against your brothers, and wound their weak conscience, it is against Christ that you sin" (1 Cor. 8:12, 13).

It is believed by some military officers that if the Germans had developed their "buzz bombs" sooner, the invasion of Europe by the Allies would have been indefinitely postponed.

The so-called "buzz bombs" were highly destructive missiles, hurled into the sky from the Continent in the general direction of England. Since it was impossible to direct their flight, no one knew where they would land. The very uncertainty of their coming was terrifying in itself, while the damage to life and property was tremendous. There was little defense against these projectiles that crashed down from the sky scattering death and destruction over the land. The only warning they gave was a buzzing sound, hence the name.

The courageous people who endured the nerve-racking experience can testify to the material damage wrought by these fiendish bombs.

But there is no one, except God, who can tell the spiritual damage done by those who give flight to the "buzz bombs" of scandal and harmful gossip. There is evident to the observer much similarity in origin, in silent striking power, and in destruction between these two diabolical weapons. But the "buzz bombs" of scandal and evil gossip are far the more dangerous because they destroy man's souls. All should be on their guard lest they be tempted to use their tongues as a launching field for such diabolical implements of spiritual ruin. "He that keepeth his mouth and his tongue keepeth his soul from distress" (Prov. 21:23).

"The devils look for instruments through which to do their work" (Origen).

"So too, it is not the will of your Father in heaven
that even one of these little ones should be lost"
(Mt. 18:14).

"Take care that you do not despise any one of these little ones: I tell you, their angels in heaven look continually upon the face of my Father in heaven; besides, it is the mission of the Son of Man to save what is lost. What do you think? When a man has a hundred sheep and one of them strays, will he not leave the ninety-nine on the hillside and go in search of the straggler? And when he succeeds in finding it, he is better pleased with it, I assure you, than with the ninety-nine that have not gone astray! So, too it is not the will of your Father in heaven that even one of these little ones should be lost" (Mt. 18:10–14).

In this lovely Gospel parable, Christ points out the value of the immortal soul. The soul of man is priceless. Christ, true God and true Man, suffered agonizing death on the cross for the souls of men. He does not want to lose even one. His abundant grace is offered to each and all. It is an unfortunate soul, indeed, who refuses His grace. "The Lord does not delay fulfilling his promise, as some estimate delay, but he is long-suffering toward you, not wishing a single soul to perish but that every last one should have a change of heart and mind" (2 Pet. 3:9).

> *"This gift exceeds all others; namely, that God*
> *should call man son, and man should call God,*
> *Father"* (St. Leo).

"If your sins be as scarlet, they shall be made as white as snow" (Isa. 1:18).

No sinner should be discouraged, for the Psalmist has told man, "The Lord is sweet to all: and his tender mercies are over all his works" (Ps. 144:9). From Scripture man has every evidence of God's love for those who fall victim to the wiles of the flesh, the world, and the devil. He simply asks that the sinner tell his sins to His representative, His priest, sincerely repent, and resolve with the help of His grace, to remain in His friendship. Christ hates sin, but He loves sinners.

The crude oil that is pumped up from the deep, dark wells of the earth is anything but beautiful as it gushes forth and stains everything it touches; yet, it contains in itself the most brilliant of colors. The refining processes turn this seemingly repugnant substance into colors so beautiful that they beggar description. If science can perform this miracle, cannot God, the Father of science, change a sinner into a saint? "Be cheered and stout of heart, all you that hope in the Lord" (Ps. 30:25).

"Our God, who is good and merciful, wishes us to confess our sins in this world so that we may not be confounded by them in the next"

(St. Augustine).

GOOD FRIDAY

"He was led like a sheep to slaughter . . . "
(Acts 8:32).

First Word: "Father, forgive them; they do not know what they are doing" (Lk. 23:34).

"Take from our hearts, O Lord, all suspicion . . . wrath and contention, and whatever may injure charity" (*Imit.,* Bk. 4, C. 9).

Second Word: "Indeed I assure you, this very day you will be with me in paradise" (Lk. 23:43).

"Even though He give punishments and scourges . . . He acts for our welfare" (*Imit.,* Bk. 2, C. 10).

Third Word: "Mother, this is your son." He then said to the disciple, "This is your Mother" (Jn. 19:27).

"I bless you, O heavenly Father, Father of my Lord Jesus Christ, for having condescended to remember me a poor creature" (*Imit.,* Bk. 3, C. 5).

Fourth Word: "My God, my God, why do you abandon me?" (Mk. 15:34).

"I became . . . the lowest of all men that you might overcome your pride with My humility" (*Imit.,* Bk. 3, C. 13).

Fifth Word: "I am thirsty" (Jn. 19:28).

"There is nothing I can give more pleasing than to offer my heart completely to my God" (*Imit.,* Bk. 4, C. 13).

Sixth Word: "It is now completed" (Jn. 19:30).

"This is my one desire, that my heart may be united with you" (*Imit.,* Bk. 4, C. 13).

Seventh Word: "Father, into your hands I commend my spirit" (Lk. 23:46).

"Oh, when shall I be with You in that Kingdom . . . which You have prepared . . . from all eternity?" (*Imit.,* Bk. 3. C. 48.)

> *"I am the good shepherd. A good shepherd lays down his life to save his sheep"* (Jn. 10:11).

The love of the Church for her children is exemplified in her daily life. A devoted pastor was called to an apartment hotel to give the Last Sacraments to a dying parishioner. When he hurriedly reached the hotel, the manager told him the sick man lived on the seventh floor and the elevator was broken.

"I'll take the stairs," the priest replied. "You can't do that, Father, you know your heart is bad. The climb will kill you," urged the manager. "I will take the stairs," the priest said simply.

He gave the last rites of the Church to the dying man. A week later, the good pastor died of a heart attack in the arms of a fellow priest.

Sometimes non-Catholics find it difficult to understand the Catholic's love for his priests. It is acts similar to this one that are performed day after day by the clergy that endear them to the laity. The faithful know that in their hour of need, their priests will not fail them. "No one can give a greater proof of his love than laying down his life for his friends" (Jn. 15:13, 14).

"The priest is constituted a mediator between God and man, God on one side, man on the other; he is less than God, but greater than man"
(Innocent III).

THE GOSPEL (MK. 16:1–7)

"When the Sabbath had passed, Mary Magdalen, Mary the mother of James, and Salome bought spices in order to go and anoint him. At a very early hour in the morning the first day of the week, they set out for the tomb and arrived at sunrise. Now they had been saying to one another, 'Who will roll away for us the slab of stone at the entrance of the tomb?' when, straining their eyes, they saw that the stone had already been rolled away. It certainly was very large.

"On entering the tomb, they saw a young man seated at the right dressed in a white robe; and they were frightened. But he said to them: 'Do not be frightened. You are looking for Jesus the Nazarene, the Crucified. He is risen; he is not here. Look, here is the place where they laid him to rest. Go now, and say to his disciples, in particular to Peter: "He is going to Galilee to await you there; there you are going to see him, just as he has told you."'"

> *"If you carry the cross willingly, it will carry and lead you to the desired goal, where indeed there shall be no more suffering . . ."*
>
> (*Imit.*, Bk. 2, C. 12).

"Who among men knows the inner thoughts of a man save the man's spirit within him?"

(1 Cor. 2:11.)

The word "pacific" means peaceful, calm. When Balboa, the great Spanish explorer, named the Pacific Ocean, he did so because of its peaceful appearance.

The surface of the sea shimmering in the brilliant sunlight presented a picture of deep serenity. It never occurred to this intrepid traveler that in the depths of these limitless waters, there existed a panorama of mighty mountain peaks, winding rivers, and sprawling canyons. Oceanographers have discovered that off the Philippine Islands the depth of the sea is 35,000 feet; that in various parts of the bowels of the Pacific Ocean, mountains rise to ten and twelve thousand feet. The casual sailor would never suspect these myriad contortions of nature below the placid surface of the Pacific Ocean.

If it be difficult to penetrate into the depths of inanimate things, it is next to impossible to delve deeply into the individual soul, for as Scripture declares, "There are many thoughts in the heart of a man" (Prov. 19:21).

Therefore, it behooves all men to treat their fellow men with respect, with consideration, and with Christian charity lest they misjudge another's exterior complacency, and discover too late, that an unkind word has deeply wounded an already sorrowful heart. ". . . would not our God have searched this out? He knows the secrets of the heart" (Ps. 43:22).

"If your heart were right, then every created thing would be a mirror of life for you and a book of holy teaching" (Imit., Bk. 2, C. 4).

*"Our help is in the name of the Lord, the maker
of heaven and earth"* (Ps. 123:8).

Most men do not wish to commit sin. They wish to be
pure of heart, enjoy a good reputation, and be friends of God.
Yet in the desire to satisfy the cravings of the flesh, to improve
their financial position, to gain honor and power, or for
some other personal reason, they act against God and their
own conscience — they sin.

Judas was a good friend of Christ. No doubt, in his own
way, he loved Christ, yet he set his heart on some objective
that could only be obtained by getting the thirty pieces of
silver he received for betraying his Lord. He loved Christ
but he loved himself more, and that is sin.

Satan is the father of liars and there is no truth in him.
By his higher intellect, he, Lucifer, can persuade man, if
man listens to him, that he, man, will be rich or powerful
or happy if he goes against God. The tempter paints a glowing picture to the tempted. Why not? It does not cost him
anything. He sometimes confuses the most learned, the most
faithful. Eve's complaint still may be heard, "The serpent
deceived me" (Gen. 3:13). Scripture advises: "Be as wise
as the serpent," yes, and remember that truthful statement:
"And he that loveth danger shall perish in it" (Ecclus. 3:27).
"Be prudent, then, like serpents, yet, for all that, as innocent
as doves" (Mt. 10:16).

> *"We have need of great vigilance, since we are
> engaged in an unceasing war to which there is
> no truce"* (St. Chrysostom).

> *"Silver and gold I have none; but what I have,*
> *that I give you"* (Acts 3:6).

One day a Little Sister of the Poor was engaged in caring for an old man in one of their houses. The man's leg had become gangrenous and the odor was sickening. The Little Sister, with a smiling face, performed her task of dressing the putrid leg with a gentleness that evoked a comment from a visiting benefactress.

"Sister," the lady said, "I wouldn't do that for a million dollars."

The good Sister, continuing her work of mercy, simply said, "Neither would I."

Countless souls, inside and outside religious houses, are dedicating their life's work to God. They are happy and content in the knowledge that their work is pleasing and profitable in the sight of their heavenly Father. They seek no other remuneration but the eternal reward that He has promised to the faithful. Their labors should be an inspiring example to all. "Trust in the Lord; do what is good; long will you live on earth, lapped in security!" (Ps. 36:3).

"The measure of our love for God is to love Him
without measure" (St. Bernard).

"Now we know that God causes all things to work together for the good of those who love him" (Rom. 8:28).

In the early history of the American colonies, before the government had protected the coastline with lighthouses, a most diabolical practice was followed by unprincipled and lawless men.

During the height of a terrific storm, when a sailing vessel, buffeted by wind, rain, and high seas, and confused by the darkness of the night, was desperately seeking shelter, human scavangers, armed with high-powered lanterns, would lure the helpless craft on to the rocks. Disdainful of the loss of innocent lives and the destruction of the ship, these heartless wretches would salvage the cargo cast upon the shore, and then sell it to the highest bidder.

As man travels through life, Satan and his followers will seek every means at their disposal to lure him to eternal destruction. As long as man keeps his eyes on the Lighthouse of God's love, shining out through the darkness of discouragement, disappointment, and even serious sin, he will be guided out of the earthly storm into the peaceful harbor of eternal life. "The Lord is my salvation and my light; whom shall I fear?" (Ps. 26:1.)

> *"Nothing seems hard, no labor difficult, to those who love God; let us also love God and all will seem easy"* (St. Gregory).

"Whoever are led by the Spirit of God, they are the sons of God" (Rom. 8:14).

A handy man called Tommy used to help about the house where there were several young boys. As boys will, they were accustomed to use the household tools carelessly.

One day, Tommy asked one of the lads to get him the ax so that he might cut down some scrub timber. The boys, after much searching, finally succeeded in locating the desired implement that had performed many services for which it was never intended.

Tommy gazed at the timber to be cut and at the axhead. He surveyed the numerous nicks in the cutting edge with a critical eye, then quietly observed, "You know, boys, if this ax didn't have a long handle, I'd think it was a saw."

Everything in life has a definite purpose. If an instrument intended for one purpose is employed for another end, the instrument is abused.

God created man for eternal life. If man uses all his God-given faculties toward an earthly end, eliminating God from his thoughts, on the final day of reckoning, God will hardly recognize him as worthy of His eternal Kingdom. All should remember that, whether they "eat or drink, or do anything else," they should do everything for God's glory (1 Cor. 10:31).

"When the smallest matters are carefully attended to, the power of discipline continues; but when the least excesses are neglected, discipline becomes gradually relaxed" (St. Ambrose).

"No trifle, in the Lord's own reckoning, is the
death of his saints!" (Ps. 115:6).

In the Martyrology of the Church, the book that records
the lives and deaths of the martyrs, the feast day of these
saints is celebrated, not on the anniversary of their birth,
but of their death.

God intends death to be beautiful.

Behold nature. The fall, when the swan song of dying
nature goes forth, is the most picturesque time of the year.
The foliage surpasses all the beauty of the spring and summer. The wild life sports its loveliest plumage and furs.
The whole countryside bursts into myriad color. In its dying
hour, nature is at its loveliest.

The faithful soul is always ready to meet his Master. In
whatever manner God may decide to call His children
home, those who "have fought the good fight" (2 Tim. 4:7)
go forth with the knowledge that their departure from this
life is but a happy step into His loving presence. Everyone
should strive every day to prepare for that most important
and certain hour. "How lovely is your dwelling place, O
Lord of hosts! My spirit pines — for the courts of the Lord
it faints with yearning" (Ps. 83:2, 3).

> *"We should not dread that which frees us from*
> *every cause of fear"* (Tertullian).

*"Anyone who loves me will treasure my message,
and my Father will love him, and we shall visit
him and make our home with him"* (Jn. 14:23).

Last year, approximately 10,000 laws were passed in this
country. This large number of edicts made in one year gives
some idea of the number of man-made laws on the statute
books.

God gave His people *only* Ten Commandments. In these
few commands are contained all the precepts that man must
follow in order to gain his eternal destiny — heaven. " ' . . . If
you want to enter eternal life, keep the commandments' "
(Mt. 19:18).

To ensure the enforcement of man-made laws, countless
federal officers, state troopers, city police, county sheriffs,
town constables, and other officials are needed. The only
check on God's law is man's conscience. To assist man in
doing His will, God offers him all the necessary grace. The
Divine Judge is patient, kind, merciful. He judges not His
children's external acts, but their motives — their intentions.

But there will come a day when God's justice will replace
His mercy. Then the unrepentant offender must be punished. "The Lord, therefore, knows how to rescue the God-
fearing from trial and keep the Godless for the Day of
Judgment, chastising them in the meantime, but especially
those who live lustful lives . . . and who despise authority"
(2 Pet. 2:9, 10). The faithful friend of God and the sincere
seeker after eternal glory with Him will be most observing in
fulfilling His commandments. "Hear, my people, what I
teach; incline your ears to the words I speak" (Ps. 77:1).

*"My Child . . . Be resigned to My will, and you
will suffer no loss"* (Imit., Bk. 3, C. 27).

*"Let me tell you that if even we ourselves or an
angel from heaven should proclaim to you a
gospel other than we have proclaimed, let him
be accursed!"* (Gal. 1:8.)

Solomon, one of the wisest of men, was called upon to
settle a most perplexing problem. Each of two women claimed
a baby as her own. Solomon was forced to exercise his greatest
wisdom in awarding the babe to its rightful mother.

After much deep thought, Solomon called the women
before him and made known his decision. He would sever
the baby's body in two equal parts and give each woman half.

One of the women readily agreed to his decision; the other
cried out that she would surrender her right to the child
that the baby might live. To this woman, Solomon awarded
the custody of the child, for as he wisely decreed she was the
true mother who would not permit her offspring to be
divided and consequently die.

Those who divide the teachings of Christ find themselves
in the position of the pseudo mother. The true Church
clings to the whole truth with a tenacity that defies division.
"For of his mercy toward us he has given fresh and mighty
proofs: the Lord's fidelity endures eternally" (Ps. 116:2).

> *"He who will not have the Church as his mother,
> cannot have God as his Father"* (St. Cyprian).

> *" . . . if they had known it, they would never have crucified the Lord to whom belongs all glory"* (1 Cor. 2:8).

Shortly after the turn of the century, a young lady in the Far West decided to take an excursion to New York City. Such a trip was most popular in those days.

She arrayed herself in the latest finery and felt quite confident that her attire was the "last word" in style. Accompanied by her aunt, she started on the momentous journey. After viewing the sights in the Big City, the tourists decided to call on relatives in Brooklyn. There they were graciously received by their kinfolks.

During the course of their conversation, a young girl in the family, after surreptitiously surveying the Western visitors, suddenly turned to her mother and exclaimed, to the embarrassment but also relief of the travelers, "Why, Mother, they look just like us!"

Distance not infrequently causes people to look upon "foreigners" as being quite different from themselves, yet once they come into contact with each other, they find that they are basically alike. Someone has said, "No one can dislike a person he really knows." The so-called enemies of Christ would cease to be His enemies if they made a sincere effort to know Him. "He guides the humble by his just demands, and to the humble shows his ways" (Ps. 24:9).

> *"Love of our neighbor is produced by our love of God, and our love of God is strengthened by love of our neighbors"* (St. Gregory).

" . . . offer up to God a sacrifice of praise"
                              (Ps. 49:14).

There is a famous medieval painting called "Our Lady's Juggler." The artist has depicted a young monk, in the privacy of his cell, performing a juggling act before a picture of the Blessed Virgin Mary.

The legend connected with this painting explains that the illiterate monk, unable to imitate his more gifted brothers in their ability to write beautiful poems, liturgical hymns, and inspiring books to the honor of Mary, determined to offer her that which he could do best. Having been a successful juggler before entering the religious life, the humble Brother, far from the applauding crowds, executed his cleverest feats before the picture of God's mother as his greatest tribute of love.

The moral of the legend is evident. Few have the capacity to write, paint, or carve masterpieces; but each, in his own way, has something to offer to those whom he loves. To others the tribute may seem insignificant, but to the one receiving it, the present, no matter how trifling it may be, is most acceptable and pleasing.

The Creator wants the creature's love. This is the most beautiful gift that His children can give to Him. A single act of sincere love for God may win eternity. "How, then, shall I requite the Lord for all that he has granted me?" (Ps. 115:3.)

> *"The wise lover regards not so much the gift of Him Who loves as the love of Him Who gives"*
> *(Imit.,* Bk. 3, C. 6).

> *"Let us, therefore, confidently draw near to God's throne, the source of grace, that we may obtain mercy and find grace to aid us when we need it"*
> (Hebr. 4:16).

All owners of material things are anxious to protect their possessions once they have managed to acquire them. The bank, the office, the mill have vaults or safes where their wealth is secured behind steel and concrete. Their purpose is, naturally enough, to preserve these desirable objects for themselves.

The combinations that open these strongboxes are secretly kept by the interested parties. Whatever they possess is theirs; it has been gathered together only after arduous labors, sleepless nights, and the acquisition of a few ulcers. They do not intend to share their wealth indiscriminately.

How differently God acts! The Golden Treasury of infinite grace acquired through the agonizing death of His Son upon the cross is opened to all! Christ invites everyone to share in this spiritual wealth. Not unlike the bankers' vaults, however, this storehouse of merit also has a combination. But it is not a secret system of numbers and letters. The combination to God's treasury, spelled with only four letters — L-O-V-E — is simple and known to all; the unlettered as well as the most brilliant can quickly learn it. The combination — love of God and love of neighbor. "Anyone who loves me will treasure my message, and my Father will love him, and we shall visit him and make our home with him" (Jn. 14:23).

"A brief commandment is given to you: Love, and do what you will" (St. Augustine).

"Well done, my good and faithful servant . . . you
were faithful in managing something small; I
will now put you in charge of something great:
share to the full your master's happiness"
(Mt. 25:21).

In ancient times, when "knighthood was in flower," there
was a slogan among the nobility that served to inspire the
members to many brave and selfless acts. "Be loyal to the
royal that is in you" was their watchword.

The sincere Christian is a true subject of the King of
Kings. He is even more than that. He is a member "of the
household of the faith" (Gal. 6:10).

Therefore, let each one be loyal to the royal that is in him,
loyal to Christ and His Mystical Body, the Church.

Loyalty is a virtue admired by all; disloyalty brings only
criticism and grief. When Judas, remorseful, returned the
money to those who had bought Christ's betrayal, he be-
moaned, "It was wrong for me to betray innocent blood";
they responded, "What does that matter to us? . . . that is
your worry!" (Mt. 27:4.)

Peter, too, denied Christ. His denial was not premeditated,
however, but prompted by fear. But his loyalty to his Master
was too deep to be shaken by human frailty. Peter repented
his failure in loyalty, and Christ gave to him the greatest trust
given to man. Christ made Peter the cornerstone of His
Church. "My eyes will search the land for honest souls; that
they may dwell with me; and only men above reproach shall
be my servants" (Ps. 100:6).

"He loves Thee less who shares his love between
Thee and something which he does not love for
thy sake" (St. Augustine).

*"Always be grateful. Such sentiments God
wills you to have in Christ Jesus"* (1 Thess. 5:18).

Mrs. Smith was a professional complainer. Just nothing
could be done for her that merited her approval. Despite
her constant dissatisfaction with life, her relatives, and her
friends, faithful Mrs. Green, her next-door neighbor, was
loyal to her. Each day Mrs. Green dropped over to visit Mrs.
Smith and to bring some delicacy that she had cooked that
day.

Finally, it dawned on Mrs. Smith that her devoted visitor
was deserving of some praise for her kindness. Yet, she could
not go against her principles entirely, but decided to lay the
accolade of honor upon the worthy shoulders of her friend
as generously as her nature would permit.

She startled her good neighbor on her next visit with a
prepared speech; "Mrs. Green, you have been very good to
me. When everyone else ignores me, you remain steadfast,
bringing me this and bringing me that; cheering me up
when I'm 'down in the boots,' and taking good care of me.
You know, Mrs. Green," declared Mrs. Smith, as though
laying a wreath upon the statue of a mighty hero, "I sometimes think you must be a *fallen angel!"*

Praise is the least expensive gift. Many hearts would be
much happier if everyone were more generous with it. "But
I will loudly hymn the Lord, and praise him in the midst
of throngs" (Ps. 108:30).

*"All works are virtuous when they are directed
to that end, which is Christ"* (St. Augustine).

*"And in doing good let us not be discouraged,
because in due time we shall reap if we do not
become careless"* (Gal. 6:10).

There are two types of sin: those of commission and those
of omission. Many people never give a thought to the latter,
although, in some cases, sins of omission are more serious
than those actually committed.

Some individuals take a negative attitude toward God.
They convince themselves that if they do not act contrary to
God's will, they are doing all that is expected of them. But
Christ taught differently from this belief.

Not to do wrong will keep a man out of jail, but will not
necessarily get him into heaven. "In the same way good
deeds are manifest, and those that are not good cannot remain
hidden" (1 Tim. 5:25).

Not infrequently, even the faithful bemoan the omission
of good deeds that should have been done but were passed
over. These good souls should not waste their time in regret,
but instead should labor to amend the omission by present
good works, physical or spiritual. St. James admonishes all,
"Is any one of you in trouble? He should pray" (James 5:13).

"My tears ran down, and it was well with me"
(St. Augustine).

". . . there is no discrimination. All have sinned and lack the approval of God" (Rom. 3:22, 23).

The young American missionary had been in China only a few months. About to start out on his first trip into the interior, he went out to the pasture to saddle the Community's horse. As soon as he drew near to the animal, it shied away from him and ran to the other end of the field. Twice more the priest attempted to quiet the horse and failed.

An elderly Chinese, who had been watching this scene, approached and graciously offered to saddle the horse for the missionary. He accomplished the task with ease.

The young priest, quite mystified, asked the Chinese why the animal was so docile to the native and so untractable to the American. After much prodding, the gentlemanly native gave the explanation. "Father," he said with great delicacy, "the white man has an odor that is most repugnant to anything Chinese."

Frequently the white man is prone to criticize those not of his own race. This lesson taught the missionary, as it should all people, that there is no superiority of color.

All peoples are created to the image and likeness of God. Each person possesses an immortal soul that he must strive to save with the help of God's grace. The Creator makes no distinction regarding the color of His children. The faithful child of God must follow the example of his heavenly Father. "Love does no evil to a neighbor. Love, therefore, is the complete fulfillment of the Law" (Rom. 13:10).

" . . . for in whatever a man seeks himself there he falls from love" (*Imit.*, Bk. 3, C. 5).

"I tell you, there is joy in heaven over one repentant sinner" (Lk. 15:7).

" . . . suppose a woman has ten drachmas and loses one: does she not light a lamp and sweep the house and search carefully till she finds it? And when she has found it, she calls her friends and neighbors together and says, 'Congratulate me, for I have found the drachma that I had lost.' For the same reason I tell you, there is joy among the angels of God over one repentant sinner" (Lk. 15:8–10).

God loves all souls. He loves the sinner while he hates the sin. Regardless of how far from Him the offender has wandered, God's love goes out to him. Neither sin nor shame nor degradation nor even depravity can hide the soul, made to the image and likeness of God, from its Creator. St. Augustine, who traveled the path leading farthest away from Christ, could not escape His love. The love of the Crucified Christ followed him everywhere even as it does each sinner today. And when that sinner returns to his Father's house, great indeed is the rejoicing: "In my distress I called upon the Lord: and to My God I cried, and in his shrine he heard my voice; and my cries came to his ears" (Ps. 17:7).

> *"Therefore, whether we pray to God in words when necessary, or in silence, we must cry out in our hearts"* (St. Augustine).

> *"The shadow of your wings is my retreat until disaster passes by"* (Ps. 56:2).

Two operations were being performed in the comparatively small hospital. In one operating room was a patient who had been preparing for this necessary surgical work for months. His heart was weak and his general condition poor, but to save his life the surgeon knew he had to undergo this operation. Every precaution was taken. All necessary emergency equipment had been moved into the white-tiled room.

In the adjoining section, a man had been brought in with an infected toe that needed lancing. The extremely ill patient sailed through the ordeal in a most satisfactory manner, but during the course of his operation, all the emergency equipment had to be rushed in to the next room to save the man with the sore toe. This patient reacted badly to the anesthesia and almost died.

Many things in life cause much worry, and unnecessarily so. Fear of this and fear of that troubles men's souls. The future, over which he has no control, oftentimes appears forboding. Past injuries upset him. Let man put his trust in God. Let him leave the past and the future in the hands of his heavenly Father. Let him take care of today with faith in God, and He will take care of tomorrow. Let him recall the words of the aged man on his deathbed, "I've had a hard and difficult life, with many cares and worries, but most of them never happened." Then say to the Lord: "My protector and my citadel: my God, in whom I trust" (Ps. 90:2).

"My child, always commit your cause to Me. I will dispose of it rightly in good time. Await My ordering of it and it will be to your advantage" (Imit., Bk. 3, C. 39).

*"Hear, O my son, and receive my words, that
years of life may be multiplied to thee"*
(Prov. 4:10).

The *Lost and Found* column advertised, "Lost, inexpensive
ring. Sentimental value only. Substantial reward to finder."
Behind this advertisement, no doubt, there was an appealing
story of great love. The lost ring, valueless in itself, symbol-
ized some priceless event, association, or friendship in the
life of the owner.

Almost everyone has cached away somewhere a few trinkets
that mean much to him alone — a few strands of baby's hair;
a bit of handwriting from a departed dear one; a frayed and
yellowed letter from one's first love; or an unfinished piece
of woodwork, the masterpiece of Johnny's handiwork in the
first grade at school. These items are dear to the possessor
because of their pleasant associations and happy memories.

And deep down in the hearts of everyone, regardless of his
violent denial or his rugged exterior, is a love for God. Only
the fool denies the existence of a Supreme Being. This
submerged love for God and the things of God should not
be permitted to lie hidden away like the trinkets gathering
dust in some forgotten bureau drawer, but should be allowed
to rise to the surface. Neither pride nor lust nor love of material things should be permitted to cover over and weigh down
this natural and supernatural desire for the friendship of God.
The hesitant soul should follow the admonition of Scripture:
"Just so let your light shine before your fellow men, that
they may see your good example and praise your Father who
is in heaven" (Mt. 5:16).

*"Every hope that depends on time is uncertain,
because time itself is uncertain"* (St. Augustine).

"God is my strong one, in him I will trust: my shield, and the horn of my salvation. He lifteth me up, and is my refuge: my saviour, thou wilt deliver me from iniquity" (2 Kings 22:3).

The story is told of a man who started a bank in a small boom town. He put up a sign over a tiny shack telling all and sundry he would accept deposits. Within a short time he had over $200,000 of other people's money on hand. The amateur banker was so encouraged by the confidence that other people had put in him, that he decided to deposit some of *his own* money. This is supposed to be a humorous story, but it contains much human philosophy.

When one realizes he has the confidence of others, he immediately perks up. Confidence begets confidence. Subordinates accomplish greater deeds when they realize they have the full trust of their superiors. The same applies to children and their parents; and particularly is this true, when husband and wife place confidence and faith in the judgment of each other. He who places his confidence in those who love him seldom goes wrong. He who puts his confidence in God never errs! "O Lord, my rock, my fortress, my deliverer, my God, the stronghold of my weal, my guard" (Ps. 17:3).

"He truly believes who, by good works, makes his life correspond to his belief" (St. Augustine).

"Consequently, brothers, strive even more to
make your calling and election secure"
(2 Pet. 1:10).

When the colonists landed on this continent, they were
faced with an almost insurmountable task. The first necessity
was to raise sufficient food to enable them to keep body and
soul together. In order to grow crops, however, they had
first to clear the land. The magnificent forests that reached
from the shore line halfway across the continent must be
removed before seeds could be planted. How was such a
tremendous undertaking to be accomplished? The secret lay
in fighting back the wood lots a little at a time.

The first year a small clearing was made. The next year,
a little more tillable land was added. Their day-by-day assault
upon the forest gradually achieved mastery over their worst
enemy, and an abundant supply of food was soon growing
where a short time before the forest held sway.

To a person held down by bad habits, the labor of eradi-
cating these evils from his soul may seem impossible. The
secret of his successful attack upon them lies in his "daily
stint"; that is, his quiet, determined battle against them each
day. In this daily assault against these sins, little or great as
they may be, he has the ever present help of God's grace.
"Where man fails God still avails" (Lk. 18:27). If a handful
of determined men could change the face of a continent with
their daily persistent efforts, the sincere soul, with God's help,
can eradicate any and every obstacle to his salvation. "Now,
who is it that is a victor over the world, if not he that believes
that Jesus is the Son of God?" (1 Jn. 5:5.)

> *"Remember your promise and never let your*
> *vigilance slacken"* (St. Ambrose).

> *"So then, both he who plants and he who waters count for nothing; God who makes the seed grow is what matters"* (1 Cor. 3:7).

In the late fall, several young boys went out into the country in search of apples. On this trip they received their first lesson in what is called "food speculation." Passing an orchard, they noted the trees heavy with the much desired fruit.

After taking counsel with themselves, they decided to ask the farmer to part with some of his enormous crop.

"Well, boys," the kindly farmer replied, "I'd be glad to let you have all the apples you could eat but them apples ain't mine. A city feller came through here last spring and contracted for all the fruit hereabouts. He paid me good for my crop. He ain't been back and I don't think he ever will, but they're his'n and nobody can touch 'em."

Out of His gracious goodness, God gives to His children the fruits of earth, and woe betide those unscrupulous individuals who deliberately defeat His purpose by depriving, for one reason or another, His children of their God-given rights. This principle holds true with all God's gifts. "Many are the things you do, O Lord! With wisdom you accomplish everything! And with your creatures teems the earth" (Ps. 103:24).

"It is not enough to refrain from evil; that which is good must be done; and it is a small thing not to injure anyone, unless you strive to be useful by good works" (St. Augustine).

*" . . . and your young men shall see visions, and
your old men shall dream dreams"* (Acts 2:17).

Who is so carefree as a boy on a bike! The world is at
his command. He is bursting with energy, with adventure,
with friendliness. He is master of every situation. He is
conqueror of worlds that lie hidden from all but himself.
Worries are unknown to him. The path ahead lies straight
and beautiful, bordered with the most gorgeous roses. He is
free! No one has ever felt or known such a life as his. He
will rule the world with love and joyousness and song. He
will bring pleasure and peace and love to all. He will be a
crusader into unknown lands and will bring back home all
the treasures of the world and lay them at the feet of his
mother and father and God. "O God, you schooled me from
my youth, and even now I still proclaim your wondrous
deeds" (Ps. 70:17).

He is free because he knows not sin, nor hate, nor envy,
nor the thousand and one vices that burden the hearts of
men. It would be well for all men to recall the visions of
those days when they were just "a boy on a bike"; to recall
their promises made to God to be a worthy protagonist of
His teachings. "O train me to observe your law, and I will
cherish it with all my heart" (Ps. 118:34).

> *"What is zeal but a certain interior incitement
> of charity, urging us to strive for the salvation
> of our brother"* (St. Bernard).

> *"So my beloved brothers, be steadfast, immovable.
> Devote yourselves fully at all times to the
> Lord's work, realizing that your toil in the
> Lord can never be in vain"* (1 Cor. 15:58).

The dentist had kept his patient coming week after week. Each time his client protested about the delay, the dilatory doctor assured him that he would need just one more "impression" and the work would be completed.

This day, the impatient patient waited an hour in the outer office while the dentist worked and talked with another patient.

Finally, the irritated gentleman was seated in the chair. The dentist, hoping no doubt to impress him with his devoted clientele, said, "You saw that woman leave the office. Well, she's one of my most faithful patients. She's been coming here for treatment since she was a little girl." The recipient of these remarks merely mumbled, "'Same tooth, I presume."

Patience is a virtue that everyone could profitably practice in his own life. People of older countries seemed to have developed this quality to a high degree. In the United States, however, "rush" seems to be the byword. Fast cars, fast trains, fast planes, fast elevators are a "must." This desire to keep going at high speeds permeates the very lifeblood of the people. An old Latin proverb should frequently be called to mind: "Make haste, slowly." "The Lord is kind and merciful, to anger slow, and full of graciousness" (Ps. 144:8).

> *"Let a Christian rejoice in adversity; because he is
> either tried, if a just man, or freed from faults,
> if a sinner"* (St. Augustine).

"Have courage, my son; your sins are now forgiven" (Mt. 9:2).

"So he entered a boat and . . . came to his own town. Here . . . some men were trying to bring before him a paralytic lying on a mat. When Jesus saw their faith, he said to the paralytic, 'Have courage, my son; your sins are now forgiven.' Immediately some of the Scribes said to themselves: 'This man blasphemes.' Jesus read their thoughts, he said, 'Why do you entertain thoughts that are absurd? Really, which is easier, to say, "Your sins are now forgiven," or to say, "Rise and walk"? Now I want you to understand that the Son of Man has power here on earth to forgive sins!' He then addressed the paralytic: 'Rise, take up your mat and return home!' He arose, and went home. As the crowds saw this, a feeling of awe came over them, and they praised God who had given such power to men" (Mt. 9:1–8).

To the afflicted, the cure of physical defects is a tremendous blessing, but still greater than this is the restoration of a sinful soul to the peace and friendship of God.

There is no greater happiness than that experienced by the sinner when he is absolved from his sins. The terrible weight of this unwanted burden is removed from his soul. Where there was darkness before, now there is light; where there was restlessness and discontent, now there is peace; from an enemy of Christ, the penitent has been restored to His love and friendship. No greater grace can be given to man. The sinner should let nothing stand in the way of his obtaining, by the Sacrament of Penance, this great happiness.

"Why are you afraid to confess what you have committed willingly and without hesitation?"

(St. Jerome.)

> *"Do you accept his person, and do you endeavor to judge for God?"* (Job. 13:8.)

A person is seldom satisfied with his own photograph. After all, the camera registers only what is before it. The artistic photographer may use his talents to improve on nature's oversights, but still the subject is not completely appeased. This attitude is quite understandable. The picture is only an inanimate representation of an animate being. That being is composed of a body and a soul and no camera can ever capture the spiritual soul. St. Paul asks: "Who among men knows the inner thoughts of a man save the man's spirit within him?" (1 Cor. 2:11.)

It is "the spirit of the man which is in him" that no photograph can reveal. The subject of the camera is alone aware of this "spirit" and he looks in vain for the revelation of this "something" in his portrait. Not finding it in his picture, he feels that justice has not been done to his personality.

The spirit of a man is known only to himself and God. Thus it is quite evident why it is God's prerogative alone to judge His creatures. The charitable and prudent person never strives to usurp the Creator's prerogative but leaves the judgment of his fellow men to God alone. "When I have set the time, then I will justly judge," says the Lord (Ps. 74:3).

> *" . . . God weighs the love with which a man acts rather than the deed itself"* (Imit., Bk. 1, C. 15).

*"In all thy works remember thy last end, and
thou shalt never sin"* (Ecclus. 7:40).

The good father used to gather his flock together each
night and all would recite evening prayers. As the children
readied themselves for bed, the father regularly reminded
the little ones, "Now, wash your faces and hands well. You
know the angels might come for you during the night and
you wouldn't want them to find you with dirty hands and
faces."

What a wonderful way to remind the little ones that they
must always be prepared to meet their God; not with fear
nor dread, but with joy and happiness, clean of hand and
heart.

The adult does not have to worry so much about the clean-
liness of his body as he does the purity of his soul. As man
grows older and meets the temptations and moral dangers
that present themselves, he must always remember that at any
time he may be required to go into the presence of his
Creator and Judge.

The faithful soul strives with prayer and sacrifice to lead
a good life, but if under the powerful stress of his passions
he falls into sin, he immediately makes amends through the
Sacrament of Penance, in order that he may receive God's
angels clean of hand and heart, with happiness and joy.
". . . I tell you, there is joy among the angels of God over
one repentant sinner" (Lk. 15:10).

> *"Blessed are they who long to give their time to
> God, and who cut themselves off from the
> hindrances of the world"* (Imit., Bk. 3, C. 1).

> *"At once they abandoned their nets, and became his followers"* (Mt. 4:20).

"Walking about by the Sea of Galilee one day, he saw two brothers, Simon, surnamed Peter, and his brother Andrew, flinging a casting net into the sea, for they were fishermen. 'Come, follow me,' he said to them, 'and I will make you fishers of men.' At once they abandoned their nets, and became his followers. Thence he went on and saw another pair of brothers, James, the son of Zebedee, and his brother John. They were in a boat with their father Zebedee, mending their nets, and he called them. Forthwith they abandoned their boat and their father, and followed him" (Mt. 4:18–22).

This account of the selection of His first Apostles by Christ appeals to the hearts of all. The direct way in which Christ spoke to His disciples and the readiness with which they accepted His invitation shows the character of these holy men. Fundamentally, they were devout and holy souls, courageous, honest, honorable, loyal, with all the failings of human nature, yet filled with a spiritual longing for the things of God. When the "call" came they were willing and determined to accept it. Their *remote* preparation had made their souls ready for the greatest of all gifts, personal friendship with Christ. Each one should endeavor to be alert to answer Christ's "come" whenever He calls him. "It is the part of man to prepare the soul: and of the Lord to govern the tongue" (Prov. 16:1).

"The nobler the cause in which we are engaged the greater the attention we should pay to it"
                                    (St. Ambrose).

"One must obey God rather than men"
(Acts 5:29).

Obedience is one of the most difficult virtues to exercise, because it means that man must submit his will and judgment to another. The true Christian must be obedient to God and His earthly representative, the Church. It is only in fulfilling the teachings laid down by God that man can obtain his ultimate end, eternal life with God.

St. Joseph gives a splendid example of complete submission to the will of God.

Scripture relates that an angel appeared in sleep to Joseph and instructed him to leave immediately with the Child and His Mother and flee into Egypt and remain there until he was told to return (cf. Mt. 2:13-15).

St. Joseph promptly followed the admonition of God's angel. He did not question his authority; he did not balk at leaving his home, his relatives, his friends; he did not protest against going into a foreign land. He did what he was told to do and thus saved the life of the Child Jesus from Herod's "slaughter of the innocents." "An obedient man shall speak of victory" (Prov. 21:28).

> *"Observe God's commandments, always obey God's will, expect from God the reward of a good will, guard the faith, avoid fraud, know that God will reward you for all your works"*
> (St. Augustine).

> *"Above all things practice constant love among yourselves; it wins forgiveness for many sins"*
> (1 Pet. 4:8).

The pastor advised the missionary about one of his parishioners who was causing much unpleasantness in his parish by continuous gossiping.

"Father, when you give your sermon on Charity tonight, I should appreciate it very much if you would *stress* the sin and havoc wrought by spreading scandal, true or false."

The missionary made it a point during his discourse to emphasize the wickedness caused by those who go about doing harm by misuse of the tongue.

The pastor was extremely pleased and hoped sincerely that the strong words of the missionary would have the desired effect on his uncharitable parishioner.

As the parish priest was leaving the church that evening, he was hailed by the person in question. She was bubbling over with praise for the grand discourse.

"And you know, Father, that powerful sermon is going to have a very beneficial effect on this parish. I am certainly glad so many of these gossips were present to hear it."

How seldom is it that anyone feels that *he* is at fault? It is always the other fellow. It is well for all to listen and to consider when an effective sermon is given, and ask themselves as the Apostles did of Christ at the Last Supper — "Is it I?" (Mk. 14:20.)

"Consider how much love you have for yourself and have as much for your neighbor"
(St. Augustine).

"But the Lord keeps faith and he will make you steadfast and will guard you from the wicked one" (2 Thess. 3:3).

In the animal world God, who is the Creator of all things, has given to the least of His creatures protection from their enemies.

Every hunter is aware of the marvelous protective coloring that nature gives to wild life so that these animals and birds merge with the surrounding countryside in such a manner that it is almost impossible to detect their presence.

If God is so considerate of the birds of the air and the animals of the field, is not He much more concerned with His spiritual children?

To adapt a phrase, He gives to man the "protective coloring" of His grace which molds man more and more into a resemblance to Himself. But unlike the animal that has no power to plead, man is given the faculty to request this grace from God. In order to protect himself from evil, he should constantly raise his mind and heart to his Father in heaven, requesting the grace of protection from his enemies. "He spread a cloud to shelter them, and gave them fire for light throughout the night" (Ps. 104:39).

"If we shall have obtained the grace of God, no one will prevail over us, but we shall be more powerful than all" (St. Chrysostom).

> *"Do not judge, that so you may not be judged"*
> (Mt. 7:1).

"Do not judge, that so you may not be judged; for the sentence you pass will be passed upon you, and the measure you use in measuring will be used to measure out your share.

"Strange that you should see the splinter in your brother's eye, and do not notice the log in your own! Or, how can you say to your brother, 'Let me take the splinter out of your eye,' when, think of it, there is a log in your own eye! Hypocrite! First take the log out of your own eye, and then you will see clearly enough to take the splinter out of your brother's eye" (Mt. 7:1-5).

How frequently is it said, "Oh, if I did not see such a bad example in so and so, I would be a better person!" It is true that the conduct of others has a great influence on those about them. Yet, each one is going to be judged on his own merits. In the final judgment, he will *only* be asked how well or badly he conducted *himself.* There is an old Latin expression, *"attende tibi,"* which translated freely means, "attend to yourself." A good motto, indeed, to follow for those who look forward to the mercy of God. "But you, why do you condemn your brother? Or, why do you despise your brother? We shall all stand at the judgment seat of God" (Rom. 14:10, 11).

> " . . . *beware of judging the deeds of other men,*
> *for in judging others a man labors vainly, often*
> *makes mistakes, and easily sins . . . "*
> (*Imit.,* Bk. 1, C. 14).

"Blessed are those who have not seen me and yet believe" (Jn. 20:29).

When a babe is born, philosophers say its mind is a *tabula rasa,* a "clean slate." All the knowledge that the baby, and every human, receives comes through their five senses: touch, taste, smell, sight, and hearing. Many people believe the first four of these senses are sufficient. They forget that the fifth, "hearing," is coequal with the others. They accept what they can feel with their hands, see with eyes, taste with their mouths, or smell with their noses. Yet, they hesitate to accept what they hear when the words are based upon the solid truth of the greatest Authority, God Himself.

Unless certain people can touch or see things, they question their truth. Even St. Thomas, doubting that his brother Apostles had seen the Lord, declared: "Unless I see in his hands the print of the nails, and put my finger into the place where the nails were, and lay my hand into his side, I am not going to believe" (Jn. 20:25).

When Christ reappeared eight days later and invited Thomas to do just what he wanted to do, "Thomas answered and said to him, 'My Lord and My God!' Jesus said to him, 'Because you have seen me, is that why you have believed? Blessed are those who have not seen, and yet believe'" (Jn. 20:28-29).

> *"Faith is the source of justice, the principle of sanctity whence all justice takes its beginning"*
> (St. Augustine).

*"And may the Lord direct your hearts to the
love of God and to patient waiting for Christ"*
(2 Thess. 3:5).

Each year in late summer and early autumn, hundreds
of farm barns throughout the land are destroyed by fire.
Those whose business it is to know such details declare that
50 per cent of these fires can be traced to spontaneous combustion in the haymow.

Not a great deal is known about this phenomenon, but
most scientists and chemists agree that spontaneous combustion is produced in a substance by the evolution of heat
through the chemical action of its constituents.

Fires of this kind can result from many materials where
chemical elements are of the proper ratio to ignite.

Spontaneous combustion is not reserved to material things
altogether, either. How frequently are men and women
destroyed by a similar phenomenon. Jealousy, hatred, lust,
envy lie hidden in their souls. There these passions are
secretly nurtured and expanded until such time as conditions
or events are ideal for an explosion.

If combustible materials are exposed frequently to air and
sunlight, the forces which cause the fire are eliminated.

The soul that relieves itself of all underground evils by
exposing them to the sunlight of God's love will avoid a
"spontaneous combustion" that may cause it eternal harm.
"A heart all pure create in me, O God; a spirit new and firm
breathe into me" (Ps. 50:12).

*"God both inspires in us the beginning of a holy
will, and bestows strength and opportunity to
complete what we have properly begun"*
(St. Prosper).

*"And this is the victory that has conquered the
world, our faith"* (1 Jn. 5:4).

Hippocrates, the father of medicine, declares that anger and
fear breed poison in the soul.

Modern medicine is gradually accepting this dictum of the
first physician. Doctors are beginning to realize the great
part that human emotions play in the health of the individual, so much so, that one outstanding medico has asserted
that 90 per cent of the ordinary ills are caused by failure to
control these emotions.

Since man is a spiritual as well as a physical being, this
assertion can be readily believed. The observing doctor has
discovered that the realization, consciously or unconsciously,
on the part of the patient that he is negligent in his duties
toward God becomes a burden that wears a man down.

The faithful and humble servant of God is confident that
God is a loving Father who will watch over him, and those
near and dear to him; and in this faith and confidence, the
faithful follower of Christ, doing God's will, will find peace
of mind, one of the primary conditions for good health.
"Restore to me the joy which your salvation brings; and
by a generous spirit make me strong" (Ps. 50:14).

> *"Nothing is to be desired by anyone so much
> as to enjoy peace of mind, and to control his
> passions"* (St. Gregory).

*"But now, set free from sin and become slaves
of God, you have your reward in sanctification,
which finally leads to life everlasting"*
(Rom. 6:22, 23).

One day, a gentleman was standing in front of a religious-goods store. In the window was a very beautiful reproduction of the Crucifixion. A young boy came along and stopped to gaze at the painting.

"Do you know the story of this picture?" the man asked the lad. "Oh, yes, sir," replied the youth. And he immediately launched into a graphic account of Christ's birth, His life, His sufferings, and finally His death on the cross, "All to save us," concluded the boy.

The gentleman, much impressed with his instructor's eloquence, congratulated him and continued on his way. Soon, he heard the boy call after him. He waited.

The lad rushed up and burst out, "But that isn't the end of the story, Mister; Christ rose again from the dead and ascended into heaven, where He continually watches over us!"

No, Christ's death on the cross was not the end of His story. His victory over death and His ascension into heaven, where He reigns forever, completes His odyssey. Too many people look toward death with fear and trembling, not realizing that death is not the end, but the beginning of life. "If we have died with him, we shall also live with him; if we endure, we shall also reign with him" (2 Tim. 2:11, 12).

*"To each one is given, without any merit on his
part, the help by which he may strive for the
reward; and to each one is given before he labors,
the help that will enable him to receive a reward
according to his labor"* (St. Ambrose).

*"After all, where your treasure is, there, too, your
heart is bound to be"* (Mt. 6:21).

"Five hundred dollars, please!" It is the custom of many
businessmen to go to their respective banks the first of each
year and borrow this or a similar amount of money. During
the following three months, the borrowers make it a point
to pay these loans back at regular specified periods. These
successful merchants have no need of the money at the time
they borrow, but they are laying the foundation for future
loans should some financial emergency arise. In other words,
they are establishing their credit rating with their banks
while they are in good financial condition, in order that
they may be able to obtain future loans should unforeseen
financial reverses make such a request necessary. "For the
children of this world are in relation to their own generation
more prudent than are the children of light" (Lk. 16:8, 9).

The "children of light," the faithful followers of Christ,
should be as prudent in their spiritual life as these successful
men are in their business undertakings. The wise soul strives
to gain merit each day by his good deeds for God and God's
children. He follows the advice of Christ, "but lay up
treasures for yourselves in heaven, where neither moth devours nor rust consumes, nor thieves break in and steal"
(Mt. 6:20).

*"He helps the unwilling man to will; He re-
mains close to the willing man that he may not
will in vain"* (St. Augustine).

> *"Do not let your heart be troubled. You have*
> *faith in God: have faith in me also"* (Jn. 14:1).

Christ constantly admonished His disciples to have faith in Him. He realized that the future with all its disappointments, its fears, and His final humiliation on the cross, would put His disciples to a great test. Thus, He wished them to recall how He had cured the sick, restored sight to the blind, raised Lazarus from the dead, in order that this faith would sustain them in the great hour of the Crucifixion. He also knew that His glorious resurrection would follow the dark hours of Good Friday.

As Jesus prepared to take His departure from His disciples, He told them, "And when I am gone and have prepared a place for you, I will come back and take you home with me. I want you to be where I shall be. The way to where I am going you know, of course" (Jn. 14:3, 4).

Thomas said to Him, "Lord, we do not know where you are going; how do we know the way?" (Jn. 14:5, 6.) And Christ makes answer, "I am the way, and the truth, and the life" (Jn. 14:6). Yes, by following the teaching and example of Christ man will know the way; he will know the truth; and he will obtain eternal life.

Comforted with these words let not your hearts be troubled, but rest serenely in belief in Christ.

"When Christ has spoken, all curious question-
ings must cease; we need not be inquisitive
when we know the Gospel" (Tertullian).

" . . . they must persevere in prayer and not lose heart" (Lk. 18:1).

"Ask, and you will receive; seek, and you will find; knock, and you will gain admission. In fact, only he who asks receives; only he who seeks finds; only he who knocks will gain admission. Really, will anyone among you give a stone to his son that asks him for bread? or a snake, when he asks for a fish? Well, then, if you, bad as you are, choose to give useful gifts to your children, how much more will your Father in heaven give what is good to those that ask him!" (Mt. 7:7–11.)

It is quite evident from this passage of Scripture that Christ wants His children to ask for what they need. It is noted that Christ places no limit on the number of requests. He does, however, demand that the petitioner exercise himself, "Ask!" "Seek!" "Knock!" All these words clearly express the need for effort on the part of those requesting favors. As St. Paul urges, "Like a good soldier of Christ Jesus join the ranks of those who bear hardship" (2 Tim. 2:3, 4).

Those who ask God for gifts should not weaken in their quests but recall that St. Monica, mother of St. Augustine, prayed unceasingly for thirty-three years for her son's conversion before her petition was granted.

> *"Without perseverance he who fights does not obtain the victory, nor does the victor obtain the palm"* (St. Bernard).

"You acted kindly toward your worshiper, O Lord, according to your word" (Ps. 118:65).

The heavily loaded passenger plane approached the airfield. The pilot asked for instructions. The voice from the tower informed him that the field had been suddenly closed in by a heavy fog. The plane must go on to the nearest landing field, 200 miles distant. Here was an unexpected emergency. The heavy plane had already consumed a tremendous amount of fuel. How was it possible for it to go 200 miles more than its scheduled flight? The answer was simple. The authorities had prepared for just such an emergency as this by requiring all passenger planes to carry sufficient gasoline to keep the plane in the air for several hours over and above the scheduled flight time. The law that makes it necessary for planes to carry much more fuel than they would ordinarily need is indeed a wise provision.

The wisdom of this provision may be profitably applied to the spiritual life of man. Faithful souls should strive to lay up for themselves treasures in heaven upon which they will be able to call in time of emergency and great spiritual need. These souls are not content to give God the minimum of their love and devotion, but they strive each day by offering up their joys, their labors, and their tears, to their heavenly Father, to prove worthy of His love and reward. "After all, where your treasure is, there, too, your heart is bound to be" (Mt. 6:21).

"Not to go forward is to fall back" (St. Bernard).

*"The path of the just departeth from evils: he
that keepeth his soul keepeth his way"*
(Prov. 16:17).

The destructiveness of the iceberg lies not in the comparatively small icecap that projects above the water. This inno-
cent-looking fortress drifting quietly down from the Arctic
Circle is a deceitful destroyer whose placid tranquillity belies
the acres and acres of death-dealing ice that lie hidden beneath
the serene surface of the ocean.

The unwary skipper who ignores the danger signals sent
out by the iceberg is doomed. These silent enemies of the
northern shipping lanes, like all enemies of man, both
material and spiritual, by their very nature broadcast their
power for destruction. A sudden drop in temperature accompanied with a peculiar coldness that cuts to the marrow of the
bone warns the captain that his ship is entering the ice fields
and that he must proceed with the utmost caution. To continue at his normal speed and to ignore the warnings is to
court disaster, as history has proved.

The prudent man soon learns that a great many things in
life are not as they appear on the surface. "A fool receiveth
not the words of prudence" (Prov. 18:2).

From the very goodness of his own heart, or from bitter
experience, the spiritual soul detects the danger signs that
warn of approaching evil. To shun those places, persons,
or things which may cause spiritual ruin is the duty of all
men. "Get wisdom, because it is better than gold: and purchase prudence, for it is more precious than silver" (Prov.
16:16).

> *"Be prudent, then. Watch in prayer and in all
> things humble yourself"* (Imit., Bk. 3, C. 24).

> *"If, then, you have risen with Christ, seek the things that are above, where Christ is seated at the right hand of God"* (Col. 3:1).

To a child few things are more pleasant and enjoyable than a ride on a merry-go-round. What can be so attractive to the little ones in this monotonous whirl, just sitting there and going around in circles? The appealing thing to the children about the merry-go-round is the opportunity it offers them to use their imagination. Their eyes see a majestic horse, flying through the wind to the accompaniment of the most beautiful songs. They rise above the garish horses, the tin-panny music, the monotonous circle, and ride in a world of their own making.

Countless people today complain about the monotony of life. The daily routine gets them down. The trip to work, the grind in the office or factory, the same trip home at night, the same meals, the same faces, the same routine tomorrow.

We older people can learn a lesson from the children on the merry-go-round. If we really understood the purpose of life, we would rise above dreary monotony. We would know that we are not laboring only for enough to eat, a place to sleep, and something to wear. We are preparing ourselves for a great and glorious eternity. We are traveling a short road that leads to the eternal presence of God, so vividly described by St. Paul, "What no eye has ever seen, what no ear has ever heard, what no human heart has ever thought of, namely, the great blessings God holds ready for those who love him" (1 Cor. 2:9).

"Never cease to yearn for that which you shall possess forever" (St. Augustine).

*"My son, go and spend today working in my
vineyard"* (Mt. 21:28).

"Now" is a small word but a most important one. "Now"
is defined as "the present time or moment." Life is made
up of three stages: the past, the future, and the present. The
past is over and gone; the future lies ahead. Man possesses
only the present, "now." What great opportunities lie in this
brief moment which God has given man to call his own!

In this day, he can make amends for the past; he can
prepare for the future.

Countless souls spend their God-given hours bemoaning
mistakes, failures, or sins of bygone days. What a waste of
time! Instead of remorse for former indiscretions, the prudent
soul avails himself of the present to compensate for these
failures by actions — good deeds, work, and prayer. St. Paul
had much to regret, yet he declares, "But one thing I do:
forgetting what is past, I strain toward what is ahead. With
my eyes fixed on the goal, I press on to the prize in store for
those who have received from above God's call in Jesus
Christ" (Phil. 3:13, 14). Paul does not handicap himself with
the burdens of the past; he profits by the present to prepare
for the future, as all faithful friends of Christ should do.

"Right now is the acceptable time! Right now is the day
of salvation!" (2 Cor. 6:2, 3.) To use the present wisely and
well is to act according to God's will, and in these daily
duties well done the humble soul will find consolation and
peace.

> *"The present is very precious; these are the days
> of salvation . . . The time will come when you
> will want . . . just one hour to make amends, and
> do you know whether you will obtain it?"*
>
> (*Imit.*, Bk. 1, C. 23).

"It is a wholesome sacrifice to take heed to the Commandments, and to depart from iniquity"
(Ecclus. 35:2).

Last year, the banks in this country paid out to the members of their Christmas Clubs approximately a billion dollars. This enormous sum of money was saved during the year for the primary purpose of buying gifts at Christmas time. For the most part, the depositors put into their accounts only a dollar or two a week. "Substance got in haste shall be diminished: but that which by little and little is gathered with the hand shall increase" (Prov. 13:11).

This billion dollars of savings is striking evidence of what can be accomplished by small sacrifices.

When a member of the club receives his check at a time when he can use the money most satisfactorily, he feels more than rewarded for his past sacrifices. This experience is so pleasant that he is determined to become a member of the Christmas Club each year.

The faithful follower of Christ can learn a practical lesson from this system of monetary recompense. By daily offering up to God some small sacrifice, the devout Christian can gain a tremendous spiritual reward, and will find himself overjoyed on the last day to discover the immeasurable merit that has accrued to his account in heaven. " . . . lay up treasures for yourselves in heaven, where neither moth devours nor rust consumes, nor thieves break in and steal" (Mt. 6:20, 21).

"Fight like a man. Habit is overcome by habit"
(*Imit.*, Bk. 1, C. 21).

*" 'Jesus, remember me when you return in your
royal glory.' 'Indeed,' he replied, 'I assure you,
this very day you will be with me in paradise' "*
                                      (Lk. 23:42, 43).

At Danemora prison in the foothills of the Adirondack
Mountains, there is a beautiful Catholic church that would
be a credit to any community. It is dedicated to "The Good
Thief" who died repentant beside Christ on the cross and
whose prayer is given in the above scriptural text.

This chapel is unique in that it was constructed by the
inmates of the prison themselves. Over a period of four years,
the prisoners performed their labor of love. Countless men
of all faiths, many experts in their various lines, worked in
the heat of summer and the biting cold of winter to rear
this imposing house of God.

Replacing the rebellion in their hearts toward men with
a supernatural love for an understanding God, these forgotten men built for themselves a fitting tabernacle where
dwells in their midst a loving and merciful Judge.

It is impossible for man really to judge his fellow men;
only God understands His children. "For the Lord searcheth
all hearts, and understandeth all the thoughts of minds"
(1 Par. 28:9.)

Thus it behoves men to follow the admonition of Christ,
Himself, "Do not judge, that you may not be judged" (Mt.
7:1). Rather everyone should bow his head before the omnip-
otent God and humbly repeat the prayer of the publican,
"O God, have mercy on me the sinner!" (Lk. 18:13.)

> *"God has placed it in our power to decide how
> we shall be judged"* (St. Augustine).

> *"If your sins be as scarlet, they shall be made as white as snow"* (Isa. 1:18).

"I've lost my keys!" What inconvenience and sense of frustration does the loss of one's keys bring about. The loser is locked out of his home, his car, his office. He has no access to his most important papers and records. His accustomed ways are disrupted. He is uneasy and restless until he recovers his keys or has duplicates made. Once again in possession of them he breathes a sigh of relief for he is now able to follow the old familiar paths with a sense of ease and peace.

When one turns his back on God and sins grievously, he has lost "his keys" to happiness and to peace of soul.

The sinner having deliberately separated himself from the friendship of God seeks in vain for the contentment and peace he once enjoyed. He finds himself locked out of Christ's friendship; "Yes, I acknowledge my iniquity; my sin at all times stares me in the face" (Ps. 50:5).

The humble, sincere soul who has lost the key to God's love will immediately seek forgiveness for his offenses. He will let nothing stand in the way of his prompt return to his Father's house, where the ever loving Christ will welcome him as the Prodigal Son was welcomed by his father. "I tell you, there is joy in heaven over one repentant sinner — more, in fact, than over ninety-nine saints that have no need of repentance" (Lk. 15:7).

"Fire tempers iron, and temptation steels the just"
                                    (*Imit.*, Bk. 1, C. 13).

*"Not everyone that says to me, 'Lord, Lord,' will
enter the kingdom of heaven; but he that does
the will of my Father who is in heaven"*
                                (Mt. 7:21–22).

"Beware of false prophets — people that come to you in
sheep's clothing, but inwardly are ravenous wolves. By their
conduct you can tell them. . . . In the same way, as every
good tree bears healthy fruit, so a sickly tree bears fruit that
is bad. As a good tree cannot bear fruit that is bad, so a sickly
tree cannot bear healthy fruit. Any tree that does not bear
healthy fruit is cut down and thrown into fire. Evidently,
then, by their conduct you can tell them" (Mt. 7:15–20).

Every court judge can recount numerous cases where the
criminal brought before him was there because of bad company. Every associate has an influence for good or evil upon
his companions.

The faithful soul, therefore, ought to be most prudent in
the selection of his friends. The wise man does not judge
another so much by his words as by his actions. If one is a
friend of God, he does the work of God. Recall the oft-
repeated adage that a bad apple will eventually destroy the
whole barrel. The sincere soul seeks the friendship of the
friends of God. "Rescue me, O Lord, from a wicked man;
screen me from a violent one" (Ps. 139:5).

> *"To be associated with the just is profitable both
> for instruction and as a proof of virtue"*
>   (St. Ambrose).

*"Make glad your servant's soul, O Lord, because
to you I lift my soul"* (Ps. 85:4).

The transcontinental plane roared down the long runway
on a dark, gloomy afternoon. Soaring into the heavy overcast
at three miles a minute, the airplane with its several score
passengers was soon riding along in the bright sunshine. The
blanket of clouds that covered the earth was only a few
hundred feet thick. Above this murky veil, the sun as usual
was sending forth its cheerful brightness and warmth.

It is well for all to remember that even on the darkest and
most dismal days, the joyful sun is shining in all its accustomed brilliance just above the somber canopy that over-
shadows them.

Just as an airplane, overcoming the earth's pull, can raise
itself aloft and penetrate the bleak clouds, and there find the
smiling sun, so too man, by prayer and sacrifice, can raise
up his spiritual self, however dark the day, and draw close
to God, the Source of all light and joy and peace.

The faithful child of God should not be disturbed by the
fickleness of the elements or the vicissitudes of life, for
regardless of the trials and troubles that may afflict him, he
knows that his changeless Friend, Christ, is never far away.
"The God who said 'Let light shine from the midst of darkness,' has shone in our hearts, to give enlightenment through
the knowledge of God's glory, glowing in the face of Christ"
(2 Cor. 4:6).

*"Enlighten me, good Jesus, with the brightness of
eternal light, and take away all darkness from the
habitation of my heart"* (Imit., Bk. 3, C. 23).

*"Blessed are those who have not seen me and
yet believe"* (Jn. 20:29).

"Thomas, one of the Twelve, called the Twin, was not
with the group when Jesus came. So the other disciples said
to him, 'We have seen the Lord.' But he replied: 'Unless I
see in his hands the print of the nails, and put my finger into
the place where the nails were, and lay my hand into his
side, I am not going to believe.'

"Eight days later, his disciples were again in the room,
and Thomas was with them. Jesus came, though the doors
were bolted, and, standing before them, said, 'Peace be to
you!' Then he addressed Thomas, 'Let me have your finger;
put it here, and look at my hands. Now let me have your
hand, and lay it into my side. And do not be incredulous, but
believe!' Then Thomas burst out into the words: 'My Lord
and my God!' 'Because you have seen me,' Jesus said to him,
'is that why you believe? Blessed are those who have not
seen me and yet believe'" (Jn. 20:29).

Christ wants man's faith. He wants His children to have
confidence and trust in Him. Nothing delights the human
father more than to have his little ones place their tiny hands
in his with a trustfulness that leaves no doubt as to their
absolute belief that he can do all things. If this joy comes
to a human father's heart from the loving confidence of his
offspring, how much more so does such faith shown by His
creatures delight the Divine Heart of the Creator. "And
whosoever believes in him shall not be disappointed" (Rom.
9:33).

> *"It is difficult for him who really believes, to
> lead a bad life"* (St. Augustine).

"Thou shalt not have strange gods before me"
(Exod. 20:3).

The beautiful masterpiece stood in a prominent place in a museum. It was a painting of Christ holding a magnificently designed chalice in His upraised hands. The artist had lavished his greatest talents on depicting a beautiful goblet so that the eyes of all admirers were immediately attracted to the consecrated cup. The painter's work was a failure. The main feature of the artist's painting had become, not the figure of the Sacrificing Christ, but rather the vessel of Sacrifice.

How often does it happen that men and women miss the point in God's teaching and adore the creature instead of the Creator! They worship, not God, but the things of God. They pay homage at the altar of brotherhood, ignoring the essential element of Fatherhood. God wants the love of His children. His command is clear, "My son, give me thy heart; and let thy eyes keep my ways" (Prov. 23:26).

"The measure of our love of God is to love Him without measure" (St. Bernard).

"What if ten should be found there? And he said: I will not destroy it for the sake of ten"
(Gen. 18:32).

Some people discount the necessity of leading a sincere spiritual life, either for themselves or others. "What's the use?" they complain. "There is too much evilness in the world. What could I do to help?"

The important part played by those devoted to God can be better understood from the biblical account of the destruction of the city of Sodom (cf. Gen. 18 and 19).

Sodom was a beautiful city but the inhabitants were extremely wicked and God determined to wipe the evil town off the face of the earth. Abraham pleaded with God to spare the city. Abraham asked Him if he were able to find fifty just men in the city, would He relent. God agreed.

Apparently fearing he had put the number too high, Abraham then suggested 45, 40, 30, 20, and, finally, 10. And God agreed, "I will not destroy the city for the sake of ten."

The city was actually destroyed, for apparently Abraham could not find the required number. But the fact that God would have spared it for the sake of just ten good men shows the tremendous influence good people have with God.

It is quite evident, then, how much one devoted soul can do for the welfare of others. The prayers, penance, and sacrifices of devoted souls are most acceptable in the sight of God and have on countless occasions served to withhold His avenging hand. The faithful soul realizes his importance and the importance of his good deeds in God's sight.

"The prayer of the just man is the key to Heaven; prayer ascends and the mercy of God descends"
(St. Augustine).

"The woman that feareth the Lord, she shall be praised" (Prov. 31:30).

Tears of joy glistened in the eyes of the lady as she read the Mother's Day greeting from her children. The message read: "Before we children were born, we held a meeting in heaven and decided to choose the most beautiful, the most devoted, the loveliest creature on earth for our mother. After we had carefully considered all the other women in the world, dear Mother, we selected you!"

Such a touching tribute to motherhood could only originate in the hearts of children who had been taught the virtues of gratitude, faithfulness, and deference. Actually, then, "bread cast upon the water" had returned.

Sometimes the reverse is true, but, ordinarily speaking, children will reflect in their lives the virtues that the parents exercise in their everyday living.

All fathers and mothers must bring up their children in the love and fear of God, so that, having trained their off-spring in the fundamental truths of the Ten Commandments, both parents and children may reap the reward of not only earthly but also eternal happiness. "A gracious woman shall find glory" (Prov. 11:16).

"Love often knows no measure, but is inflamed above all measure" (Imit., Bk. 3, C. 5).

"O come to me, all you who are weary and over-burdened, and I will refresh you. Take my yoke upon you, and master my lessons, I am gentle and humble of heart. Thus you will find refreshment for your souls. My yoke is easy and my burden light" (Mt. 11:28–30).

While much evil has come from horse racing, at least a lesson can be learned from its procedure.

In order to match the horses as evenly as possible, the faster horse is proportionately handicapped. This handicap consists of adding a certain number of pounds of lead to the horse's saddle. The added weight may seem insignificant, but in the gruelling race that the horses endure, even a few extra pounds can spell the difference between defeat and victory.

St. Paul compares man's life to a race with the ultimate victory being heaven. There are few people who escape the knowledge that life is at times a severe race and that the contenders need God's grace in abundance in order not to weaken and fall.

It seems very foolish for a soul struggling to win the prize to take on the awful burden of sin which may handicap him to such an extent that he will wind up in this most important of all races an "also-ran."

St. Paul advises the participants struggling in this most important of all contests, for the prize of heaven, "So run that you will surely win" (1 Cor. 9:25).

> *"The nobler the cause in which we are engaged, the greater should be the attention we pay to it"*
> (St. Ambrose).

> *"How will a youth preserve his innocence? By cherishing your words"* (Ps. 118:9).

Don't worry about honest mistakes — even the best ball player seldom bats 400. Many souls waste their time and energy mulling over wrong judgments or unintentional errors. At the time, their action seemed prudent and just but in the light of future events they clearly see where they have erred. Hindsight is always better than foresight. Under similar circumstances, and with the same knowledge, these people would, no doubt, act in the same manner again. It is only the added knowledge of the present that proves the past action unwise.

To limit one's mistakes to a minimum, one must have recourse to God who sees all things: past, present, and future. St. Peter admonishes, "Keep awake and pray, all of you, that you may not succumb to temptation" (Mk. 14:38).

One of the most beautiful prayers of the Church is directed to the Holy Ghost for guidance and direction, "O God who has taught the hearts of the faithful with the light of the Holy Spirit, grant that by the gift of the same Spirit we may be always truly wise and ever rejoice in His consolations through Christ our Lord." "There is no wisdom, there is no prudence, there is no counsel against the Lord" (Prov. 21:30).

"The more humble [a man] is and the more subject to God, the wiser and the more at peace he will be in all things" (Imit., Bk. 1, C. 4).

"'Who are you, Lord?' he asked. Jesus replied,
'I am Jesus, whom you are persecuting'"
(Acts 9:15).

St. Paul was a zealot in seeking to persecute the Christians. He had obtained a commission from the highest authority to go to Damascus and there carry out his plan to destroy this newborn "sect."

En route, he was miraculously thrown from his horse, and while lying on the ground, a voice addressed him saying: "Saul, Saul, why do you persecute me?" And Saul asked, "Who are you, Lord?" Jesus replied, "I am Jesus, whom you are persecuting." "Arise and go into the city, and you will be told what you must do" (Acts 9:7).

Paul was struck blind but shortly after recovered his sight through the instrumentality of Ananias whom the Lord sent to him. From a confirmed and determined persecutor of Christ, Paul, when he was made aware that Christ was the true God, became one of His greatest missionaries.

God does not perform such a miracle for all as He did for Paul — this is not necessary today — for through His Church, He daily offers to all men the knowledge and understanding and grace to become His devoted followers. The sincere searcher after truth has a duty to investigate the teaching of Christ in His Church, and the earnest follower of Christ must strive to know Him better. "O Lord, make known your ways to me, and teach me all your paths" (Ps. 24:4).

> *"The grace of God surpasses not only all the*
> *stars, and all the heavens, but even all the angels"*
> (St. Thomas).

"I bring my reward to requite each one according to his deeds" (Apoc. 22:12, 13).

"It's the little things in life that really count" — trite but true. Everyone has a tendency to look for heroic things to do while he passes by the countless "little" acts that would make him strong and great.

St. Therese, the Little Flower, performed no outstanding deeds. She was an invalid practically all the time she was a nun. She died when she was only twenty-four years old. Yet, she was canonized as a saint by the Church a few short years later.

Her whole philsophy of life is probably summed up in one of her oft-repeated sayings, "Pick up a *pin* from the *motive* of *love,* and you may thereby save a soul." It is not the deed that matters but the motive that prompts it. There are not many things more insignificant than a pin, yet St. Therese declares if one picks it up out of love of God, this humble act may be the means of saving a soul. What a tremendous reward for such a simple act!

The Little Flower's whole life was an accumulation of little deeds; today she is a saint in heaven. "O holy souls, joy in the Lord exceedingly; hearts good and true, exult!" (Ps. 31:11.)

"The just please and move God more by small acts than some who do many things. For God does not look to the act, but to the fervor of the will; and He considers not what is done, but the devotion and good will with which it is accomplished" (St. Ephrem).

*"If one eats of this bread, he will live forever;
and furthermore, the bread which I give is my
flesh given for the life of the world"* (Jn. 6:51).

At Capharnaum, a centurion, a high Roman military officer, made known to Christ that his servant, no doubt a trusted and much loved individual, was grievously ill. Evidently, he believed that Christ out of His charity would cure him. Christ, however, surprised the centurion with His answer, "Am I to come and cure him?" Then the centurion replied: "Sir, I am not fit to have you come under my roof. No, only utter a word, and my slave will be cured."

When Jesus heard the man's words, he "marveled" and said to His followers, "I tell you frankly, I have never found such lively faith anywhere in Israel." Then He said to the centurion, "You may go. In answer to your faith, your wish shall be granted," and the Gospel continues, "The slave was cured that same hour" (Mt. 8:7-13).

The very fact that man is so unworthy to receive Christ into his heart emphasizes His love for souls when He enters into the hearts of the faithful in Holy Communion. Surely man is unworthy that Christ should "come under his roof," but the love of Christ for man passes all understanding. "I am the living bread that has come down from heaven. If one eats of this bread, he will live forever; and, furthermore, the bread which I shall give is my flesh given for the life of the world" (Jn. 6:51, 52).

> *"Although He (God) is omnipotent, He could
> not give more"* (St. Augustine).

> *"The good man's lips speak words of wisdom;*
> *his tongue expresses what is right. The law of*
> *the Lord reigns in his heart; his steps are never*
> *faltering"* (Ps. 36:30, 31).

Many people favor law and order as long as they are the ones to make the laws and give the orders.

The legitimate lawmaker and the one who lawfully commands must realize that they have a tremendous responsibility before God and man.

Christ clearly identified the source of all laws when He was taken before Pilate: and Pilate said to Jesus, " 'What is your origin?' But Jesus gave him no answer. 'You will not speak to me?' Pilate said to him. 'Do you not know that I have power to set you free and power to crucify you?' 'You have no power whatever to harm me,' replied Jesus, 'unless it is granted to you from above' " (Jn. 19:9–11).

God alone is the First Cause of all law and all order. Those who exercise authority must realize that they are but instruments in carrying out His will. Thus it behooves those who are in any and every position of trust to seek divine guidance in all their acts. In following the law of God in the exercise of his power, the wise and humble administrator will find confidence and happiness and peace. "There is one Lawgiver and Judge, he who can save and destroy" (James 4:12).

> *"Behold all things are yours, even those which I*
> *have and by which I serve you"*
> (*Imit.*, Bk. 3, C. 10).

*"As long as you remain united with me, and
my teachings remain your rule of life, you may
ask for anything you wish, and you shall have it"*
(Jn. 15:7).

The artisan was a notorious borrower. Doing some carpenter work in the building where there was a small cabinet-
making shop, he asked the owner for the loan of a special-type
saw. The proprietor reluctantly allowed him to have it.

After keeping the saw all day, the carpenter finally returned
it. The cabinetmaker was justly upset at the delay and spoke
sharply. "I am glad to get that saw back. Do you know I had
to borrow one myself?"

Not the least bit perturbed by the rebuke, the carpenter
nonchalantly said, "Well, I hope it was better than the one
you loaned me!"

The professional borrower is frequently an ingrate. The
ordinary person, however, is grateful for any kind of loan and
strives to return the borrowed article in the same condition,
or even better than it was when he became the temporary
proprietor.

Whatever man has in this life, God has loaned to him. No
further proof of this statement is needed than the fact that
"he can't take it with him" — unless it is spiritual.

However, each one will be obliged to account for the use
of these temporary loans, spiritual, material, or physical, as
the case may be. Therefore, the prudent man will exercise
the greatest zeal in making sure that he uses them wisely and
returns them in the most perfect condition.

*"Fail not in prayer; God will grant what He has
promised; and if He delays He does not refuse"*
(St. Augustine).

"God resists the proud but gives his grace to the humble" (1 Pet. 5:5).

The passenger in the plane was amazed at the change in the flourishing countryside beneath him. Spread out as far as his eyes could see was a multicolored carpet of luxuriant vegetation, interspersed with immense barns and picturesque farmhouses.

The traveler had made this same trip several years before. At that time, this particular section of the country was barren, desolate, uncultivated, uninhabited. What miracle had changed this desert into a farmer's paradise? A fellow passenger explained the phenomenon. The land had been irrigated.

From a mighty river, hundreds of miles away, fresh, cool, life-giving water had been brought into this seared and unproductive region, and had transformed the thirsty soil into productive and profitable farm land.

Just as water can change barren ground into fertile and lucrative soil so too the grace of God can transform a sinner into a saint. Christ is most generous with His gifts to all that do His will. "Anyone who loves me will treasure my message, and my Father will love him, and we shall visit him and make our home with him" (Jn. 14:23).

"Let Your grace, therefore, go before me and follow me, O Lord, and make me always intent upon good works, through Jesus Christ Your Son" (Imit., Bk. 3, C. 55).

"Repose upon the Lord, and trust in him"
(Ps. 36:7).

A gentleman of exacting routine had formed the habit of shaving each morning before a small mirror hanging from the wall in his room. He performed the customary ritual this particular day, but after he had finished shaving he discovered the mirror was not there! A careless cleaning woman had broken the looking glass the previous day.

St. Thomas declares, "A habit is a quality we acquire by repeated acts." There are two kinds of habits, as all know, good and bad.

Good habits are just as easily formed as bad ones. Therefore, it is up to youth especially to make every effort to start their lives correctly by putting into practice the admonitions of their superiors. By the constant repetition of good deeds, strong habits will be formed that will remain with them all their lives.

Children are quick to observe and to imitate. Wise parents not only admonish their offspring always to do what is right in the sight of God but they also must set a good example for them. The concerned father and mother are most anxious to demonstrate in their own lives the virtues which they hope to see develop in their young ones. "Show yourself in every respect an example of good deeds. In teaching, manifest integrity and dignity. Let your speech be sound and blameless" (Titus 2:7, 8).

"My Child, walk before Me in truth and seek Me always in the simplicity of your heart"
(*Imit.*, Bk. 3, C. 4).

"So you were not able to keep awake one hour with me?" (Mt. 26:40.)

Christ is true Man as well as true God and, being the perfect Man, He suffered in proportion to His perfection. Being human, He longed for the company of His fellow men.

We all want to be near someone whom we love, and this is especially true in time of sickness or sorrow. In the agony in the Garden, Christ instructed His Apostles to wait for Him while He went on a bit to pray. When He returned to seek the consolation and the company of His followers, He found them *asleep.*

Christ's lament still echoes down the ages; it still goes forth from every tabernacle where He is "a Prisoner of love"; it seeps into every human soul: "Were you not able to keep awake one hour with Me?"

Christ waits in His tabernacle of love in every Catholic church throughout the world for His faithful to come in and visit Him. In every city and town, thousands pass the church daily, and few indeed have the time to drop in and pay a call on Christ. Those who do "call on Christ" find a source of consolation and strength that is unknown to those who thoughtlessly pass Him by. "How lovely is your dwelling place, O Lord of hosts: My spirit pines—for the courts of the Lord it faints with yearning" (Ps. 83:2).

"The mind that is occupied with the thought of God has little room for other thoughts, especially evil ones" (St. Ignatius).

*"Were not the ten made clean? . . . But where are
the other nine?"* (Lk. 17:17–18.)

Christ always rewards gratitude. Being Man, as well as
God, He appreciates the acknowledgment of His good deeds.

All people desire to be thanked for favors done. A word
of gratitude will carry one through the day on wings of
happiness.

St. Luke gives a fitting example of Christ's appreciation
of gratitude in the parable of the ten lepers whom He
miraculously cleansed of their awful affliction and restored
to human society.

"He was about to enter a village when ten lepers came
his way. They stopped at some distance, and with raised
voices cried out: 'Rabbi Jesus, take pity on us.' Noticing
them, he said: 'Go, and get yourselves examined by the
priests!' and . . . while still on their way, they were made clean.
Now one of them . . . turned back, loudly praising God;
he threw himself at Jesus' feet and thanked him. And this
was a Samaritan! 'Were not the ten made clean?' Jesus asked;
'Where are the other nine? . . .' He then said to him, 'You
may rise and go home. Your faith has cured you'" (Lk.
17:12–19).

To the stranger who returned to express his gratitude to
Christ for healing his body, Christ, it would seem, in appreciation gave him the infinite grace of saving his soul.
God daily gives countless blessings to His children. The
acknowledgment of these gifts from God by the recipient is
an assurance of greater gifts to come.

> *"Thank God! No saying can be shorter than
> this, nor can any act be more profitable"*
> (St. Augustine).

*"Blessed are the promoters of peace for they will
rank as children of God"* (Mt. 5:9).

Parthia was an ancient independent kingdom northwest
of Iran.

The name of this little country comes down today in a
rather unique way. The Parthians were great warriors and
developed unusual skill in a particular style of warfare. These
horsemen would retire from their enemy, as if in retreat.
Suddenly they would whip about on their racing steeds and
send poisoned arrows into their pursuing foe. Thus, from
this method of battle has been derived the phrase, "Parthian
shot."

Not infrequently, when bitter arguments have been quieted
down and peace has been restored, one of the departing contestants lets go with a verbal thrust, a "Parthian shot," and
tempers flare again.

This method of dealing with another is anything but
gentlemanly and its very use is bound to disrupt peace and
contentment.

The "Parthian shot" is only one of the many means of
rending asunder the happy home. Peace of mind is the
most desirable of possessions. Those who do not contribute
toward this condition in their family and among their friends
are failing in their duty before God and man. "O mark how
pleasant and how good it is when brethren dwell together in
perfect unison" (Ps. 132:1).

*"Nothing is to be desired by anyone so much as
to enjoy peace of mind, and to control his passions"* (Gregory Nazianzen).

"The sun has its own degree of splendor, the moon its own, and the stars their own. Yes, star differs from star in splendor. It is the same with the resurrection of the dead"

(1 Cor. 15:41, 42).

One day, St. Therese, the Little Flower of Jesus, expressed surprise to her sister Pauline that God did not give an equal amount of glory to all the souls of the elect in heaven. Therese was fearful that not all the saints would be quite happy if a distinction was to be made among them.

Pauline took her father's large tumbler and Therese's small drinking glass and filled each to the brim with water. Then she asked Therese which one was more full. The Little Flower replied that each contained all the water it could hold.

"In this way," said Therese, "Pauline made it clear to me that in heaven the least blessed would not be envious of the spiritual happiness of the greatest."

Those souls who are closest to God on earth will be closest to Him in heaven, "for star differs from star in glory." Everyone should strive here to be as close as possible to God hereafter. "He will appeal to me, and I will hear his prayer: in tribulation I shall be with him" (Ps. 90:15).

"All human glory, all temporal honor, all worldly position is truly vanity and foolishness compared with Your everlasting glory" (Imit., Bk. 3, C. 40).

"Whoever are led by the Spirit of God, they are the sons of God" (Rom. 8:14).

"Then Herod secretly summoned the Magi and, after carefully ascertaining from them the time during which the star had been visible, he sent them to Bethlehem with this injunction: 'Go and make careful inquiries about the child, and, when you have found him, report to me. I, too, wish to go and do homage to him'" (Mt. 2:7, 8).

Herod was a crafty and deceitful man — and a cruel one. The purpose of his apparent solicitude for the Christ Child was to hoodwink these godly men into thinking that his intentions were honorable, and that he too did wish to worship the newborn King.

Clever men can frequently fool their fellow men, but they can never fool God.

After adoring the Babe, these holy wise men from the East "advised in a dream not to return to Herod . . . departed for their country by a different route" (Mt. 2:12).

In order that faithful souls may not be ensnared by worldly deceptions, it is necessary that they turn constantly to God for guidance and direction. The wise Christian turns frequently to the Holy Ghost for enlightenment. "May God, the source of hope, fill you with all joy and peace based on faith, that you may abound in hope by the power of the Holy Spirit" (Rom. 15:13).

"The Holy Spirit gives the pledge of salvation, the strength, the life, the light of knowledge"
                                        (St. Bernard).

"And in doing good let us not be discouraged,
because in due time we shall reap if we do not
become careless" (Gal. 6:9).

The young man was helping to earn his college expenses by clerking in a shoe store on Saturdays. One dull afternoon, a young mother came into the store with her little girl. The child was exceptionally beautiful and all were attracted to her. The young clerk remarked to an elderly co-worker, "My, what a pretty child!"

The older man was silent for a moment, then gave his junior a bit of advice that is worth passing along.

"Yes," he said thoughtfully, "the child is beautiful. But you know she is an exception. Many children are not so well dressed, not so attractive, not so pretty. Those are the ones you want to give attention and consideration to. That child will always have admirers."

A little consideration and kindness shown to those who are passed over by the crowd will bring much happiness to these souls, and a great deal of consolation to one's self. "My brothers, do not practice your faith in our glorious Lord Jesus Christ with partiality" (James 2:1, 2).

> *"That is true humility by which one thinks little*
> *of oneself, and praises the good qualities of an-*
> *other without envy or jealousy"* (St. Augustine).

*"May all my spoken words and deepest thoughts
please you, O Lord, my savior and my rock!"*
(Ps. 18:15.)

Today, most persons are bent on doing something or anything that will keep their minds off themselves. People do not want to be idle a moment lest they take stock of their lives and be obliged to reproach themselves for their sins of commission or omission.

The movies are an ever present antidote against boredom. The sports arenas are crowded with those who like to lose themselves in a crowd. The fraternal organizations furnish a meeting place when the weather is inclement. The cocktail lounge and corner tavern are gathering places for the lonely. Home is a place to eat and sleep.

What a change would take place in the average life if each one gave even a few minutes of meditation to God each day! There is plenty of opportunity: on the bus, in the railroad station, on the streetcar or train, to and from work, while waiting for the traffic lights to change, while waiting for dinner, a few moments spent in the nearest church. A thousand opportunities present themselves each day to praise God. The sincere seeker after God uses them wisely. "I always keep the Lord before my eyes: and on my right is he; I shall stand firm" (Ps. 15:8).

The faithful will be surprised how much happier they will be if they give to God *more* of their time and attention. "At all times, I will bless the Lord and ever be his praise upon my lips" (Ps. 33:2).

*"He who created us without our help, does not
make us holy without our help"* (St. Augustine).

*"So you, too: at present you are in sorrow; but I
shall see you again, and then your hearts will rejoice, and no one will take your joy away from
you"* (Jn. 16:22).

"Going home!" There is no saying more satisfying and
joyous than this one. Whether it is the schoolboy on his
holidays, the patient discharged from the hospital, or the
weary traveler who turns his steps homeward; to each,
the happiness that wells up in his heart at the prospect of
going home brings universal delight.

The little lad who spends his first night away from his
mother and the familiar family surroundings experiences
pangs of homesickness the memory of which lingers the rest
of his life. Despite the ensuing years, the masculine appearance and robust frame, deep down in the heart of all men
is that longing for home.

Man cannot be completely happy in this life because it
is not his home. He is but a traveler, ever drawing closer
and closer to the end for which he was created, eternity with
God. St. Paul summons up the longing of the sincere seeker
after heaven, "desiring to depart and be with Christ" (Phil.
1:23).

Life is short — eternity long. Therefore, it behooves the
faithful traveler here always to keep his thoughts on "Home,"
that by his sacrifices and love, he may assure himself of a
glorious welcome by his heavenly Father. "O Lord, I love
the house in which you dwell, the place in which your glory
is enshrined" (Ps. 25:8).

> *"What ought we to love? That which can be
> with us for all eternity"* (St. Augustine).

"May he be pleased with my poor utterance: for me, I will rejoice in the Lord (Ps. 103:34).

"Well, Bill, what do you really think of my acting?" The two Thespians were having a heart-to-heart talk on matters pertaining to the stage.

"If you honestly want to know the truth, I think you are terrible. Your diction is poor, your gestures are awkward. . . ."

"Just a minute," interrupted the seeker after praise, "I don't think you are much of an actor yourself!"

Thus ended a beautiful friendship.

Few like criticism, even when they ask for it. The prudent man knows this and will avoid telling the harmful truth. It is difficult enough for one who is obliged to criticize another to speak out, for he knows that he is going to hurt that individual.

It is surprising how resentful of criticism most of us are, and yet, how quick we are to make known our poor opinion of another, especially when the object of our unkindness is not present.

St. James declares, "We all commit many faults" (3:2). It is better to remain silent and endure than to wound another's heart. Leave criticism to those whose obligation it is to perform such delicate duties. When one is constrained to undertake such a task, he should make sure that it is not selfishness that prompts his action, but rather sincere love for his fellow man. "Everyone should be quick to listen, slow to speak, slow to get angry. By anger man does not achieve the holiness that God requires" (James 1:19, 20).

"First keep peace with yourself; then you will be able to bring peace to others" (Imit., Bk. 2, C. 3).

" . . . whoever hears these words of mine and acts
accordingly is like a sensible man who built his
house upon rock" (Mt. 7:24).

" . . . whoever hears these words of mine and acts accordingly is like a sensible man who built his house upon
rock: the rain poured down and the floods came and the
winds blew and beat against that house; but it did not
collapse. It was founded upon rock. And whoever hears
these words of mine and does not act accordingly is like a
foolish man who built his house upon sand: and the rain
poured and the floods came and the winds blew and beat
against the house, and it collapsed. In fact the collapse of
it was complete" (Mt. 7:24–27).

During the war, Gibraltar was surrounded upon all sides
by the enemy but never once did they attack. The "Rock"
was too solid a fortification to be overcome.

Christ assures us that those who hear His words and
"act upon them" shall be like the wise man who built his
home upon a rock. Note that Christ says it is not sufficient
simply to know His teaching; this teaching must also be
put into practice. In the application of the word of God
to his own life, the faithful soul will find a firm foundation
for his faith; and no assault from the world, the flesh, or
the devil can ever steal away this precious gift. "They cried
to you, and they were saved: they hoped in you, and were
not put to shame" (Ps. 21:6).

> *"The house of God is founded on faith, built*
> *upon hope, and made perfect by charity"*
> (St. Augustine).

*"How privileged am I to have the mother of my
Lord come to visit me!"*
(Lk. 1:43, words of Elizabeth.)

The Patrician Coriolanus camped before the gates of Rome.
He was determined to destroy the city for the ill-treatment
he had received from the inhabitants. One emissary after
another had been sent out from the doomed city to beg him
to relent and to spare Rome and its people. All the pitiful
pleas were relentlessly ignored. Coriolanus was adamant.
Rome must be destroyed.

Finally, his mother went to him and with tear-dimmed
eyes begged him to reconsider his decision. The sight of
his mother in tears succeeded when every other petition
had failed. Coriolanus cried out, "O Mother, thou hast conquered. Thy tears have saved Rome!"

Practically the last act of Christ as He hung on the cross
was to present His Mother to us as our Mother. Therefore,
the weary travelers in this world can turn to their Mother in
heaven with the utmost confidence that she will intercede in
heaven with her divine Son for the souls on earth. She is
the world's Ambassador at the Court of Heaven. Have
unfailing confidence in the powerful intercession of the
Mother of God. "Lord, hear my prayer, and listen to my cry;
and to my tearful plea do not be deaf" (Ps. 38:13).

*"It cannot happen that the son of so many tears
should perish"*
(St. Ambrose, quoted by St. Augustine).

*"Let us, therefore, make every effort to enter that
Rest, in order that no one may fall by giving the
same example of disobedience"* (Hebr. 4:11–12).

Julian, the apostate Roman emperor (361–363), was reared
a Christian. Gradually he fell away from Christianity. As
soon as he ascended to the throne, Julian threw aside all
pretense of being a Christian and persecuted the followers
of Christ unmercifully, referring to them contemptuously as
Galileans. He attempted to rebuild the temple of Jupiter
at Jerusalem, but fire and earthquake prevented this undertaking. In 363, Julian was wounded in the side by an arrow
in a small cavalry skirmish and died during the night. Both
Christians and pagans believed the legend that he cried out
when dying, "Thou hast conquered, O Galilean."

Many unfortunate souls follow in the footsteps of Julian.
Out of greed, immorality, or pride, they turn their backs
on the teachings of Christ and seek wealth or pleasure or
prestige among His enemies. Fearing that they will not be
accepted as *true* opponents of Christ unless they cry out
against Him, not infrequently, these sad souls strive to do
all things harmful to the loving Christ. And yet they must
know, as Julian must have known, that Christ will eventually
conquer. Repenting all past evils, these former friends should
hasten to the outstretched arms of the patient, sorrowful,
long-suffering Christ. Here, at last, these unhappy, restless
souls will find refuge and rest. "Then the peace of God
which surpasses all understanding will guard your hearts and
your thoughts in Christ Jesus" (Phil. 4:7).

*"You will find, apart from Him, that nearly all
the trust you place in men is a total loss"*
(Imit., Bk. 2, C. 7).

*"A child I was, and am an old man now; I
never saw a good man yet left in the lurch, nor
did I see his children begging bread"*
(Ps. 36:25).

The conversation of the three friends had become serious.
"I was just thinking the other day," said the first, "that it's
tough to be old."

The second added, "It's worse to be old and sick!"

The third observed, "But worst of all, is to be old and
sick and poor!"

All these observations were right in a limited sense, looking at these subjects from a purely natural standpoint.

As age creeps up on the individual, his youthful vigor and
vitality wanes because the human body naturally begins to
deteriorate. This certainly awaits all who live long enough.

To the faithful friend of Christ, however, these natural
evils mean nothing. To the aged person who can look back
over a life spent in the company and service of God, sickness or poverty are but guarantees of heavenly awards.
"Trust in the Lord; observe his law: and he will prosper your
possession of the land" (Ps. 36:34).

The richest people in the world are those whom advanced
age has placed on the doorstep of heaven, secure in the
humble knowledge that they have fought the good fight.
Everyone, young and old, should keep before his mind daily
the pleasant prospect of gazing backward over a lifetime of
faithfulness to his Creator. "You are my expectation, O my
God; O Lord, you are my hope from childhood up" (Ps. 70:5).

*"You are my hope. You are my confidence, You
are my consoler, most faithful in every need"*
(Imit., Bk. 3, C. 59).

*"He guides the humble by his just demands, and
to the humble shows his way"* (Ps. 24:9).

The Roman Caesars were proud men. These leaders of the
mighty Roman Empire surrounded themselves with solemn
pomp and ceremony. They reared gorgeous pagan temples
to false gods and it was their fondest hope that these
architectural triumphs would serve as everlasting monuments to their distinguished names and great military accomplishments. Today, the only memorials to these haughty
monarchs are the ruins of the magnificent edifices they so
hopefully erected.

God has promised to humble the proud and exalt the
humble. Meditate upon this truth in the case of St. Agnes.
She was a young girl, thirteen years of age, when she was
martyred during the fourth century. This young virgin mar-
tyr, who was put to death by the command of the arrogant
Roman emperor, sought not self-aggrandizement nor worldly
glory — she sought only eternal glory with God. Yet, today,
in Rome a magnificent basilica declares to all ages the young
saint's undying love for God and the things of God. The
name of the august Roman Caesar who ordered Agnes'
execution has been lost in history. " . . . the Lord loves his
race; and crowns the humble folk with victory" (Ps. 149:4).

> *"To glory in adversity is not hard for the man
> who loves, for this is to glory in the cross of the
> Lord"* (*Imit.*, Bk. 2, C. 6).

> *"In answer to your faith, your wish shall be granted"* (Mt. 9:29).

"As Jesus walked on from that place, two blind men followed him, shouting the words, 'take pity on us, Son of David!' When he got indoors the blind men came up to him. 'Do you believe,' Jesus said to them, 'that I have power to do this?' 'Yes, Lord,' they replied. Then he laid his hands on their eyes and said: 'In answer to your faith, your wish shall be granted.'"

The faith of these blind men was richly rewarded. Christ, it is noted, put the condition of their cure upon their own faith in Him. God desires man's faith in Him at all times. In times of sickness, strife, turmoil, hardship, Christ wants us to have confidence in Him. He will requite the faithful with consolation and help.

The little child has absolute confidence that his father can do all things. It never occurs to the youngster that there is anything that "Daddy" cannot accomplish. While, in most cases, the accomplishments of his earthly father are extremely limited, the faith of the child is limitless.

Man's all-powerful Father in heaven, however, can accomplish all things. Thus, man should have childlike faith in Him. This type of faith is most pleasing to "our Father who art in heaven."

"If my hope is in man, my hope will falter when he falters; but if I hope in God, I shall never grow weak" (St. Augustine).

"Keep awake and pray, that you may not suc-
cumb to temptation" (Mt. 26:41).

The coal miners, working several hundred feet below the
surface of the ground, completely ignored the cheerful singing
of several canaries whose cages hung from the jagged roof.
Suddenly, the singing stopped. As one man, the miners turned
their heads in the direction of the birds. The little singers lay
dormant on the bottoms of their cages. The exodus out of
that mine was almost comic.

What had happened? These sweet-singing canaries were
kept in the mines to detect gas. Their sensitive organs were
more quickly affected by the deadly fumes that frequently
gathered in the pits than those of the miners. When the
birds stopped singing, no time was to be lost in getting away
from that place.

There are all kinds of signs, best known to each individual
person, that point out spiritual dangers which will destroy his
soul. He should be as wary of perils in his spiritual life as
these miners were in their daily labors. St. Paul declares, "If
God is for us, who is against us?" (Rom. 8:32), but he also
states, "Yet we carry this treasure in earthen vessels, to show
that its superabundant power comes from God and not
from us" (2 Cor. 4:7, 8).

> *"You carry a load of gold, that is good works;*
> *you must avoid the robber, that is, vain and*
> *empty glory in the eyes of men"* (St. Jerome).

> *"Then the king will say to those at his right:
> 'Come, the elect of my Father! Take possession
> of the kingdom prepared for you at the beginning
> of the world'"* (Mt. 25:34).

Life is a series of separations from the day man is born.
Gradually he becomes less dependent upon his mother. He
grows away from the family fireside. School claims his attention; college takes him from the bosom of his dear ones.
Eventually, he marries and sets up a home of his own. Age
slowly deprives him of his youth. He slows up; his hearing
fails, his sight becomes impaired. Death eventually claims
him. Only his soul remains untouched. Finally, after all these
changes and separations, he reaches his true home where
there is no more separation, no more sorrow, no more sin,
but only if he has fought the good fight.

The faithful soul during this long series of separations
from the cradle to the grave makes sure of one thing — that
he is not separated from God. Mortal sin is the only instrument that breaks the tie that binds the creature to his
Creator. All things pass away. God and man's soul alone
remain eternal. "For our present light affliction is producing
for us an eternal weight of glory that is beyond all measure"
(2 Cor. 4:17, 18).

> *"We cannot go to heaven in ships, or in chariots,
> or on foot; for not only to start on the journey
> but also to reach the journey's end, is nothing else
> than to wish to go thither; to wish it with a
> strong and firm will, not in a careless manner, as
> if at the same time wishing it and not wishing it"*
> (St. Augustine).

"Therefore, whoever believes he is standing firm,
should beware lest he fall" (1 Cor. 10:12).

The old priest was intently reading his breviary as the plane rushed across space.

The gentleman, sitting next to him, finally spoke, "Excuse me, Father, but I must ask you why you continue to say so many prayers. You have worked hard for God. You have led a spiritual, sacrificing life. You have devoted yourself to others. Why don't you just take a 'spiritual vacation' in your declining years?"

The priest smiled and turned to his traveling companion, and asked, "How fast do you think this plane has been going since we took off?"

"Oh, I should say a couple hundred miles an hour, why?"

"Well," continued the priest, "what do you think would happen to us if the pilot decided to give it a rest — cut the fuel supply and just coast along? You and I would start looking for a nice landing strip!"

"I see your point, Father," replied the questioner, meditatively.

Man must constantly pray. There is no such thing as a "vacation" in the spiritual life. To the sincere, faithful Christian who keeps in constant contact with God, his vacation comes after death. "The fervent prayer of a holy person is very powerful" (James 5:16).

> *"It is no great thing to begin good thing, but to complete it, that alone is perfect."*
>
> (St. Augustine).

"Carry it into action; do not be a mere listener. Otherwise you deceive yourselves"

(James 1:22, 23).

The art of oratory consists in convincing the hearer's intellect, and then persuading his will to action. It is comparatively easy to convince a person what is good for him but it is an entirely different thing to move his will to act.

Christ sought constantly to convince His hearers of His supernatural powers by His words and His miracles but many were unwilling to accept and act upon what their senses and minds told them was the truth. Pride, tradition, jealousy, hatred, anger; all these passions conspired to hold their wills in check.

St. James tells his readers, "Carry it [God's word] into action; do not be a mere listener. Otherwise you deceive yourselves. If anyone listens to the doctrine and does not carry it into action, he is like a man who looks into a mirror at the face nature gave him. He looks at himself, yes, but then goes his way, and at once forgets what he looks like. But he who has looked carefully into the perfect law that imparts liberty, and observes it, who is not one that listens and forgets, but puts it into practice, this type of person is to be congratulated for observing it" (James 1:22-26).

"God did not create man to pass his life in idle and sluggish desires; but, on the contrary, to occupy himself with honorable labor" (St. Basil).

*"Anyone who loves me will treasure my message,
and my Father will love him, and we shall visit
him and make our home with him"* (Jn. 14:23).

When a traveler passes from one country to another, the main handicap is lack of knowledge of the language of this foreign land. The stranger always feels a stranger until he has acquired a facility in expressing himself in the mother tongue of his new country. The wise man, realizing he is going to change his place of living, prudently prepares for this journey by seeking to master the language beforehand.

Everyone in this world knows that sooner or later he is to make his departure from these familiar surroundings and enter into a distant country, "We see now by means of a mirror in a vague way, but then we shall see face to face. Now my knowledge is incomplete, but then I shall have complete knowledge, even as God has complete knowledge of me" (1 Cor. 13:12, 13).

The faithful soul daily strives to acquire an adeptness in the language of his future home. The mother tongue of this new country is the universal language of Love, love of God and love of neighbor. "If I should speak the languages of men and of angels, but have no love, I am no more than a noisy gong and a clanging cymbal" (1 Cor. 13:1, 2).

> *"The countenance and image of Christ, by which
> we are known to be His, is engraved in us; it
> is the glory of charity"* (St. Cyril).

" . . . strive even more to make your calling and election secure . . . " (2 Pet. 1:10.)

Man by his nature, it seems, loves to gamble. Many foolish persons are forever spending in their imagination the "jack pot" they expect to win on the radio or with the treasury slip or at the race track. Disappointment, generally, is their only reward; yet these devotees of chance keep on spending and hoping.

Many souls use this same "system" of gambling in seeking to win their eternal reward. Making no real effort to gain eternal happiness, they hope that by some "lucky break" they will manage to grasp, in their dizzy whirl through life, the "brass ring" that will assure them eternal bliss. Countless disappointments in the past have not served to persuade them of the great risk they are taking. "Look, humble souls; rejoice; you look for God; then may your hearts revive" (Ps. 68:33).

The faithful and prudent soul adheres to St. Paul's admonition, "work out your salvation with fear and trembling" (Phil. 2:12), and endeavors to assure himself of eternal happiness by his daily devotion to God. "Life eternal he will give to those who by persevering in good deeds seek glory, honor, and immortality" (Rom. 2:7, 8).

"God questions the rich and the poor regarding their heart, not about their coffers or their houses. For what would it profit you to be destitute of riches, if you are inflamed with cupidity"
                                             (St. Augustine).

"Whatever you do, work at it heartily, as for the Lord and not for men, in the realization that from the Lord you will receive the inheritance as your reward" (Col. 3:23, 24).

Bruce, the king of Scotland, wanted his heart buried in the Holy Land. A company of Christian soldiers carried out this mission. En route, the convoy was attacked by a superior band of Saracens, and was gradually driven back. In danger of being overcome and taken prisoners by the enemy, the leader of the Christians hurled the golden casket containing Bruce's heart among the pagans and cried out, "There goes the heart of Bruce!"

The captain's declaration fired the courage of the weakening soldiers. Determined to regain the coveted heart of their king at all cost, the Christians fell upon the Saracens with such violence that they quickly conquered the enemy and retrieved their prize.

If men would make such a superhuman effort for the heart of a man, what should they not do to win the Heart of Christ? The Sacred Heart of Jesus is the Symbol of His love for man. Someone has said that a man's religion is that which he thinks most about. The true follower of Jesus must be daily devoted to the Heart of Christ, and in this devotion, he will find the key to life and the key to eternity. "Who shall separate us from Christ's love for us?" (Rom. 8:35).

"For Jesus' sake we have taken this cross. For Jesus' sake let us persevere with it"
(Imit., Bk. 3, C. 56).

> *"A mild answer breaketh wrath: but a harsh word stirreth up fury"* (Prov. 15:1).

The practical joker arranged for an introduction between two of his friends. He falsely informed each one that the other was stone-deaf. When the meeting occurred, the loud words of greeting shouted by each could be heard for some distance. Unconsciously, one of the men dropped his voice into its normal register. Perceiving that the other understood, the bright light of understanding shone on the speaker's face. It dawned on both, simultaneously, that they had been tricked by their mutual friend.

Passing over the embarrassment caused by this deception, a lesson can be learned from the men's conversation.

It will be observed that, generally speaking, one will reply in the same tone of voice in which he is addressed. If an angry individual speaks harshly, he cannot expect a soft answer. Immediately, the person so spoken to goes on the offensive, and believes that equal vehemence must be expressed in his voice in order to defend his position. It is true that "a soft tongue shall break hardness" (Prov. 25:15), but to assure peace in the home, as well as elsewhere, the Christian thing to do is to speak gently at all times, and thus feel reasonably certain that the answer will be in kind. "O may my mouth proclaim the praises of the Lord, may all men bless his holy name forever and for aye" (Ps. 144:21).

"Pride deprives me of God, envy robs me of my neighbor, and anger robs me of myself"
                                        (Hugh of St. Victor).

*"Instruct me in the ways your law commands,
and on your wonders will I meditate"*
(Ps. 118:27).

If anyone has the opportunity to visit the assembly line of a large automobile plant, he will be greatly impressed by the mechanical achievements of the present age. As the car advances along this rapidly moving line, each part and bolt and nut, ready and waiting, is quickly fixed into place.

Not the least astounding feature of the trip, is that as soon as the last operation is completed, a waiting attendant enters the car, steps on the gas, and drives the assembled vehicle to the parking lot.

This mechanical miracle of our age is awesome and makes one compare it with his own life. It would be pleasant to contemplate that when one's journey is completed, he could enter into his heavenly home as perfectly adjusted as the modern auto. But being human, he has much to undergo; a cleansing and perfecting period in purgatory, before gaining the end for which he was created, eternal salvation.

The prudent person will strive to shorten this period in Purgatory as much as he can. By penance and prayer, he will make amends for the temporal punishment due to his many sins. By fulfilling the conditions laid down by the Church, he will try to gain as many indulgences as he can. He will lay up these merits in heaven to be used after death. "Who shall separate us from Christ's love for us? Shall tribulation, or distress, or persecution, or hunger, or nakedness, or danger, or the sword?" (Rom. 8:35, 36.)

*"Grace does not work without the cooperation of
our will; but when we will, it works with us"*
(St. Augustine).

> *"Here indeed we have no lasting city, but we
> are in search of the city that is to come"*
> (Hebr. 13:14).

The real-estate agent had a difficult problem to decide. He had just taken an option on a valuable piece of property. The question before him was whether or not he should pick up his option. This necessitated a heavy investment. Was the risk worth it? If he bought the property, he would have thousands of dollars tied up. Could he make a quick sale at a substantial gain? What would be the prudent thing to do? Was it wise to risk all the money he possessed to gain more? The important point was, he held the option.

Through His grace Christ has given us an option on heaven. He purchased that option, not with silver or gold, but with His own precious Blood; with His suffering, His humiliation, with His agony on the cross. That option is given each one and each one must decide whether or not he will take it up. If he *wills* to purchase heaven, there is no risk involved, but he must pay the purchase price; with faithfulness to Christ, with tribulation, with suffering, and with tears. Christ has warned His followers, "If anyone wants to become my follower, he must renounce himself and shoulder his cross; then he may be a follower of mine" (Mt. 16:24).

With God's help, man can buy heaven with his good deeds! What a great prize for such little suffering — "What no eye has ever seen, what no ear has ever heard, what no human heart has ever thought of, namely, the great blessings God holds ready for those who love him" (1 Cor. 2:9).

*"No labor can seem hard, no time long, by which
eternal glory is gained"* (St. Jerome).

*"It is great glory to follow the Lord: for length
of days shall be received from him"*
(Ecclus. 23:38).

Two hundred fifty thousand articles, worth $2,000,000, are
left behind on railroad trains in this country each year by
careless passengers. These lost items, the return of which costs
the railroads a million dollars a year, include traveling bags,
mink coats, suits, overcoats, false teeth, gems, and money.

The reader, no doubt, is amazed to learn that there are
so many negligent people in the world. He would be the
first to declare that under no circumstances would he be
so neglectful as to lose his best clothes or a fortune in gems
or cash. Yet, the hard, cold records of the American railroads
bear testimony to the carelessness and thoughtlessness of his
fellow men. If one is amazed at such heedlessness on the part
of men concerning material things, what must be God's
concern over man's indifference to spiritual values?

By deliberately turning his back on God and His commandments, the unrepentant sinner casts away not a mere
material fortune, but a spiritual kingdom. It is written in
the Book of Ecclesiasticus (27:3), "Sin shall be destroyed with
the sinner."

The faithful and prudent soul clings tenaciously to God's
love. Should he have the misfortune, through human frailty,
to lose this gift, he immediately turns back and strives at
all costs to regain possession of God's priceless friendship.
Christ declares to all men, " . . . I tell you, there is joy among
the angels of God over one repentant sinner" (Lk. 15:10).

*"Remember me, my God, and lead me by the
right way into Your kingdom"*
(*Imit.,* Bk. 3, C. 57).

> *"As for yourselves, the very hairs on your head have all been numbered"* (Mt. 10:30, 31).

"Do not two sparrows sell for a penny? And yet, not one of them can drop dead to the ground without the consent of your Father. As for yourselves, the very hairs on your head have all been numbered. Away, then, with all fear; you are more precious than whole flocks of sparrows" (Mt. 10:29–31).

Christ is speaking to His children when He says these things. It sometimes happens that things are written and spoken that are inspiring and consoling and serve their purpose as such. But when Christ speaks, he speaks for a definite reason. He means what He says and says what He means. Thus, anyone reading this passage from Scripture is assured that God's love for men is so great that He is interested in their most minute welfare. How can anyone who reads this passage doubt the love that Christ has for him alone? "Just as the Father loves me, I love you" (Jn. 15:9, 10).

The value of one immortal soul is so precious in the sight of Christ that He would have gladly died on the cross to save that one soul. In St. Peter's epistle it is written, "The Lord does not delay fulfilling his promise, as some estimate delay, but he is long-suffering toward you, not wishing a single soul to perish but that every last one should have a change of heart and mind" (2 Pet. 3:9).

> *"There is nothing more pleasing to God, and therefore more deserving of care, than the salvation of souls"* (St. Chrysostom).

"How many are the things you do, O Lord!
With wisdom you accomplish everything!"
(Ps. 103:24.)

Over five hundred billion matches are used in this country each year! However, perhaps in no place in the world does the match play such a lifesaving role as in the Arctic region. In this land of snow and ice, the careless traveler on the trail, who forgets his supply of matches, is doomed.

No one realizes this fact more than the Oblate missionary who spends half his life behind dog sleds. On the trail, fire for tea and warmth and protection from wild animals is paramount. Hence, the missionaries have established safety practices. Five matches are always tied together as a unit. The firewood is damp and it requires the heat from all five matches to ignite the timber. The missionary is indeed grateful for the match which serves him so well in his arduous spiritual duties.

Here one sees a good example of the use of material things toward a spiritual end. In all walks of life, man can and should find a way to use these things which God has so generously given him for a salutary purpose, namely, for God's honor and glory, and for his own eternal salvation. "The Lord hath made all things: and to the godly he has given wisdom" (Ecclus. 43:37). The wise use all things well.

> *"Above all things and in all things, O my soul,*
> *rest always in God, for He is the everlasting rest*
> *of the saints"* (Imit., Bk. 3, C. 21).

"I tell you the plain truth, inasmuch as you did this to one of these least brethren of mine, you did it to me" (Mt. 25:40).

"Then the King will say to those at his right: 'Come, the elect of my Father! Take possession of the kingdom prepared for you at the beginning of the World, for I was hungry, and you gave me to eat; I was thirsty, and you gave me to drink; I was a stranger, and you took me into your homes; I was naked, and you covered me; I was sick, and you visited me; I was in prison, and you came to see me.' Then the saints will be surprised and say to him: 'Lord, when did we see you hungry and feed you? or thirsty and give you to drink? And when did we see you a stranger and take you into our homes; or naked and cover you? When did we see you sick or in prison and come to visit you?' And in explanation the King will say to them: 'I tell you the plain truth, inasmuch as you did this to one of these least brethren of mine, you did it to me'" (Mt. 25:34-40).

Much is written and spoken today about care of the old, the sick, and the abandoned. Countless millions are spent in carrying out these programs. This good work is to be commended. But real Christian charity is had only by those who willingly treat the unfortunate, not as public charges, but as individuals, with an immortal soul, made to the image and likeness of God, whose dignity as men is only a little less than that of the angels, and whose destiny is eternal glory. "Beloved, let us love one another, because love takes its origin from God" (2 Jn. 4:7).

"Virtue should strive, not for honor and glory, but for virtue" (St. Augustine).

*"In all thy works let the true word go before thee,
and steady counsel before every action"*
(Ecclus. 37:20).

The woodsman is often amazed at the clever actions of wild animals. The adroit work of the beaver is a striking example. These busy little animals will construct a dam in one night that draws the applause of the best engineers. The purpose of the dam is to hold back the rushing water in order that the beavers may have an ideal spot for living quarters for their families.

Destroy this dam and the beavers will return the next night and build another one on the same spot. These apparently intelligent little creatures work from instinct. Reason is not there to admonish them that their nightly labors are in vain. The marvelous works they perform are prompted by their particular nature, the instinct which persuades them to perform actions necessary for their preservation.

If man were to build a dam in a given spot, and that dam for one reason or another were repeatedly destroyed, he would seek another location. His intelligence would convince him that he was wasting his time.

Unlike the animal that acts from instinct, man who has free will is accountable to God, his Creator, for his every deed. Hence, it behooves man to pray constantly to God for wisdom and prudence and understanding that he may do all things well. "Those will be shamed who lightly break their faith. O Lord, make known your ways to me; and teach me all your paths" (Ps. 24:4).

"The beginning of all temptation lies in a wavering mind and little trust in God . . . "
(*Imit.*, Bk. 1, C. 13).

> *"And I, once I have been lifted up from the earth,*
> *will draw all men to myself"* (Jn. 12:32).

Almost everyone has seen in the newspaper, magazine, or movies, a picture of mountain climbers seeking to ascend some rugged and precipitous mountainside.

These men were properly outfitted for their hazardous undertaking. They wore heavy spiked shoes, their clothes were warm but light, they carried ice picks and axes, but the most essential feature of their equipment was the strong rope which bound them together; upon the unfailing strength of this tie depended their very lives. Consequently, the experienced climber made sure that this "bond" was of the highest quality. He knew the good reputation of the man who made it; he tested and examined it for the slightest flaw. He was morally certain the rope would not break should one of the party have the misfortune to slip and fall. He was sure the rope would hold, should he be forced to dig in and pull his friends back to safety. Without the security of this "bond" no climber would venture to ascend the dangerous mountainsides.

As faithful Christians strive to ascend the rugged and arduous road that leads to eternal life, they need the assistance and help of others. They have the help of Christ; but bound together with Christian love, the weary pilgrims ascend to the heights of glory, with greater security and with greater joy. All faithful "climbers" should be bound securely together with the love of God and the love of neighbor. "The Lord upholds all those who fall: and raises up all the depressed" (Ps. 144:14).

"Our love is proved by what we do"
                    (St. Gregory).

*"Instruct thy son: and he shall refresh thee and
shall give delight to thy soul"* (Prov. 29:18).

The Greek inscription on the weather-beaten headstone
intrigued the young seminarians as they wandered through
the ancient cemetery. They were out for a hike on a pleasant
summer afternoon and had noted the small family plot,
overgrown with tall grass and vines, along the roadside.
Reverently they entered and read the lovely mottoes chiseled
into the markers by the loved ones of those deceased.

Slowly one of the students translated the Greek words.
The simple statement carved on the headstone was the
noblest tribute any child could ever pay to a loving and
self-sacrificing mother. Translated, the inscription read, "She
was a good mother."

Orators, poets, and artists have dipped their pens and
brushes into the very blood stream of their hearts to paint
a worthy picture of motherhood, and many have succeeded
in portraying this state in life in all its beauty and loveliness.
Yet none has paid a more beautiful tribute to any mother than
this simple statement, "She was a good mother."

The love that exists between a good mother and a devoted
child beggars description. It cannot be expressed; it can
only be understood. It is a golden chain that encircles their
hearts and binds them so closely together that neither depths
nor heights nor sin nor shame nor sickness nor health nor
even death itself can ever separate them. This love transcends
earth and ascends to the throne of God Himself, for it is a
reflection of His own love.

> *"Youth is pliable and soft as wax, which easily
> receives the image of whatever forms are pressed
> on it, and yields without difficulty"* (St. Basil).

"Whoever exalts himself will be humbled; and he who humbles himself will be exalted"
(Lk. 14:11).

Pride is a hateful sin in the eyes of man as well as God. Most people sin against humility because they do not clearly understand what pride is. "Pride is an *inordinate* appreciation of one's own excellence."

Pride was the first sin and the cause of all evil.

When Lucifer, the "Light Bearer," the greatest of all God's angels, was put to the test, it was pride, the false belief that he was equal to God, that prompted him to cry out, "I will not serve." God promptly cast Lucifer and his followers from heaven (Apoc. 12:7, 9). Since then Satan and his cohorts have sought to lead men away from God. Sin weakened man in the Garden of Eden when Satan deceived Adam into believing that by eating the forbidden fruit from the tree of knowledge he would become as great as God. The pitiful lament of Eve is self-explanatory, "The serpent deceived me" (Gen. 3:13).

Some men have great talents; all men have some talents; but small or great they all come from God. Man should be grateful and use his talents to the best of his ability, but he should thoroughly understand and humbly acknowledge that they have come to him from the bountiful hand of God. "With all my heart I wish to hymn your praise, O Lord, my God, and glorify your name eternally" (Ps. 85:12).

"Nothing makes a man so like to God as meekness" (St. Chrysostom).

" . . . lay up treasures for yourselves in heaven,
where neither moth devours nor rust consumes,
nor thieves break in and steal" (Mt. 6:20, 21).

The safety-deposit section of the modern bank is sometimes referred to as the "Squirrel Cage." The appellation is
not a derogatory term, but rather graphically describes this
department. The entrance to this vault which contains thousands of small boxes for personal valuables is heavily barred.
Hence the designation "cage." The fact that so many people
hide away so many prized possessions in these containers
reminds one of the industrious squirrel concealing his next
winter's food supply.

It is surprising the valueless articles some people consider
valuable. Those who are familiar with these safes declare
that every conceivable object, from a man's lunch to his
shaving equipment, have been stored in the "Squirrel Cage."

Generally, however, these little boxes are repositories for
man's most precious possessions: his bonds, his stocks, his
jewels, his money. Here he hides away from the thief and
the burglar and consuming fire those material things he
has spent so much energy and toil to acquire. Here, in a
small box, are hidden the total sum of a lifetime of labor.

What paltry pay for lifelong drudgery!

If the individual had worked half as zealously for the
welfare of his soul, he would lay up treasures, not in a
"Squirrel Cage," but in heaven, where these merits would be
safe in the hands of God, a guarantee of eternal life. " . . . we
brought nothing into the world, and certainly we can take
nothing out of it" (1 Tim. 6:7, 8).

> *"Those are true riches, which once possessed,*
> *cannot be lost"* (St. Augustine).

"Not that we are competent of ourselves to take credit for anything as originating from us. Really our competency is from God" (2 Cor. 3:5).

The telephone man got out of his truck and surveyed the tall pole. The former towering monarch of the forest reared its head high above the city street. At the very top was a crossbar supporting some intricate mechanism connected with the mysteries of telephones.

It was quite evident that the workman intended to climb the lofty pole to adjust some faulty wires. To the onlooker, ascending the pole seemed an almost impossible feat, for the creosoted tree was bare of any means of ascent.

After appraising the situation, the mechanic reached into the truck, pulled out a pair of climbers which he adjusted to his feet and strapped to his legs. Then, he casually ascended the slippery pole as if he were taking a Sunday afternoon stroll in the park.

Many people would like to be better than they are. They would like to ascend higher in the spiritual life; they would like to draw closer to the mountaintop. These doubting souls fear to try, however, lest they slip and fall back; and these people are right, if they try to rise unassisted. But if they put on the "spurs" of God's love, they can ascend as easily as the properly equipped telephone man. They obtain this necessary assistance by prayer to and faith in God. "O may it please you, God, to rescue me; make haste to help me, Lord" (Ps. 69:2).

"God does not command impossibilities; but in commanding He admonishes you to do what you can, and to seek for help in what you cannot do, and He assists you to do it" (St. Augustine).

*"He who follows me will not walk in the dark,
but have the light of life"* (Jn. 8:12, 13).

His friends had nicknamed him, "The Exponent of the Evident" because of his unorthodox sense of humor. His ingenuous questions, such as "Have you noticed how the sun only shines on bright days?" or "Do you know that most people in Paris speak French?" was always good for a chuckle from his audience.

The surprising thing is, however, that there are not more exponents of the evident; not of the humorous type, but of the serious sort. It is amazing how few people actually take note of affairs about them.

This fact is particularly true in the moral order. The newspapers carry frequent articles about supposedly intelligent men and women who lose their fortunes through schemes and machinations which seem, to the outsider at least, to be self-evidently harmful.

It is frequently clear to one's neighbor that his friend is becoming entangled in some illegal or immoral affair, while the one involved seems to ignore completely all the danger signs. When the unfortunate individual finally comes to his senses, he asks himself, "How could I have been such a fool?" "The prudent man seeing evil hideth himself: little ones passing on have suffered losses" (Prov. 27:12). The faithful who wholeheartedly strive to follow God's laws are safe from the pitfalls of life. Christ declares, "I am the light of the world" (Jn. 8:12).

> *"My child, walk before Me in truth and seek Me
> always in the simplicity of your heart"*
> (*Imit.,* Bk. 3, C. 4).

"I keep my feet from every evil way, that I may keep your laws" (Ps. 118:101).

Imitation, it is said, is the sincerest flattery, and there is some truth in the saying. Many people unfortunately take this maxim too literally and strive to make their lives a living replica of their "heroes." This is quite evident, and often ridiculously so, in the case of the young girl copying her favorite movie star. It is frequently tragic when a person sets about to imitate his neighbor, whether in manner or morals or in a material way, when that individual is not worthy of imitation.

Each one should remember that he is a distinct individual, different from everyone else, a replica only of God, to whose image and likeness he is made. Man should strive only to perfect himself by developing those qualities and gifts that God has given *him*. "Envy not the unjust man, and do not follow his ways" (Prov. 3:31).

Instead of wasting time and energy striving to make himself like unto "the Joneses next door," the wise man will work to develop those special talents that God has given to him personally. Each one has his own particular gifts. When the faithful are called to give an account of their stewardship, each will be held accountable only for those talents God has given to him. "And every man shall associate himself to his like" (Ecclus. 13:20).

"To be associated with the just is profitable both for instruction and as a proof of virtue"
(St. Ambrose).

" . . . there is more wisdom in the 'absurdity' of God than in all the 'wisdom' of men and more might in the 'weakness' of God than in all the might of men" (1 Cor. 1:25).

St. Paul declares that he preaches "a crucified Christ" (1 Cor. 1:23). Paul does not offer to his hearers great riches, or high social position, or the applause of men. He holds out to them only the "failure of the cross"; for before the eyes of many the crucifixion of Christ was the consummation in ignominy of a Life that had failed.

But the "failure" of Good Friday was necessary for the triumph of Easter Sunday.

Those in this life who prefer Christ's cross to the standard of men are considered unsuccessful according to the world's norm of judging, but in the eyes of God they are the victors, for "he who freely parts with his life for my sake will win it in the end" (Mt. 10:39).

In the drama of Calvary, there is a lesson for infinite meditation. The faithful who dwell upon the suffering of Christ will find in this lesson a peace that "surpasses all understanding" (Phil. 4:7), for in the mystery of the death of Jesus Christ on the cross is hidden the key to life and the key to heaven. "I must be perfectly frank with you: you will weep and lament while the world rejoices. You will be plunged in sorrow, but your sorrow will be turned into joy" (Jn. 16:20, 21).

> *"With good reason, then, ought you to be willing to suffer a little for Christ, since many suffer much more for the world"* (Imit., Bk. 2, C. 12).

"Consequently, brothers, strive even more to make your calling and election secure" (2 Pet. 1:10).

After his ordination to the priesthood in a missionary community, a young man returned home on a visit. Among his old friends whom he called upon was a store proprietor who had often befriended him in his college days. The store owner was not of his faith. Jim Jones was delighted to see the young priest. "Where is your parish, Father?" he asked.

"I haven't a parish, Jim," responded the priest. "I am a missionary. Our work for the most part consists in going from parish to parish preaching two-week missions for the faithful."

"Oh, I see," declared Jim seriously, "you're in the *wholesale* end!"

This true story may seem funny, but it brings out an important point. There is no such factor as "wholesale" in saving one's soul. It is strictly a "retail" business. No one but the individual himself can save his own soul. His loved ones may help him; his enemies may hinder him; but in the final analysis, he and he alone, with the help of God's grace can win eternal life. "Now he who plants and he who waters the seed work in harmony, yet each will receive his own salary befitting his efforts" (1 Cor. 3:8).

*"Keep your heart free and raise it up to God,
for you have not here a lasting home"*
                              (*Imit.*, Bk. 1, C. 23).

*"Again, the kingdom of heaven reminds me of a
merchant in quest of beautiful pearls; as soon as
he discovers one pearl of great value, off he goes
and promptly sells all his possessions and buys it"*
(Mt. 13:45, 46).

The pearl is one of the most beautiful of gems. It is surprising that such a lustrous jewel should have its native
habitat deep down in the dark caverns of the restless oceans.
In order that these precious stones may bedeck milady, pearl
divers risk their lives daily beneath the surging seas. "And
I will give thee hidden treasures and the concealed riches of
secret places" (Isa. 45:3).

It is interesting to note that pearls lose their enchanting
blue-gray color, if not worn frequently; so much so that the
wealthy owners sometimes employ young ladies to wear them
in order that these delicate adornments may retain their
beauty.

Not unlike these pearls, the jewel of sanctifying grace
which adorns the souls of the faithful must be carried constantly if these souls wish to increase this priceless blessing
and to keep it bright and beautiful. By adding to it daily
acts pleasing to God, sanctifying grace is made to shine forth
in all its loveliness, a joy to God, a spiritual adornment to
the possessor, and an inspiration to one's neighbor. "Yes, it is
by grace that you have been saved through faith; it is the gift
of God; it is not the result of anything you did" (Eph. 2:8, 9).

*"The grace of God surpasses not only all the
stars, and all the heavens, but even all the angels"*
(St. Augustine).

*"And all their works are as the sun in the sight
of God: and his eyes are continually upon their
ways"* (Ecclus. 17:16).

The master of ceremonies on a radio "quiz" program asked
a woman contestant her occupation. Having heard the previous contestants aver that they were world travelers or show
people or writers, the lady answered somewhat timidly, "Oh,
I am just a housewife."

"A housewife!" What position or profession could ever
surpass the dignity of such a noble calling: wife, mother,
homemaker? She the very co-operator with God Himself,
in bringing into this world children made to His own image
and likeness, whose destiny is eternity.

Mother of the family, Queen of her domain, whose adoring
subjects stretch out to her their tiny hands for protection
and guidance and love! Maker of a home for a faithful,
loving, and hard-working husband who finds in his happy
family circle his greatest joy and contentment!

"Housewife!" What an honor! What a dignity! What a
glory!

It is well for all housewives to meditate frequently upon
the exalted position which they hold, and to prove worthy,
by their daily deeds of sacrifice and love, of the reverence
in which they are held by those both inside and outside their
beloved families. "As everlasting foundations upon a solid
rock, so the commandments of God in the heart of a holy
woman" (Ecclus. 26:24).

*"It is a great honor, a great glory to serve You,
and to despise all things for Your sake"*
                                    (*Imit.*, Bk. 3, C. 10).

*" . . . He was awaiting the city with foundations
whose architect and builder is God"*
(Hebr. 11:10).

"I like New York but I don't like Philadelphia." "I like
Philadelphia but not New York." Each traveler expresses his
like and dislike for certain cities in no uncertain terms.

Upon further inquiry, the listener will discover that the
visitor who liked New York had an enjoyable time there.
He met new friends who welcomed him. His relatives en-
tertained him royally. Now he holds the most pleasant
memories of his trip to Manhattan. He had the reverse experience, however, during his stay in Philadelphia; thus, his
lack of appreciation for that city. The tourist who liked
Philadelphia, liked it for similar reasons.

People remember with pleasure those places where they
enjoyed themselves. They have only unhappy memories of
those localities where they were lonesome or ill-used. "Oint-
ment and perfumes rejoice the heart: and the good counsels
of a friend are sweet to the soul" (Prov. 27:9).

In this life, "we have not here a lasting city." All are travelers seeking an everlasting home in the Kingdom of God.
It is well for each one, by his faithful fulfillment of God's
law here, to assure himself of a glorious welcome in heaven.
"To him, then, who is powerful enough to keep you from
stumbling and to bring you blameless and exultant to the
presence of his glory, to this only God, our Savior through
Jesus Christ our Lord, belong glory, majesty, dominion, and
authority, before all time and now and throughout all ages"
(Jude 24, 25).

> *"In truth, the loss or gain of God's kingdom is
> no small matter"* (Imit., Bk. 3, C. 47).

*"Now he who plants and he who waters the seed
work in harmony, yet each will receive his own
salary befitting his efforts"* (1 Cor. 3:8).

The high school graduation exercises were advancing satisfactorily. The speeches were quite interesting and the renditions of the orchestra and chorus most pleasing. Finally, Willie Jones arose to play a solo on the piccolo. At best, Willie was not a good player, and now his evident "stage fright" deprived him of even his ordinary ability. Despite his best efforts, the instrument gave forth toots when it should not, and refused to toot when it should have. After a gruesome exhibition, Willie sat down, quite aware of his failure, and very disconsolate. The gentleman who sat next to him sought to console the young man, "Now, don't feel bad, Willie. You did the best you could. After all, it wasn't your fault, but the nincompoop who *asked you!"*

Some people seem to think that if they succeed in persuading another to do evil, that they are in nowise responsible. They seek to shift the blame to the doer, not realizing that by being the primary cause of the act, they are more guilty than the one who actually performs the deed.

The best policy to follow is never to ask another to do something that one would not do himself. Christ who set the precedent for all faithful Christians has commanded his followers, " . . . for I have set you an example, so that what I have done to you, you, too, should do" (Jn. 13:15).

*"To serve God is to reign. Let him who loves
to reign remain firmly subject to the one God,
who reigns over all"* (St. Augustine).

"See," God said, "that you make everything ac-
cording to the model shown you on the moun-
tain" (Hebr. 8:5).

The years had taken their toll of the elderly gentleman.
As he gazed into the mirror, he noted his white hair, his
wrinkled face, his artificial teeth. Gone were his coal-black
hair, his smooth round features, the sparkle in his eyes. He
pondered thoughtfully as he turned away from the old family
mirror, and muttered aloud, "That looking glass ain't what
it used to be!"

The mirror was the same as always, but the man who
stood before it had changed. Youth had surrendered to age —
but the mirror was the same old "looking glass."

Man sometimes looks back upon the origin of the Church
and says, "If only I lived in the early days of Christianity —
I would be more fervent, more zealous, more devoted to the
principles of Christ. But the years have changed the teachings of the Church." St. Paul declares: " . . . if ever we
ourselves or an angel from heaven should proclaim to you
a gospel other than we have proclaimed, let him be accursed"
(Gal. 1:8, 9).

No, the Church has not changed! Her principles remain
the same! God is truth, and His Church is truth, and the
truth never changes. Men's ideas may change. The Church,
never! "Your reign outlives all time, and your dominion
lasts from age to age" (Ps. 144:13).

"Christ teaches; let us listen to Him with a holy
fear and do what He tells us" (St. Augustine).

> *"And this is the sum of eternal life — their knowing you, the only true God, and your ambassador Jesus Christ"* (Jn. 17:3, 4).

Everybody loves a parade. The martial music, the gorgeous floats, the snap and stride of the marchers appeal to all, for, instinctively, the human heart longs for the beautiful. Man was created not for sordidness and baseness, but for an eternity of light and beauty, for the Supreme Good, the glorious presence of God Himself.

Man craves beauty. To a limited extent, through the kindness of the Creator, the creature finds it here, but the most beautiful things of this life cannot fill his soul. They but serve to whet his appetite for the beauties that await the faithful soul beyond the grave.

In watching a parade, the onlooker instinctively pictures himself marching along in the front line, the cynosure of all eyes, receiving the applause of the thousands that line the pavements.

The human heart desires to be important, to be singled out, to be noticed. And why not? The soul has a great dignity. God has created it to His own image and likeness. He has sent it forth into the world to work out its salvation here and to receive its eternal reward hereafter. He values that soul so highly that He sent His only-begotten Son into the world to die the shameful death of the cross to save it. Yes, the human soul is important. To the faithful soul craving love and beauty and dignity, God holds out a satisfying reward — Himself.

> *"If we meditate seriously on those things that are promised to us in heaven, all the goods of this world become vile"* (St. Gregory).

*"Make known to me my end, O Lord — what is
the measure of my days"* (Ps. 38:5).

Occasionally, when one wakes during the night he hears
the distant whistle of a locomotive. The sound seems quite
near at first but gradually fades away in the distance as the
train hurries along. There is something impressive and appealing about a train whistle when heard at night that never
affects one during the day. Perhaps the darkness prompts one
to philosophize more.

The wail of the whistle brings to mind a thought of the
sleeping passengers. What are their varied purposes? Some
are bound on pleasure trips; others on sorrowful journeys;
many are engaged in business. But whatever their reasons
for riding the train, each one has some definite objective,
some purpose for traveling, and each has a definite destination. As the heavy train roars through the darkness of the
night, beckoned on by the green signal lights, it is rapidly
bringing its sleeping cargo to their various dates with destiny.

The sleepless listener to the train whistle may not realize
it, but he too, like all mortal beings, is hurrying on to his
eternal destination. He may not think the pace is fast but
each breath he takes brings him closer and closer to that final
rendezvous. Since man knows that his eternal destination is
not too far off, frequently closer than he thinks, it is only the
part of wisdom to prepare himself well each day so that
when he arrives at his eternal home he may be able to give a
meritorious accounting of his journey. "Blest be the Lord
day in, day out; our Savior God our burden bears" (Ps. 67:20).

> *"Blessed will be that man who is influenced in
> all he does by the thought of the divine judg-
> ment"* (St. Hilary).

"With gladness serve the Lord" (Ps. 99:2).

Many years ago, when the movies were in their infancy, a small theater, somewhat ahead of the times, strove to emulate the Broadway movie palaces. The owner invested heavily in a gorgeous doorman's uniform which was to add bizarre dignity to the entrance of the town's "Bijou." However, the proprietor found it very difficult to display this work of art, for in choosing an employee it was not a question of the applicant having the suit made to fit him, the job seeker must fit the suit. Since the tailor who constructed the garment had monumental ideas, the measurements required a body just short of Atlas! and since giants were few and far between in that community, the lavish outfit spent most of its life expectancy hanging from a hook in the owner's office.

Many will smile at the incongruity of this story; but perhaps these very ones are a bit inconsistent themselves. Countless people believe in God, but in practice they want God's teaching to conform to their idea; they will not conform their will to that of God's. They repeat the "Our Father" daily, but when they say, "Thy will be done," they really mean, "My will be done." The true child of God strives to do his Father's will and in the doing finds great peace and happiness. "O hear, my people, what I teach; incline your ears to the words I speak" (Ps. 77:1).

"And you will find rest for your souls; wonderful novelty! He who takes the yoke finds rest"
                                        (St. Basil).

*"Deep peace alights on those who love your law;
for them there is no stumbling-block!"*
                                    (Ps. 118:165.)

Modern offices and manufacturing plants strive to do what they can to make their employees comfortable. A great deal of money is spent on improvements. In summer, the place of employment is artificially cooled and in winter nicely warmed. To add to the composure of the workers, in many places, cheerful music is piped into the shop or office. The proprietor has not gone to this expense from a purely altruistic motive. He knows that his employees work better and produce better in an agreeable atmosphere.

Everyone knows that he does his best work, mental or physical, when his soul is at peace — peace with God and man. The Creator understands this even better; for did He not create the creature?

Instead of sending merely external means of comfort, God sends the best of all, internal solace and peace. "O come to me, all you who are weary and overburdened and I will refresh you" (Mt. 11:28) is not a meaningless invitation. This invitation and commandment is extremely efficacious, as those who have accepted and obeyed know. Those who do the will of God and receive His blessings do not lose these benefits when they step out of the air-conditioned, music-supplied office or shop, but carry them with them wherever they go. These faithful souls are always at peace because they live in the peace of Christ. "Peace is my legacy to you: my own peace is my gift to you" (Jn. 14:27).

> *"If you hear Me and follow My voice, you will be able to enjoy much peace"* (Imit., Bk. 3, C. 25).

"The greeting is in my own hand — Paul's . . ."
(2 Thess. 3:17).

Phoenicia was an ancient Semitic country north of Palestine which lost its autonomy in the second century before Christ. Yet to this small country of traders, modern civilization owes a tremendous debt. It was the Phoenicians who invented the modern alphabet. The ingenuity of the natives of this rather insignificant nation in translating the hieroglyphics of ancient times into the symbols which form the basis of today's alphabet deserves the highest praise.

The place that writing occupies in the scheme of current-day living is apparent to all. The enormity of the postal service throughout the world testifies to man's desire to correspond with his fellow men.

Of all the letters ever written those of St. Paul are the most important. The great missionary kept in contact with the Christian world by means of the written word. His opening sentence in his Epistle to the Ephesians is typical: "Paul, by the will of God an Apostle of Jesus Christ, to the saints and faithful at Ephesus in Christ Jesus: to you grace and peace from God our Father and the Lord Jesus Christ" (1:1, 2).

In all his fourteen Epistles, St. Paul preaches the doctrine of Christ. In his First Epistle to the Corinthians, he declares, "Woe to me if I do not go on preaching the gospel!" (9:16.)

"Truth, not eloquence, is to be sought in reading the Holy Scriptures; and every part must be read in the spirit in which it was written"
(Imit., Bk. 1, C. 5).

*"Now therefore, ye children, hear me: Blessed
are they that keep my ways"* (Prov. 8:32).

The members of the golf club had had a set of tumbling
rings built to keep the caddies out of mischief during their
spare time. The boys would run along a bench set against
the caddy-house wall, grab the rings, and do a few somer-
saults. One day one of the lads attempted this feat, but as
he grabbed the rings his hands slipped and the next thing
he knew he was trying to recover his wind which had been
knocked out of him by his three-point landing.

The cause of the accident was soon evident. That morning
the postman had delivered several samples of salve to the
caddy master. One of the older boys managed to obtain some
of the salve and smeared it on the rings, with the most
satisfactory results — to himself.

This incident is a forceful example of the misuse and
abuse of a good thing. The salve in itself was a very salutary
medicine in case of sunburn and similar complaints. When
applied to the rings, however, a use for which it was never
intended, the salve performed a most unpleasant work.

Whatever God has given to man is good. Only when it is
misused or abused does it become evil. The true servant of
God strives to use the talents God has given him for a good
purpose, realizing that, as the Gospel parable so graphically
relates, he will have to render an account of the use of these
talents when he appears before the Supreme Judge. "Thus
your life will be a credit to the Lord and will please him in
every respect . . . " (Col. 1:10, 11).

> *"No one can in one and the same thing serve
> the omnipotent God, and be pleasing to His
> enemies"* (St. Gregory).

> *"At all times I will bless the Lord: and ever be his praise upon my lips"* (Ps. 33:1).

Frequently, it is said about some chronic complainer, that he doesn't know how well off he is. It is not necessary to make that statement about another; each individual can take the assertion to his own heart. Through the mercy and love of God, everyone has escaped countless hardships.

Thirty young airmen, who had finished their tour of duty in the Pacific area, anxiously waited as the B-24 that was to carry them to the port of embarkation was warmed up.

Finally, the men were seated in the plane and their "last trip" was a reality. The plane after fighting much bad weather succeeded in making a safe landing in time for the worried passengers to make the homeward-bound boat. As the airmen piled out of the plane, some actually kissed the burnt coral of the New Guinea island. Others simply moved their lips in silent prayer.

Soon all were safely aboard ship and the bomber prepared to take off for the return trip. As the plane arose a few feet from the runway, the number three engine "conked out." Through the skill of the pilot, the bomber was safely air-borne and soon made the home field. "Good work," exclaimed his copilot. "Lucky," murmured the pilot, "but," he continued, "not half as lucky as the boys that got off the plane! If this had happened on the take-off with that load aboard, none of us would have lived." Each one should be grateful to God for those things that could have happened but never did.

> *"Be grateful, therefore, for the least gift, and you will be worthy to receive a greater"*
> **(Imit.,** Bk. 2, C. 10).

"So, my beloved brothers, be steadfast, immovable. Devote yourselves fully at all times to the Lord's work, realizing that your toil in the Lord can never be in vain" (1 Cor. 15:58).

Bridge building is one of the most interesting and most dangerous of undertakings. To span a roaring river, or a deep gorge, or thundering rapids, demands skill and daring.

The building of the new bridge at Niagara Falls was a most hazardous task. To watch the engineers and steel-workers scramble over the weblike fabrications, high above the tumultuous waters, inspired one with the greatest admiration for their courage and ability. Yet in a comparatively short time from the date the heavy foundations were laid, thousands of sight-seers and honeymooners were safely enjoying the view from this magnificent structure.

In order that any bridge may be safely laid, the most essential feature of the work is the solid foundation to which the cables and underpinnings are attached. If these foundations are weak and defective, the bridge cannot withstand the weight of traffic or the pressure of gales or the hundred and one obstacles that may war against it.

Each soul, by his daily labors, tears, toils, and joys, is building a bridge to span the space between his temporal home here and his eternal home hereafter. He should make sure that the foundation of that bridge is based on the solid rock of God's teachings so that when his time comes to cross it, he will be able to pass over the span with safety. " . . . the sure foundation which God has laid stands firm . . . " (2 Tim. 2:19).

> *"A little of the time that is being wasted is the price of eternity"* (St. Jerome).

"Take my yoke upon you, and master my lessons,
for I am gentle and humble at heart."

(Mt. 11:29, 30).

The story is told of a man who was unemployed for a long time and finally secured a job as a motorman on a streetcar. When he returned after his first trip, the starter asked how he made out. "All right," the novice replied, "but I had no passengers." "What do you mean?" demanded the official. "Didn't anyone even wave at you to stop?" "Sure, quite a few waved, but I paid no attention. Those people wouldn't recognize me when I didn't have a job!"

It is humorous to observe the antics of certain people striving to bask in the glory of some prominent personage. The manner in which these individuals humiliate themselves is appalling. It is human nature to desire to be noticed, but when this recognition is purchased at such a stiff price of humiliation, it should prove most embarrassing.

Lawful ambition is to be commended, but flattery and servility are repugnant. The celebrity, not infrequently, exhibits a marked disdain for those who admire him, and accepts the applause of the multitude with practiced disinterest.

How differently does the Creator act toward His creatures! Those who seek to be near Him are welcomed with great love and kindness. They share, not His reflected glory, but the pure, unadulterated brightness of His friendship and love. They are raised up and honored beyond all worldly comprehension. In His presence, true humility is the highest virtue. "What else is there in heaven for me but you? And, if I am with you, the earth has no delights for me" (Ps. 72:25).

"My God, my life, who didst pursue me when I
was forgetful of Thee" (St. Augustine).

*"After all, where your treasure is, there, too, your
heart is bound to be"* (Lk. 12:34).

The visitor to the city stepped out of his hotel. As he
waited for a cab, he asked the starter what the imposing
structure just across the street was.

"Why, that is the City Club," the cab-starter responded.
Then he added as though anxious to speak on the subject,
"That is the most exclusive club in town. You could have
several million dollars, yet, if you did not descend from the
'first families' of the city, you could not become a member.
That's one place where money doesn't count — family background is everything."

As the visitor rode away in his taxi, he pondered upon
the strange ways of men; their desire to separate themselves
from their less gifted fellow men and to seek sociability
among their own classes.

How differently does the Creator act! He invites all to
become members of His "most exclusive club" — heaven. Yet
how careless are His children in ignoring His invitation to
become associated with Him here in His work in order that
they may enjoy the privileges of His divine company for
eternity. The wise and thoughtful soul makes sure, with
the help of God's grace, that he will be admitted as a member of that "most exclusive of all clubs" — heaven. " . . . he
will send forth his angels sounding a mighty trumpet, and
they will assemble his elect from the four winds . . . "

> *"Ponder deeply on the nature of God; it con-
> tains all things, fills all things, embraces all
> things, surpasses all things, and sustains all
> things"* (St. Gregory).

*"For their hope is on him that saveth them: and
the eyes of God are upon them that love him"*
(Ecclus. 34:15).

The long, graceful limousine, the enameled white refrigerator, the hundred and one appealing items that fill even the five and ten cent counters are evidence that today is rightly called the machine age. In order to supply the demand of the public for luxuries or near luxuries, the ingenious assembly lines run twenty-four hours a day.

The first problem that faces a manufacturer considering a new article is to discover how quickly and inexpensively it can be produced. The research departments of industrialism are tireless in finding ways to speed up mass production.

The results of these efforts, it is true, have made America an easier place in which to live.

The interesting point for man to note, however, is that while mass production holds sway in material things, the saving of his soul is still a personal matter. Many would like to shunt aside their personal responsibility toward God, but man is still an individual with an intellect and a free will, and is wholly accountable for every one of his acts. In his relationship with his Creator, the creature should rejoice in the knowledge that God has a personal interest in his spiritual and temporal welfare. Even "the very hairs on your head have all been numbered" (Mt. 10:30). Each one should rejoice in the fact that God loves him so much. His words are sweet, "Come to me, all you who are weary and overburdened, and I will refresh you" (Mt. 11:28).

*"Thou hast made us for thyself, O Lord, and our
heart is restless until it reposes in thee"*
(St. Augustine).

"Thou shalt call me, and I will answer thee"
(Job 14:15).

"You go. I'll stay." The two brothers were having a conference regarding the question as to which should leave home. Both were anxious to leave the family fireside to seek their fortunes in the big, wide world. The older brother generously made the sacrifice in behalf of the younger boy, and remained at home with his parents.

The sacrificial offerings laid upon the altar of the home are countless and are most pleasing to Almighty God. There are great numbers of brothers and sisters who have surrendered their own ambitions and desires in order that other members of the family might be able to follow out their vocations. But God is never outdone in generosity. He richly rewards those who have generously forfeited their rights to another member of the family.

The brother or sister who builds his future happiness upon the sacrifice of another is always indebted to this person and should be conscious of the fact that his dear ones share deeply in whatever success may come to him. He should never forget to show his appreciation by his love, his material assistance, and his prayers.

Christ made the supreme Sacrifice of the cross that the faithful might enjoy eternal bliss; every soul should demonstrate his appreciation for Christ's love by repaying Him with love and devotion. "Then will I freely sacrifice to you, and hymn your name, O Lord; for it is good" (Ps. 53:8).

"Thank God! No saying can be shorter than this, nor can any act be more profitable"
(St. Augustine).

*"From the lips of infants and of babes you have
drawn a fitting hymn of praise"* (Mt. 21:16).

The two young boys were most faithful in serving Mass
each morning at six o'clock. And each morning, the good
Sisters of the convent, out of the kindness of their hearts,
had a breakfast of hot cocoa and buns ready for the young
acolytes.

One of the little lads had the misfortune to suffer from
diabetes and, consequently, had to be careful of what he ate.

After Mass one morning the priest asked the boys if they
enjoyed their breakfast. Both quickly replied, "We don't take
much, Father. The cocoa and buns are too sweet!" They were
advised to let the Sister sacristan know and she would rectify
this condition.

One boy held back and whispered to the priest, "Johnny
can't eat on account of his diabetes, Father. Everything is all
right for me, but I won't make him feel bad by eating in
front of him!"

Surely, out of the mouths of children come much wisdom.
If every person exercised as much consideration for his
neighbor as this young boy did for his friend, there would
be fewer wars and rumors of wars. It would do all much
good to meditate upon this happy incident frequently. "I
cherish your commands and your decrees; for in your sight
I live my daily life" (Ps. 118:168).

"He does much who loves much"
        (*Imit.,* Bk. 1, C. 15).

*"Right now is the acceptable time! Right now is
the day of salvation!"* (2 Cor. 6:2.)

Perhaps the greatest tightrope artist of all times performed
one of the greatest feats of all times over Niagara Falls. On
a wire stretched across this awe-inspiring monument of
nature, this gentleman held thousands of spectators enthralled
as he went through his various acts. Some of the deeds done
by this death-defying performer brought cries of fear and
apprehension from the audience. A defect in the apparatus
or a slip on the part of the artist would have brought him
death in the roaring cataracts a hundred feet below.

This man was not foolhardy. He was a master in his
business; he had taken every precaution against accident;
he had absolute confidence in himself. Yet the onlookers were
amazed that anyone should hold his life so lightly.

Despite their opinion of the tightrope walker, there were
undoubtedly many in that crowd who were in a far more
precarious position than he, and did not realize it. A person
who has committed mortal sin, who has cut himself off from
the friendship of God and refuses to repent, is in a hazardous
position indeed. He is skirting the brim of eternity, into
which he may fall at any minute, carrying with him the
heavy burden of sin. "Keep awake therefore; you know
neither the day nor the hour" (Mt. 25:13). Should he fall
into the abyss, unrepentant and unsorrowful, only an eternity
of remorse and regret awaits him. God holds out His hand
to all sinners. Those balancing themselves on the edge of
eternal damnation should hurry to receive His assistance.
"O God, have mercy on me the sinner!" (Lk. 18:13.)

> *"If God did not love sinners, He would not come
> down from Heaven to earth"* (St. Augustine).

"Beloved, let us love one another, because love takes its origin in God . . . " (1 Jn. 4:7).

A magnet is a body capable of exerting magnetic force and attracting certain substances to itself. Everyone has seen a magnet. School children use them for toys and delight in the drawing power displayed by these little playthings. In the shop and factory, huge magnets are employed to lift mighty loads of iron and steel. In the manufacturing plants, magnets are used to trace down and recover costly and delicate machine parts that would be difficult to locate with the human eye.

Man was created for the honor and glory of God, as well as for his own eternal happiness. Since man was made for God, there is always present in him an attraction toward his Maker. God's love, which is above and beyond man's understanding, constantly reaches out toward the creature. He cannot get away from it whatever he does, wherever he goes, whatever he thinks. Listen to St. Paul, "I am sure that neither death, nor life, nor angels, nor principalities, nor things present, nor things to come, nor powers, nor height, nor depth, nor any other creature can separate us from God's love for us, which is in Christ Jesus our Lord" (Rom. 8:38, 39).

The drawing power of the hugest magnet pales into insignificance compared with the love of God for man. The creature should indeed glory in this limitless love of the Creator for him. "And I, once I have been lifted up from the earth, will draw all men to myself" (Jn. 12:32, 33).

"Turn where you will and as often as you will, you find all things burdensome; in God alone is peace" (St. Augustine).

"Because he clings to me I will deliver him,
and shield him; for he knows my name"
(Ps. 90:14).

Attila, called the "Scourge of God," had sacked practically all of Italy. He now advanced on Rome, determined to plunder, pillage, and destroy the Eternal City.

The inhabitants cowered behind their questionable fortifications; that is, all except the great Pope Leo. Dressed in his papal robes, the Pontiff moved to the city gates to meet the vicious leader of the Huns. To the astonishment of all, St. Leo prevailed upon the terrible Attila with this great prize within his grasp, to turn his horde of barbarians back toward the Danube.

Cheated of the coveted spoils, his angry lieutenants demanded to know why Attila had acted so strangely. The Hun leader answered that he had seen two venerable personages — believed to be St. Peter and St. Paul — standing behind Pope Leo.

Christ assured St. Peter, "you are Peter, and upon this rock I will build my Church, and the gates of hell shall not prevail against it" (Mt. 16:18, 19). If the perils of the Church are as great today as they were in Pope Leo's time, the solicitude of Christ for the successor of Peter is not less.

The constant prayer of all the faithful should be directed to St. Peter and St. Paul, pleading for their intercession, and God's protection in this trying hour. "So that we may confidently say, "The Lord is my helper; I have nothing to fear. What can man do to me?" (Hebr. 13:6.)

> *"Who are you, then, that you should be afraid of*
> *mortal man? Today he is here, tomorrow he is*
> *not seen"* (*Imit.,* Bk. 3, C. 36).

*"Such being the promises we have, beloved, let
us cleanse ourselves from all bodily and spiritual
defilement, putting the finishing touches on the
work of our sanctification out of reverence for
God"* (2 Cor. 7:1).

One of the outstanding examples of resisting temptation
is for a customer to walk through a department store without making a purchase. The purpose of the successful merchant is to overcome buyer resistance. Therefore, he makes his
offerings so attractive that the temptation to buy is almost
overpowering.

The prospective customer with a limited purse and a
definite purchase in mind sees on all sides so many beautiful
things that he would like that he must exercise great will
power to overcome the temptation to buy these appealing
items and to accomplish the original object of the shopping trip.

The faithful Christian knows that he has one essential
purpose in life — the saving of his immortal soul. As he
continues along his earthly journey, he must keep this fact
uppermost in his mind. On all sides he will behold tempting,
attractive, alluring objects — all his for a price — the price
of sin, the price even of his immortal soul. But by keeping
before his eyes the glorious rewards of heaven, all the glitter
and glamour and glory of earthly things becomes dull and
uninviting. "God is faithful and will not let you be tempted
beyond your strength. On the contrary he will, . . . supply
you a way of escape, so that you will be able to hold your
own" (1 Cor. 10:13).

*"Our victory is within us: let the Christian strive
manfully to conquer as Christ conquered"*
                                        (St. Augustine).

*"Not that we are competent of ourselves to take
credit for anything as originating from us. Really
our competency is from God"* (2 Cor. 3:5).

Peter was selected by Christ to be the foundation stone of
His Church. Christ nominated him for this position in the
presence of His other apostles. His words are clear and concise, "And I . . . say to you, you are Peter, and upon this
rock I will build my Church . . . " (Mt. 16:18, 19).

Yet when Christ was taken prisoner the evening before
His death, Peter, who had declared, "At your side, Lord, I
am ready to go to prison and to death" (Lk. 22:33, 34),
denied that he knew Christ. The third time Peter shouted,
"I have nothing to do with this man you are talking about!"
At that moment a cock crowed a second time "Then Peter
recalled the prediction — how Jesus had said to him: 'Before
a cock crows twice, you will disown me three times.' And
he broke out into sobs and tears" (Mk. 14:72).

Perhaps the reason why Christ permitted this awful humiliation to befall Peter was to make him humble. Peter
was so confident of his loyalty and devotion to Christ that
he was sure no temptation nor trial could weaken him. He
had been warned by Christ that he would fall, yet he had
relied upon his own strength and courage to overcome all
obstacles. He had forgotten that all virtue comes, not from
man, but from God. In the future, Peter depended solely
upon Christ. From this sad experience of the first Apostle,
all men can learn a lesson of deep humility — "Severed from
me, you can do nothing" (Jn. 15:6).

> *"We cannot fulfill the precepts of justice in
> every particular, unless we are helped by God"*
> (St. Augustine).

"Cast all your anxiety on him, because he takes care of you" (1 Pet. 5:7, 8).

Everyone has read of the great benefits derived by thirsty, weary travelers from the oases of the deserts. What a sense of relief and restfulness must enter the heart of the travel-worn pilgrim as he sees the swaying palm trees rising majestically from the midst of the burning sands. The promise of a cooling drink of water in that sun-baked region enkindles in the wayfarer renewed energy and hope.

Few, however, know that deep in the Antarctic where perpetual snows, biting winds, and barren skies hold forth the year around, there is an open lake of comparatively warm water.

Here is evidence of God's solicitude for His children. Even in the hottest desert and the most frozen outposts of the world, the Creator has not forgotten His creatures.

In His love for His children, God has given them every material assistance. He is even more generous to the spiritual traveler working his weary way across the desert of life. Along this roadway which He Himself first traveled, as an example to men, Christ constantly walks again to assist the weak, the struggling, and the strong. He has placed His Church in strategic spots where He personally waits to receive the homeward-bound pilgrim, to strengthen him, to refresh him, to guide him on his way. Everyone should take advantage of this kindness of Christ. "The Lord remembers us, and blesses us" (Ps. 113:12).

"The more human help fails, the more strongly should we hope in the divine mercy"
(St. Ambrose).

"My son, from thy youth up, receive instruction:
and even to thy grey hairs thou shalt find wis-
dom" (Ecclus. 6:18).

The patient had several small unexplainable blisters on the sole of his foot. The young intern was zealously seeking to diagnose the cause of the trouble. Finally, he asked the young man if he played golf. "Oh, yes, quite frequently." A smile lighted up the neophyte's face. "Well there's your explanation! The spikes in your golf shoes are irritating the skin."

"But," responded the owner of the aching foot, "I don't wear spikes. I use rubber-soled shoes."

The crestfallen intern promptly prescribed a cure-all that healed the blisters in due time.

The point, of course, is that most people, especially the inexperienced, jump to conclusions. The older one grows the more he realizes that simple solutions to problems are rare.

The roots of most difficulties, whether of the mind or the body lie deep. "Counsel in the heart of a man is like deep water: but a wise man will draw it out" (Prov. 20:5).

The prudent person will proceed slowly in advancing toward any and every conclusion. The wise captain will sound the depths of the water before he takes his ship into strange seas. The sincere Christian will follow the advice of St. James (1:19, 20): "Everyone should be quick to listen, slow to speak, slow to get angry. By anger man does not achieve the holiness that God requires."

> *"Do not yield to every impulse and suggestion*
> *but consider things carefully and patiently in*
> *the light of God's will"* (Imit., Bk. 3, C. 45).

> *"In short, have done fretting about the morrow.
> The morrow, surely, can do its own fretting. One
> evil a day is burden enough"* (Mt. 6:34).

A man called on his neighbor to ask him for the loan of his garden hose. "I'm sorry," replied the neighbor, "I can't let you take the hose today because I must shingle the garage roof."

Somewhat mystified by the refusal, the man departed — hoseless.

The hose owner's wife, overhearing her husband's excuse, said, "That certainly was a silly answer. What has shingling the roof got to do with using the hose?" "Well," replied her spouse philosophically, "when you don't want to do something, one excuse is as good as another."

Ridiculous though this may sound, it is not half as ridiculous as the excuses sometimes advanced by people when they do not wish to carry out some obligation. In fact the so-called reasons given by many people for failing to worship God, makes the hose owner's excuse sound sensible.

Man has no choice when it is a question of serving his Creator. He has an obligation of paying homage to God and of fulfilling His law. Many times he will fail in this obligation, since he is human, but the obligation remains, just the same. The faithful soul should fulfill his duties each day and leave the future in the hands of God. "If, in fact, the good will is there, it is welcome according to what it has to give, not according to what it does not have" (2 Cor. 8:12).

*"The Heart of man is of so great a dignity that
the Supreme Good alone can satisfy it"*
                                        (St. Augustine).

"Clearly, what will it profit a man to gain the whole world when his life is forfeited in any case?" (Mt. 16:26.)

There is an ancient proverb which declares, "Be careful what you set your heart on, because you will surely get it." If one honestly, sincerely, and determinedly sets his heart on gaining some definite objective, he is practically certain of accomplishing his purpose.

All too often men set their hearts upon some position or deed or honor which they believe will bring them complete happiness. Then once obtained, the coveted object turns to wormwood and gall. How many people complain in their old age, "If I were to live my life over again, I certainly would do differently." Hindsight is always better than foresight.

To make sure of having no regrets as one surveys the past, the only certain way to follow is that prescribed by Christ Himself, "If you want to enter eternal life, keep the commandments" (Mt. 19:17).

In the final analysis, the only thing that counts is the salvation of one's soul. When the faithful Christian definitely sets eternal salvation as his main objective in life, he has taken out the securest insurance against an eternity of regret. "My safety and my glory rest with God, my rock and strength: my refuge is in God" (Ps. 61:8).

> *"If you have a heart, understand that the necessity of saving your soul is greater than any other"*
> (St. Ambrose).

*"You filled my heart with keener joy than when
a man abounds in wheat and wine . . ."* (Ps. 4:8).

It is quite commonly observed in life that people gradually begin to resemble their associates. Many persons like to be often in the company of younger friends because they declare the associations make them feel and look less old than they really are. Not only heredity, but, oftentimes, the close association of family life, causes the members to resemble each other so closely that their relationship is immediately apparent.

It has been observed, too, that many castoffs from society follow a definite pattern in their facial expression. Yet when these unfortunates are restored to contact with their family and friends, their whole expression changes. The hard stare in their eyes softens, the rebellious attitude becomes quieted, a contented countenance replaces the crafty and worried look. "For God created man incorruptible, and to the image of his own likeness he made him" (Wisd. 2:23).

It is an error, of course, to judge people by their faces, but it not infrequently happens that certain types resemble each other closely.

The soul is made to the image and likeness of God. The closer the association of that soul with its Creator, through prayer and the Sacraments, the more Christlike the individual becomes. That Christlike interior is bound to evidence itself externally. The sincere soul desires to be closely associated with Christ here in order that he may be forever associated with Him hereafter. "You are my friends, provided you do what I command you" (Jn. 15:14).

*"This is the glory of man to persevere and remain
in the service of God"* (St. Irenaeus).

*"I called upon the Lord, the worshipful, and from
my foes I shall be safe"* (Ps. 17:4).

When Joseph was told in his sleep by an angel to take
the Child and His Mother and to flee into Egypt, he
obeyed immediately and thus saved the Child from Herod's
vengeance.

To undertake such a long journey into an unknown land,
where there were no members of his own family or close
friends to assist him, required great fortitude; and also a
certain amount of money to defray expenses.

St. Joseph had the gift of absolute confidence and faith
in God. But from where was the money to come? As a
carpenter, Joseph never acquired much wealth. According
to some scriptural writers, Joseph financed the trip of the
Holy Family into Egypt with the gold that was given to
them by the Wise Men. "Then give us help against the foe,
for vain is any help of man" (Ps. 107:13).

It is evident from these events that God gives the necessary
assistance to His children to carry out His will. When one
undertakes to do great things for God, he may be sure that
God's help will not be wanting to him. "Yes, as co-workers,
we also exhort you that it be not in vain that you have received the grace of God" (2 Cor. 6:1, 2).

> *"Help me, O Lord God, in my good resolution
> and in Your holy service. Grant me, now, this
> very day, to begin perfectly, for thus far I have
> done nothing"* (Imit., Bk. 1, C. 19).

> *"Bodily training is of little profit, while piety*
> *is profitable in all respects, since it holds promise*
> *for the present life as well as for the next"*
>
> (1 Tim. 4:8, 9).

In the lawless days of the western migration, notorious gunmen fought for survival in a very precarious pursuit. These men, lacking all virtue, had developed a skill in self-preservation and destruction that captures the imagination of the adventurous even today. The speed and efficiency with which these hardened bandits could draw their death-dealing weapons have intrigued generations.

To the neophyte, anxious to ape the master's art, only one bit of advice was given, "Watch the other fella's eye!" In the tenth of a second, before his hand moved toward his gun, the destroyer revealed through the "windows of his soul" the evil intent that dwelled within.

Everyone wants to make a good impression on his fellow men. That is human nature. In order to win the approval of his neighbor, it is necessary that he demonstrate to him a good, kind, solid character. In order to show this character, he must first of all possess it. Therefore, it behooves him to put into practice the teaching of Christ, the foundation stone of all virtues. One's neighbors do not judge him by what he says, but by what he is; by what they see peering out from the "windows of his soul." In order to have the conscientious approval of one's neighbors, it is necessary first to have the approval of God. "Restore to me the joy which your salvation brings: and by a generous spirit make me strong" (Ps. 50:14).

> *"You are what you are, and you cannot be said*
> *to be better than you are in God's sight"*
>
> (*Imit.*, Bk. 2, C. 6).

*"After all, it is the mission of the Son of Man
to seek and save what is lost"* (Lk. 19:10).

Scripture tells man that "The Lord is patient and full of
mercy" (Num. 14:18). Of all God's attributes, His mercy
for the sinner is supreme. Consequently, Christ constantly
dwells upon this virtue. In His parables in the New Testament, the most consoling of all appertain to His love for the
sinner; the good shepherd who left the flock and went off
in search of the lost sheep; the story of the widow and the
lost groat; and that most beautiful of all stories, the parable
of the Prodigal Son.

Even in the death of the sinner, His mercy passes understanding. Someone has penned these beautiful lines, "Between
the saddle and the ground, mercy sought and mercy found."

Forgiveness for injuries is one of man's most difficult
achievements. Yet Christ, who died on the cross for man,
will patiently endure his insults and sins for years, in the
hope that the sinner will amend his ways and return to
His Father's House. "The Lord is kind and merciful, to
anger slow, and full of graciousness" (Ps. 144:8).

Let no one despair of the mercy of God, "know ye that no
one hath hoped in the Lord, and hath been confounded"
(Ecclus. 2:11).

While Christ despises the sin, He loves the sinner. He
simply asks the sinner to forsake his evil ways and come
to Him with a sincere and contrite heart. "The Lord is
good to all, toward all his creatures merciful" (Ps. 144:9).

> *"So great is the mercy of God that it cannot be
> explained in any words, understood by any cre-
> ated intelligence, or conceived by any mind. It
> is above human reason"* (St. Chrysostom).

"I can do all things in him who strengthens me"
(Phil. 4:13).

The small sailboat was coming into the slip. As the two-man crew was about to lower the sail, a sudden gust of wind caught the men unprepared and capsized the boat, throwing the sailors into the water. Neither man could swim, and struggling to keep afloat in the cold water, they cried for help. Several boys were sitting on the dock where the accident occurred, and two of them swam out and brought the scared and exhausted crewmen to safety.

It seems strange that these sailors had never learned to swim. They had been around boats all their lives, but for one reason or another had never learned to protect themselves in an emergency such as had just occurred.

The wise and prudent man strives to prepare himself well for eventualities that may call upon him for all his reserve knowledge and energy. "I pondered on my ways: and I direct my steps toward keeping your decrees" (Ps. 118:59).

The faithful soul, realizing the pitfalls of life and the terrifying temptations that may attack him at any time, struggles manfully to be ready when these attacks bear down upon him. He prays constantly for God's grace, he receives the sacraments often, he assists at the Holy Sacrifice of the Mass frequently. He builds up in his heart such a love for God that the most virulent temptations cannot lure him away to destruction. He follows the advice, "In time of peace prepare for war." "The learned in word shall find good things: and he that trusteth in the Lord is blessed" (Prov. 16:20).

"The devil can bark, but he can bite only him who is willing to be bitten" (St. Augustine).

*"But I have called you friends, because I have
made known to you all that I have heard from
my Father"* (Jn. 15:15).

Libraries are a great boon to mankind. They furnish an
unlimited source of information. Their ponderous volumes
instruct man how to build a bridge, to erect a home, or to
wield the scalpel. The appealing novel gives him many hours
of entertainment. The papyrus and parchment manuscripts
reveal the early story of Christ and His Church. Librarians
have spent years of labor and unlimited wealth gathering
these sources of knowledge and entertainment.

Yet there is a little paper-covered, inexpensive booklet that
contains all the information and all the knowledge and all
the wisdom that lies within the quiet confines of all the
libraries of the world. This booklet is the "penny" Catechism.

Holy Mother Church, in her love for her children, has
reduced to the simple formula of a comparatively few questions and answers the whole history of mankind and given
to her little ones the *essential* knowledge and understanding
of life's purpose and its end. A thousand books could not
answer this question more completely. "Why did God make
me?" "God made me to know, love, and serve Him in
this world and be eternally happy with Him in the next."
Every faithful soul should know his Catechism. "The Lord's
ways are all kindness and fidelity: to such as keep his precepts and his covenant" (Ps. 24:10).

> *"Invincible ignorance will not be imputed to you
> as a fault; but ignorance ceases to be invincible
> and will be imputed as a fault, when you can
> acquire the necessary knowledge, and neglect to
> do so"* (St. Augustine).

> *"My eyes I lift to you who dwell in heaven above"*
> (Ps. 122:1).

The customs officer was quite brusque. "What is your name?" "Citizen of what country?" "Where were you born?" "Anything to declare?" "Unlock the trunk of your car!" "Open up your bags!"

Even the most honest citizen feels a chill run up and down his spine when he endeavors to answer these questions or to obey these commands.

First of all, he is entering a foreign country. The familiar and stable ground on which he is wont to trod as "king" is gradually slipping out from under him. Strange faces, strange customs, strange lands lie ahead. This introduction on the part of the border agent does not add to his sense of security.

However, once he has received the official "nod" and has entered the desired country, his sense of balance returns, and he feels flattered that he has won the approbation of the stern-visaged representative of the new land.

Everyone knows that sooner or late he must leave the familiar scenes of this life, and enter into another world.

Unlike the unrepentant, the faithful follower of Christ looks forward to this journey without fear, trepidation, or worry, but with hopeful expectation that he will be safely "passed," through the kindness of God, into the land of eternal security, perpetual peace, and unending happiness. "Go forth from your country and from your kindred, and come into the land that I will show you" (Acts 7:3, 4).

"Faith is the source of justice, the principle of sanctity, from which all justice takes its beginning" (St. Augustine).

*"For in him we live and move and have our
being"* (Acts 17:28).

Acting is one of the most ancient and noble professions.
The religious drama, the forerunner of the modern stage,
goes back to the beginning of history. The sincere, honest
actor who is successful in his chosen profession surrounds
his work with the highest ideals. The end of his endeavors
is not the colossal paycheck or the gleaming limousine or
the magnificent home; all these happen to be the incidental
rewards. What the successful actor thrives on is the enthusiastic approval and appreciation of his efforts. An appreciative audience brings out the best in him.

Man by his very nature desires approval of his labors. A
word of appreciation from the most humble individual is
music to the ears of the hearer.

Many people wonder why men and women separate
themselves from the activities of the world and enter into
the hidden life of the monastery and the convent. It is not
because they love the companionship of their family and
friends less, but because they love the company of Christ
more. In the silence of the religious life, they hear more
clearly the voice of God. The sweet voice of the Redeemer
is music to their ears. They know that in their humble labors
they have the approval and appreciation of Him who is to
be their final Rewarder. To them, the applause of the
theater of life is as nothing compared to the approval of
God. "He who in this way serves Christ pleases God and
is approved by men" (Rom. 14:18, 19).

> *"I have striven hard to find You outside Your-
> self, and yet if I desired You, I would find You
> dwelling in my heart"* (St. Augustine).

"You may go. In answer to your faith, your wish shall be granted" (Mt. 8:13).

Today, an ocean-going boat under a foreign flag tied up at the dock. Longshoremen were busily engaged loading the vessel with goods to be carried back to its home port.

The thought came to the mind of the onlooker, "How can such a comparatively small boat find its way on the trackless and stormy ocean? Yet, it takes the most direct route and is seldom driven off its course."

The answer is known to every schoolboy. The laws of nature's God will guide it home. The captain reads his position from the heavens; he knows the constant drift of the currents; he knows the proper ship lanes.

The Church, under God, gives man the proper guidance to reach his eternal home. "The steps of man are guided by the Lord. But who is the man that can understand his own way!" (Prov. 20:24.)

An abandoned ship tossed about by the winds and waves unguided by a wheelsman is called a "derelict." This word comes from the Latin and means "thoroughly to relinquish." A soul that relinquishes its hold on God becomes a derelict in the sea of life, without guidance, driven about by every wind that blows, without a star to guide him into a port of refuge. The wise and prudent and faithful soul never relinquishes his hold on God. "But near you are, O Lord; all your commands reveal your faithfulness" (Ps. 118:151).

"What is His worship but love of Him?"
(St. Augustine.)

" . . . for there exists no authority not ordained by God. And that which exists has been constituted by God" (Rom. 13:1).

Confidence begets confidence. When the employer singles out a certain individual employee and says to him, "Joe, I am sending you out on this job. I have every confidence in you that you will make a success of it," the employee is determined to justify the trust that has been put in him. The fact that he was chosen among all the other men in the office gives him a lift. Joe is now a man with an important job to do. The very fact that his employer has confidence in Joe inspires confidence in Joe himself.

Each creature is sent into this world by God to do some particular work, and every duty is of the utmost importance from the very fact that it originated in the divine will.

Man should have great trust in God who puts such trust in him. St. Paul assures his followers, "So, my beloved brothers, be steadfast, immovable. Devote yourselves fully at all times to the Lord's work, realizing that your toil in the Lord can never be in vain" (1 Cor. 15:58).

The employee rejoices in the fact that his employer has seen fit to honor him with his trust, but what a frail honor this is compared to being selected by God, as each faithful soul is, to do the work of the Creator of the universe! "Rejoice in the Lord, O universal earth! With gladness serve the Lord" (Ps. 99:2).

> *"Time is as valuable as God himself . . . God is gained by time well spent"* (St. Bernard).

*"Gladly, therefore, will I boast of my infirmities,
that the power of Christ may spread a sheltering
cover over me"* (2 Cor. 12:9).

Pencils are rather insignificant things. They are so common in this country that no one pays much attention to them. Yet the manufacture of a pencil requires twenty-five different materials and two hundred different operations. Even after all this labor and expense, the pencil is not able to perform its intended duty. The tremendous work it does each day in the home, the office, the shop, the studio could not be accomplished without the writer first preparing that instrument by the final necessary operation — sharpening. Some wood that holds the lead in place must be removed before it can do what it was intended to do.

Man, the creature of God, is an instrument in the Creator's hand. He is sent into this world to perform the will — the work of God, "only he who does the will of my Father who is in heaven will enter the kingdom of heaven" (Mt. 7:21, 22). Before he can fulfill this end, however, he must be perfected by trials, temptations, sufferings. The waste material of his life must be cut away — often painfully. The burdensome characteristics of his personality must be separated from his soul by the sharp instrument of humility. When God has prepared him for his task by taking from him that which would prevent him from rightly performing his duty — only then is he ready for profitable and meritorious undertakings. "And . . . through many tribulations we must enter the kingdom of God" (Acts 14:21, 22).

*"Let a Christian rejoice in adversity; because he
is either tried, if a just man, or freed from faults,
if a sinner"* (St. Augustine).

"Be assiduous and attentive in prayer with thanks-
giving" (Col. 4:2).

The office manager was "down in the boots." He felt he
was thoroughly abused. Here it was a beautiful summer
afternoon and his "boss" had asked him to get out some
special work.

As the employee groaned over his unhappy lot, he pulled
from his desk the unfinished report that it was necessary to
complete that day. As he did so, out came a canceled check.
Casually he glanced at it. Oh yes — the $100 the boss gave
him the time his wife was sick. Pretty thoughtful of the old
man! Soon a chain of good deeds performed by his employer
was running through his mind. That annual three weeks'
vacation with pay; the Christmas bonus; the nice weekly pay
check. Say, his employer wasn't such a bad fellow after all.
Oh well, working one Saturday afternoon wasn't so bad.

Man's tendency is to be a "receiver" not a "giver." He
soon forgets the good deeds that have been done to him
and for him and looks around for more. It would be well
for each one to sit back occasionally and count up all the
good things he has received from God, that he "may not
forget the works of God, and observe whatever he enjoyed"
(Ps. 77:7). God has given to His children life, good health,
grace, parents, a family, a home, and countless other blessings.
God has given them everything that they possess. Then let
each one ask themselves: "What have I given back to God
in return?" — "How, then, shall I requite the Lord for all
that he has granted to me?" (Ps. 115:12.)

> *"But alas! Men forget God at the very time when*
> *they are enjoying His blessings"* (Lactantius).

"Glory to God in the heavens above, and on earth peace to men of good will" (Lk. 2:14).

Frequently enough these days, when we look into the sky we can see a large transport plane hurrying along on its scheduled trip. This heavy machine has succeeded in overcoming the law of gravity and raising itself high above the earth. Sometimes as passengers in these planes one looks down upon the beautiful countryside, resembling a patchwork quilt of brilliant colors. The roar of the engines assures him that all is well. If the engines failed to perform their appointed task, this mammoth ship would immediately crash to the ground, wreck itself, and bring death to its occupants.

Man's soul is the engine that lifts the mortal bodies of men above the things of earth. Not unlike the plane's engines, men's souls need fuel — spiritual fuel. They must be kept clean and properly adjusted. Countless hours are spent in keeping the plane engines in perfect shape. How much time do you give to keeping your soul in condition? "As deer will yearn for running brook, so yearns my soul for you, O God" (Ps. 41:2).

"As the soul is the life of the body, so God is the life of the soul. You are not filled with charity if you mourn over a body from which the soul has departed, and do not mourn over a soul from which God has withdrawn" (St. Augustine).

*"In case one member is in pain, all the members
share it. In case one member is honored, all the
members share its satisfaction"* (1 Cor. 12:26).

The visitor to the large city found his hotel room stuffy
and hot, so he decided to take a stroll in the nearby park.
As he walked across the avenue, a speeding truck struck him,
knocking him unconscious. In the hospital, no means of
identification could be found on the stranger. He had left
his coat and wallet with his money and papers in his room.
Here was a man in deep distress, unknown, seriously injured,
and without friends. Suddenly, one of the doctors observed
a fraternal locket attached to the watch chain. The doctor
himself belonged to this same prominent organization. The
sick man was without friends no longer. A short time later
he was identified and his family was called.

Not infrequently, the Catholic who wears a medal around
his neck is accused of idolatry or superstition by his non-
Catholic neighbor. This is due to the fact that the neighbor
does not understand why the medal is worn. The person
wearing the medal has placed himself under the special
protection of Mary or one of the saints, and in doing this,
he has asked for her or his intercession in obtaining grace
from God; either to avoid distress, or if distress comes, to
have the powerful help of the one in whose honor he wears
the insignia. "It follows that you are no longer foreigners
and guests; no you are fellow citizens with the saints and
members of God's household" (Eph. 2:19, 20).

> *"Make friends for yourself now by honoring the
> saints of God, by imitating their actions, so that
> when you depart this life they may receive you
> into everlasting dwellings"* (Imit., Bk. 1, C. 23).

" . . . rejoice to the extent that you share in the suffering of Christ, so that you may also rejoice and exult when his glory will be revealed" (1 Pet. 4:13, 14).

No one likes to be in debt. When misfortune strikes, however, and financial obligations mount up, the burden of debt may become great indeed. The loan shark even may be visited with consequent increase in the already staggering obligations. It seems as if this overwhelming load can never be lifted. Yet eventually, through the grace of God, all debts are paid. What a tremendous relief for the borrower to be free of the crushing weight that has borne him down. He is truly a new man.

Every man is a debtor to God. He owes Him his life and health and all that he possesses. The creature has the obligation of paying back his Creator in the currency that is the standard of exchange in heaven — love. While finite man cannot repay the infinite God for His immeasurable graces, he has the obligation of paying up the debt as fully as he is able. Yet God is a merciful noteholder. One act of sincere sorrow for a penitent heart can win an eternal place in the eternal kingdom. The wise and penitent soul strives to store up in heaven those meritorious deeds that will be credited against his debts when he personally appears before God to give an account of his stewardship. "Come, bless the Lord, all you who serve the Lord" (Ps. 133:1).

"The strength of desires enables us to bear toil and sorrow; and no one willingly undertakes to endure what gives him pain, unless it be for that which gives him pleasure" (St. Augustine).

"We exercise mutual love because he first loved us" (1 Jn. 4:20).

In the not so distant past, many families secured their drinking water from the family well. In dry seasons, when the water was low, it was necessary to "prime the pump." Priming consisted of pouring sufficient water down the pipe to displace the air and thus cause suction. When the necessary suction was established, the cool, refreshing water was easily pumped to the surface.

Deep down in the hearts of all men, regardless of their rough exterior or apparent evil nature, there is great goodness. To bring this charity to the surface, frequently, the hearts of these people must be first "primed" with kindness. Human nature reacts quickly to compassion, consideration, thoughtfulness, forgiveness, mildness, mercy, and all the other qualities that have their foundation in love. The kind soul who "primes" the hearts of others with his own charity is delighted to behold reciprocal kindness gushing forth from the depths of these grateful neighbors.

St. John admonishes the faithful, "let us therefore love, because God first loved us" (1 Jn. 4:19, 20). God has, as it were, "primed" our souls with His own love. By meditating upon the life of Christ, and especially His greatest Act of Love, His death on the cross for men, there will pour forth from the hearts of the grateful souls a superabundance of love for God and for their fellow men. "Yea, I have loved thee with an everlasting love: therefore have I drawn thee, taking pity on thee" (Jer. 31:3).

> *"Jesus Christ must be loved alone with a special love . . . For Him and in Him you must love friends and foes alike . . . "* (Imit., Bk. 2, C. 8).

"Blessed are the promoters of peace, for they will rank as children of God" (Mt. 5:9).

Every religious community has its own pious customs and traditions. Many nuns wear a ring, a band of silver that signifies their undying devotion to their beloved Spouse, Christ. Inside this ring, it is customary to have inscribed a motto, some particular phrase that serves to inspire the wearer to strive for greater perfection. This inscription, known only to the Sister and God, is a constant reminder of the good nun's determination to do all things, suffer all things, endure all things for Christ. "I will extol you, O my God, my king: and bless your name forever and for aye" (Ps. 144:1).

This custom could be profitably imitated by newly married couples. What inscription could they use? Any one of hundreds that would serve to remind them of their first love and nuptial vows. Perhaps the best would be one that would bring to mind their resolution never to speak harshly to their life partner. If the first harsh word is never spoken, peace will remain forever in the home. Such a slogan might be "No harsh words." "Anyone who loves me will treasure my message, and my Father will love him, and we shall visit him and make our home with him" (Jn. 14:23).

Whether or not this resolution is inscribed in the wedding ring, it most certainly should be written in letters of gold in the heart of each newlywed—and in the hearts of older married people as well. "Then the peace of God which surpasses all understanding will guard your hearts and your thoughts in Christ Jesus" (Phil. 4:7).

"When concord, and peace, and the bond of love exist between husband and wife, all good things come to them at the same time" (St. Gregory).

"Therefore, whoever believes he is standing firm,
should beware lest he fall" (1 Cor. 10:12).

Man is a creature of God and as such is completely dependent upon the Creator. Not infrequently, however,
people decide for themselves that they are sufficient unto
themselves and need no help from God. It may be that they
feel secure in their wealth, their power, or their puny wisdom.
They become proud. Like Lucifer of old, they refuse to
acknowledge the Supreme Being as their Creator, Saviour,
and Final Judge. These people are riding to a fall.

How differently St. Paul! In his humility he refers to
himself in the third person when he writes: "And I know
that this person . . . was caught up into paradise and heard
unutterable utterances which no man is permitted to repeat"
(2 Cor. 12:3, 5).

Here is seen a great saint, to whom was given the immeasurable grace of being permitted to behold the glories
of heaven, and yet who constantly humbled himself, lest
he glory in his preaching and good works. Paul knows
human nature and he knows particularly his own frailty, so
he writes to the Corinthians, "I buffet my body and make
it my slave, lest, perhaps, after preaching to others, I myself
should be eliminated" (1 Cor. 9:27). After reading these
words of Paul, what man can feel proud?

> *"Humility makes men like to angels, and pride*
> *changes angels into devils . . . it is the beginning,*
> *the end, and the cause of all sin; because not*
> *only is pride itself a sin, but there has not been,*
> *there is not, and there will not be a sin without*
> *pride"* (St. Augustine).

"You will point out to me the way of life — the plenitude of pleasures close to you; aye, bliss at your right hand for all eternity" (Ps. 15:11).

There is a saying that, although an optimist may be wrong as often as a pessimist, he has more fun.

According to the dictionary, an optimist is "one who hopes for the best." If a popular vote were taken, there is no doubt that the overwhelming majority of people would choose as their companion the optimist.

No soul can be close to God and not possess the qualities of cheerfulness and hopefulness. In contact with the Source of all goodness, the faithful follower of Christ imbibes the spirit of joyful expectation. He understands that all trials and difficulties in this life are simply preparations for the everlasting joys of eternity. Jesus has said, "The kingdom of heaven reminds me of a treasure buried in the field; as soon as a person discovers it . . . he goes in his joy and sells all his possessions and buys that field" (Mt. 13:44).

The faithful Christian realizes he has an option on heaven; God has given him the grace to obtain the prize and he is ready and willing to suffer all things to pay the purchase price. In his labors for this great reward, he is always joyful because he has unshakable confidence that Christ will compensate him for his faithfulness with those consoling words, "Well done, my good and faithful servant . . . you were faithful in managing something small; I will now put you in charge of something great: share to the full your master's happiness" (Mt. 25:21).

" . . . keep your conscience good . . . for a good conscience . . . can bring joy even in the midst of adversity" (*Imit.,* Bk. 2, C. 6).

*"Any kingdom torn by civil strife is laid in ruins,
and no city or household split into factions can
last"* (Mt. 12:25, 26).

The Eskimo has managed to exist in the Barren Lands of
the Arctic for generations. To win a livelihood out of that
wasteland between northern Canada and the Pole bespeaks
the astuteness of the natives. Perhaps their ability to overcome the elements is best demonstrated by the Eskimos'
cleverness in building his home with the materials at hand.

With a wide-bladed knife, they cut out solid blocks of the
frozen snow and cleverly mold these blocks into a snug igloo.
The natives crawl into the igloo, light a fire, and are as
comfortable and warm as their Southern neighbors are in an
insulated apartment on Fifth Avenue. These people have
managed to survive because by their own initiative they have
overcome the terrifying obstacles of that barren land.

From the Eskimos' determination to survive, all men can
learn a lesson. It is not necessary for the inhabitant of the
crowded cities to build a material home for his family with
his own hands, but each one *must* build for himself a spiritual
bulwark to protect himself against the onslaught of the world,
the flesh, and the devil. If he builds this citadel well, with
the help of God's grace, he can find peace and contentment
and joy, secure in his own abode and unafraid of the tumult
and turmoil that storms around him. Here he will be truly
king in his own castle. "And I declare to thee, that the Lord
will build thee a house" (1 Par. 17:10).

> *"If you are wise, if you have sense, if the light
> of your eyes is with yourself, cease pursuing
> those things the gaining of which is misery"*
> (St. Bernard).

> *"As is quite proper among the saints, let there
> not so much as be mention among you of fornica-
> tion or any kind of impurity or lustful desires"*
> (Eph. 5:3).

"Evilness is given too much publicity" is a statement particularly true today. St. Paul knew human nature — its
weaknesses as well as its strength — therefore, he admonished
his disciples not to scandalize their neighbor with "shameful
conduct or senseless talk or suggestive jesting. These are all
unbecoming" (Eph. 5:4, 5).

Advertisers pay hundreds of millions of dollars a year to
keep their names before the public and to bring attention to
their wares. These men know the value of publicity; they
know that men and women, and children, too, are influenced
by what they read and see and hear. The repetition of their
sales talks has a subconscious effect upon the individual that
will urge him to buy a "name brand" when he steps into
the store to make a purchase.

Someone has said, "Any publicity is good publicity." This
means, of course, as long as his name or his product is kept
before the public, it is "good business."

The free advertising given to "evilness" is appalling —
the moral harm done by this cheap publicity is incalculable.
The *conscientious* person and newspaper and periodical are
too smart to be unwitting press agents for Satan. "The
prudent man saw the evil, and hid himself: the simple
passed on, and suffered loss" (Prov. 22:3).

> *"Enlighten me, O good Jesus, with the brightness
> of internal light, and take away all darkness from
> the habitation of my heart"* (Imit., Bk. 3, C. 23).

"A camp the angel of the Lord erects about his worshipers, and thus delivers them" (Ps. 33:8).

And the angel answered and said to him, "I am Gabriel, and my place is in the presence of God" (Lk. 1:19). St. Luke relates these words in telling of the announcement to the aged Zachary of the birth of his son, John the Baptist.

The modern world in its pursuit of material things loses sight of the close relationship between heaven and earth. Scripture relates many instances in which God has sent His angels (messengers) to men to inform them of His will.

According to the teaching of the Church, God's angels watch over every immortal soul. Christ warns, "Take care you do not despise any one of these little ones: I tell you, their angels in heaven look continually upon the face of my Father in heaven" (Mt. 18:10, 11).

What a tremendous consolation it is to know that in the struggle against evil, each one has close at hand an invisible legion of defenders! All should pray daily to their Guardian Angels to aid them in avoiding temptations, and when the tempter does intrude, to vanquish him. "Then war broke out in heaven: Michael and his angels had to fight the dragon . . . That huge dragon . . . was hurled down, he who is called the devil and Satan" (Apoc. 12:7, 9).

> *"It is only a temptation that troubles you, a vain fear that terrifies you"* (*Imit.*, Bk. 3, C. 30).

*" . . . he who does not love his brother whom
he sees cannot love God whom he does not see"*
(1 Jn. 4:20, 21).

Of all the devastating weapons, outside physical or military
means, which man uses to overcome his enemies, the most
diabolical is ridicule. The dictionary says that ridicule is
"to make fun of," "to deride."

No self-respecting person likes to be made fun of, especially
in public. It seems that the most sensitive one of all is he
who ridicules the most. As the saying goes, when the tables
are turned "he can't take it."

It is bad enough for a man to ridicule his enemies, but
it is far worse when he ridicules his friends. Some men, for
example, seem to delight in making fun of their wives in
public. This humiliation not infrequently causes serious results.

Any person who uses ridicule as a pastime is no gentleman. Newman defines a gentleman as "one who never inflicts
pain." What is more painful than being ridiculed?

The Pharisees and Sadducees tried frequently to ridicule
Christ and each time they suffered a humiliating setback.
They sought to embarrass Him when they craftily asked
what the greatest commandment was, and Christ answered:
"Love the Lord your God with your whole heart, and with
your whole soul, and with your whole mind. This is the great
and first commandment" (Mt. 22:37–39). Then he added, for
their benefit perhaps: "Love your neighbor as yourself." A
loving soul will not treat another in a manner in which he
himself would not like to be treated.

*"Let him who reproves have truth as a witness,
have mildness as a father, have justice as a judge"*
(St. Bernard).

"Know that the Lord is God; 'tis he that made us; his we are . . . " (Ps. 99:3).

The captain of a ship has a tremendous responsibility. He has a serious obligation toward his employers as well as toward his passengers. If he should deliberately endanger his ship to the detriment of its owner, he is guilty of the serious crime called barratry.

Man might be compared to a captain guiding his ship across the stormy sea of life. Despite the fact that the creature is automous and has a free will, he is not at liberty to damage his body or his soul, for he will be held responsible for his every act to his Creator. The Creator has jurisdiction over the created. While man has an independent intellect and a free will, this does not mean that he may expose himself to danger or willfully injure himself by sin or anything else without being held to account by God. "A man cannot be the slave of two masters. He will either hate the one and love the other, or, at least be attentive to the one and neglectful of the other." (Mt. 6:24).

Man may not follow after the desires of his heart and flesh nor give reign to the passions which will bring about his temporal and eternal destruction.

The creature is bound to follow the Law given him by his Creator. Sooner or later he must go before his Judge to give an accounting of his stewardship. The faithful captain strives to present an acceptable log of his trip to his admiral. "O guide me to obey your true demands; teach me; you are my Savior God. In you I always trust" (Ps. 24:5).

> *"Direct your zeal . . . first upon yourself; then you may with justice exercise it upon those about you"* (Imit., Bk. 2, C. 3).

"The patient man is better than the valiant; and he that ruleth his spirit, than he that taketh cities" (Prov. 16:32).

To display his great strength to his Saracen enemy, Richard the Lion-Hearted, on the Crusades in the twelfth century, drew his gigantic sword and severed a hardened steel bar in half.

Saladin, not the least bit perturbed by this exposition of his adversary's powers, quietly drew his long, thin, resilient, Damascus blade, tossed a silken scarf into the air, and neatly severed the falling kerchief in twain.

In the subsequent battle between these two mighty warriors, Saladin, the subtle leader, overcame and defeated Richard, the robust attacker. "A wise man is strong: and a knowing man, stout and valiant" (Prov. 24:5).

The man who uses brute force to gain his objective generally dashes himself to pieces against some immovable object, while the patient, determined, prudent individual avoids conflict, or if battle is necessary, wears down his opponent with the persevering patience of Christ. "My strength and courage is the Lord; a Savior he has proved himself to me" (Ps. 117:14).

"It is sometimes well to use a little restraint even in good desires and inclinations, lest through too much eagerness you bring upon yourself distraction of mind; lest through your lack of discipline you create scandal for others, or lest you be suddenly upset and fall because of resistance from others" (Imit., Bk. 3, C. 11).

*"Keep yourselves in the love of God, while you
await the mercy of our Lord Jesus Christ, which
will bring you to eternal life"* (Jude 21, 22).

It is consoling to know that Holy Mother Church has, in
her solicitude for her children, designated a saint known as
the "Patron of Difficult Cases." The intercession of this saint
has been experienced in wonderful ways by those who have
sought his help. In maladies defying human skill, in sickness
without apparent remedy, in anguish of soul, distress of
heart, in poverty, misery, and even in despair, the faithful
have turned to St. Jude, the Apostle, cousin of our Lord,
and have found surcease from their sorrows.

The opening words of St. Jude's epistle are most consoling,
"Jude, servant of Jesus Christ and brother of James, to
those who have been called, who have been loved by God the
Father, and guarded for Jesus Christ. May mercy, peace, and
love be extended to you in abundance" (Jude 1, 2).

St. Jude, "Patron of Difficult Cases," is most generous in
obtaining from Christ, "mercy and peace and charity," as
all his faithful clients know. Have confidence in him.
"Where man fails God still avails" (Lk. 18:27).

> *"Convert us to You, that we may be thankful,
> humble, and devout, for You are our salvation,
> our courage, and our strength"* (Imit., Bk. 3, C.8).

"And when the chief Shepherd appears, you will come into unfading glory as your reward"
(1 Pet. 5:4).

It is one of man's peculiarities that he becomes very much attached to his old hat. He may buy a whole new wardrobe, but to the consternation of his wife, he refuses to part with his old battered fedora. To separate himself from this faithful companion of the years would be a catastrophe.

His beloved spouse, on the contrary, is constantly on the alert for new headgear — a startling contraption that "will do something for her" — meaning mostly, that it will attract the gaze, and perhaps envy, of her hat-loving sisters.

This discrepancy of opinion between men and women regarding hats brings to mind the importance of headgear.

Throughout the ages, the mark of royalty and kingship has been the crown.

The saints are always pictured with a halo, a luminous circle, about their heads to convey the fact that they have received the eternal reward of their sanctity and have been decorated by the King of Kings with the crown of eternal life. "Every contestant submits to all sorts of privations, and that to win a perishable crown, but we an imperishable one" (1 Cor. 9:25, 26).

The faithful must be steadfast in their labors for Christ that they, too, may one day receive the prize for which they have striven so urgently — "the life-giving crown which the Lord has promised to those that love him" (James 1:12).

"The reward of the saints is so great that it cannot be measured, so abundant that it cannot be limited, so precious that it cannot be valued"
(St. Ambrose).

*"Whoever are led by the Spirit of God, they are
the sons of God"* (Rom. 8:14, 15).

The chaplain of the pilgrimage returning from Rome
was talking with one of the liner's passengers.

"I've enjoyed this trip tremendously, Father," the man was
saying. "Every minute was precious to me so I made the
most of my time. This vacation was purchased at a great
sacrifice, too; perhaps that is why I enjoyed it so much.
It has taken me years to save up enough money to take
this journey. I've been tempted at times to forget all about
my determination to see Europe and Lourdes and Rome, and
our Holy Father, and just enjoy myself with the money I had.
Each time, I overcame the temptation with the thought of
the pleasure I should have in visiting the great shrines and
seeing the cathedrals and monuments so closely associated
with my religion. I am glad I made the sacrifices. I have
pleasant memories that will stay with me all my life."

The enlightened and contented countenance of the passenger was visible proof of what he had said.

When the man left him, the priest used the next half hour
with the pilgrim's words for his meditation.

Heaven is man's for a price — the price of labor and toil
and endurance and vigilance, and love for Christ. The gaining of eternal glory is worth every sacrifice; and the greater
the sacrifice, the greater the glory. "See how we call them
blessed for having remained patient" (James 5:11).

> *"Do you wish to see God? In the first place, then,
> think of purifying your heart, and cast out what-
> ever you see is displeasing to Him"*
>
> (St. Augustine).

> *"And my delights were to be with children of men"* (Prov. 8:31).

Older people are wont to look back upon their youth and bemoan the passing of those glorious and carefree days. These elders forget that the intervening years have heightened the high spots and covered up the shadows. Each phase of life has its own particular worries and problems. Sometimes the problems of youth are even greater than those of age, because of the intensity of youthful nature.

Someone has categorized the various ages of youth as follows:

The "knee age" when a boy is guided by his mother.

The "we age" when he goes in for team sports and needs social guidance.

The "she age" when he meets girls and first finds an interest in them.

And finally, the "thee age" when he begins to think of others and to help them.

Each age has its own peculiar cares and worries; and since it is extremely difficult for another not of that particular period to understand the problems which present themselves to the growing youth, it is of the utmost importance that these young souls turn to God for help and guidance. God thoroughly understands the individual soul at all times — for He has created it. Thus, all youth should be constantly in the company of God. "Your reign outlives all time, and your dominion lasts from age to age" (Ps. 144:13).

*"Patience, O Lord God, is very necessary for me
I see, because there are many adversities in this
life"* (Imit., Bk. 3, C. 12).

*"Moreover, grow in grace and in the knowledge
of our Lord and Savior, Jesus Christ"*
(2 Pet. 3:18).

"Knowledge is power" — an intriguing slogan. This maxim
has a special appeal to proud human nature and especially
so to the ambitious youth. Knowledge may indeed be power,
but undisciplined learning can be a power for evil.

"Knowledge" is different from "education." The dictionary
defines "knowledge" as *information, learning, scholarship* —
i.e., something acquired, something from outside the individual.

"Education," on the other hand, comes from within the
person. The very word comes from the Latin, *e* "out" and
ducere "lead": thus it means to bring forth; to lead out of
the soul all the good that lies hidden there. Its definition is
clear: *to teach and discipline, so as to develop the potentialities
of the student.* Note carefully the words "to discipline" for
only that knowledge that is properly guided and controlled
becomes really powerful for the good of all.

God has given to man, as one of His choicest gifts, the
intellect. The Creator expects the creature to use his intellect
for a definite purpose: to honor God and to employ his
knowledge toward gaining eternal salvation, the end for
which the creature was created. In using knowledge, *to conquer and control himself,* man can exercise a tremendous
influence for good upon the whole world. "O teach me
judgment, teach me sense, because in your commands I
trust" (Ps. 118:66).

> *"You have time to engage in worldly affairs, but
> you have no time to gain a knowledge of Christ,
> that is, to learn the wisdom of God"*
> (St. Paulinus).

> " . . . *but I shall see you again, and then your*
> *hearts will rejoice, and no one will take your*
> *joy away from you"* (Jn. 16:22, 23).

The contract was carefully scrutinized by both parties. Finally, after much thought and meditation, the party of the first part and the party of the second part officially placed their signatures upon the document.

Not long after the contract went into effect, a serious court trial was underway between the signers. The interpretation of the contract must be decided by the judge. What had happened? One of the contractors apparently neglected to read the "fine print." As is the case in making formal agreements, the main agreement is set forth in bold type, but extenuating clauses are sometimes slipped into fine print, which, if overlooked by the unwary, may cause him untold embarrassment, financially and otherwise.

How differently God deals with his children. The agreement He offers to the party of the second part is open and clear and concise — there are no hidden clauses or cleverly concealed "ifs." When the young man in the Gospel asked Christ how he might save his soul, our Lord spoke *clearly,* "If you want to enter eternal life, keep the commandments" (Mt. 19:18). God freely gives the initial grace necessary for the contracting party to undertake his work, and if man fulfills his part of the agreement, and carries out the Commandments of God, he is assured of a glorious place in heaven. "The Lord is true in all his words: and holy in all his deeds" (Ps. 144:13).

"A heavenly treasure must be chosen by us, that
we may have our heart in it" (St. Basil).

*"I certainly am not ashamed of the Good News,
for it is the power of God to bring about salvation
for everyone that has faith"* (Rom. 1:16).

The passenger on the Europe-bound liner was deathly sick. It was his first ocean crossing and the weather was unusually rough. The unfortunate man weakly called his wife. "Marie, I certainly am going to die and there is one final request I want to make. When I die, I insist that you bury me in Europe, because dead or alive I never want to cross this ocean again."

This bit of humor brings to mind the fact that resolutions made by people in time of danger, illness, or distress are infinite. The wicked firmly resolve to change their ways, the good are determined to become better.

Christianity is not a religion based on emotionalism. Christianity is based solidly on faith and reason. Faith in the omnipotence of almighty God, confidence in His love, mercy, and protection; and this faith and confidence are based firmly on the Rock of Peter—the Church. God has given His creatures an intellect to understand His teachings and a will to follow them. Out of His infinite love, He freely gives to His children the great gift of faith, and He expects and commands them to put their trust in Him. With humble confidence in God, the faithful soul faces even the most unexpected and awesome events with equanimity. "Well for the man who fears the Lord, and in his laws takes great delight" (Ps. 111:1).

"Our mind will more bravely despise the terrors of temporal things the more truly it subjects itself, by fear, to the Author of things"
(St. Gregory).

*"By God's grace I am what I am and the grace
which entered me was not fruitless. On the contrary, I have worn myself out on toil more than
any of them. No not I, but the grace of God
working with me"* (1 Cor. 15:10, 11).

The Japanese were not defeated by the atomic bomb, as
dreadful as this weapon of war was, according to some
authorities. The dropping of the bombs at Hiroshima and
Nagasaki was the occasion for the surrender, but the cause
of the defeat was starvation.

Regardless of how well or how courageously men may
fight, they cannot continue to struggle without the necessary
means. This is true not only in a war among men, but doubly
true in the continuous battle between man and evil.

In the struggle to save his soul, man has a "worthy adversary" — "worthy" in the sense that the Evil Spirit is
intellectually superior, extremely clever, and absolutely devoid
of any principles of morality. In order to vanquish this
enemy, man needs great spiritual assistance. He needs spiritual
Food to keep him strong. He needs enlightenment to outwit
his attacker. He needs encouragement. God gladly gives all
the necessary requisites to wage a tireless and victorious war
against the enemy, as long as man keeps open the supply
line to the Source of all these graces. "The God of peace
will speedily crush Satan under your feet" (Rom. 16:20).
By prayer, the Mass, the Sacraments, by sacrifice, by love,
loyalty, devotion, and penance, man assures himself of God's
protection, and "My grace is sufficient for you." (2 Cor. 12:9).

*"Not the grace of God alone, nor man alone, but
the grace of God with man"* (St. Augustine).

*"Would that today you listened to his voice: O
harden not your hearts . . . "* (Ps. 94:8).

Frequently it is heard said, "I can never remember a face,"
or "I can never remember a name," and sometimes even, "I
can never remember a face or a name." Yet there is no
greater way of winning friends and putting others at ease
than by recalling their names after once having met them.

Those who have acquired the faculty of "remembering" have
a wide range of associates. Note the words, "acquired the faculty," because in most cases, this characteristic is developed.

Each person has many distinguishing qualities about him
that the new acquaintance should take time to observe and
note. It is not sufficient for him just to say "Hello" and move
on to the next introduction. The one who wishes to remember makes a mental note of the name and person of his
new-found friend. The next time these two meet, there are
no embarrassing excuses about "poor memories."

The successful artist is a man of observation. He must first
"see" what he places on canvas. The average individual uses
powers of observation to a very limited degree.

The reason why so many souls are not friends of Christ is
that they do not know Christ. They have never really
"looked" at Him. These souls never study Scripture; they
never listen to sermons; they never pray. In order that they
may learn to love God, they should first strive to *know*
Him. "But all men are vain, in whom there is not the
knowledge of God" (Wisd. 13:1).

> *"Nothing contributes so powerfully to purity of
> life and manners, or to diligence in the divine
> service, as an earnest desire to hear the word of
> God"* (St. Chrysostom).

> *"And I saw that wisdom excelled folly, as much as light differeth from darkness"* (Eccles. 2:13).

It was a beautiful sunshiny day. The faces of the people were bright with smiles; the flowers were lovelier than ever; the azure sky had spread a blanket of blue from horizon to horizon. All this transformation was brought about by the light of the sun. Just as the fragile flowers reach out their tender petals toward nature's "radiator," so man brightens perceptibly and waxes cheerful on a bright summer day.

The good man instinctively turns toward the light. "In him was life, and the life was the light of men" (Jn. 1:4).

In the earliest days of creation, man discovered that he could make a spark fly from flint; shortly after this, he used the candle to penetrate darkness, then crude oil, and gas, and finally, in his never ending search for light, he discovered electricity, which served not only to lighten his home, but his streets, and even his city.

Man desires and seeks external light to cheer his senses, but above all he craves an internal light that will brighten up his soul. This light comes from God's grace and presence. God is the Source of all light and the soul is ever attracted toward Him. The faithful soul who knows the joy of the light of God's presence, will endure all things rather than suffer that Light to be snuffed out. "O mark and taste the goodness of the Lord! Well for the man that confidently flies to him!" (Ps. 33:9.)

"The cause of our love of God is God himself"
(St. Bernard).

"In all thy works keep the pre-eminence"
(Ecclus. 33:23).

Scholars can thank the learned monks, laboring lovingly over their parchment manuscript in the "scriptoria" of their monasteries, for preserving for modern Christian civilization its priceless heritage. Not content with simply copying Scripture with pen and parchment, these holy men embellished their documents with magnificent and delicate scrolls and miniature pictures, which retain their beauty even today.

The remarkable feature of these illuminated manuscripts is their freshness. Although hundreds of years old, the script and decorations are as bright and live as if recently fashioned.

The artist was performing his task for God; therefore, only the most superb handicraft would do and only the best of materials could be used. The gorgeous dyes employed in this work have never faded. The blues and Tyrian purples and golds have a freshness and purity about them that emphasizes the loveliness of the message they express. The modern chemist would be pleased to know the formula for producing such brilliant and enduring dyes, but the secret lies buried in the hearts of those devoted men who loved God so greatly.

From the handiwork of these lovers of Christ, modern man can learn many lessons. Foremost among the patterns these spiritual men have set, is their determination that whatever the deed undertaken for God, the workmanship must be worthy of Him. "Lay open thy works to the Lord: and thy thoughts shall be directed" (Prov. 16:3).

> *"I consider fervor to be an ardent, firm, constant desire of pleasing God in all things"*
> (St. Basil).

> *"How little faith you have! . . . what made you doubt?"* (Mt. 14:31.)

"Peter said to him: 'Lord, if it is you, tell me to come to you over the water.' 'Come,' he replied. So Peter climbed out of the boat and, starting in the direction of Jesus, walked on the water; but when he felt the stiff breeze, he took alarm and, since he began to sink, cried out: 'Lord, save me!' Jesus immediately reached out his hand and took hold of him. 'How little faith you have!' he said to him; 'what made you doubt?' Then they climbed up into the boat and the wind subsided. The men in the boat prostrated themselves before him and said: 'You are indeed the Son of God'" (Mt. 14:28–33).

This account of Christ and Peter is one of the most inspiring and consoling stories in Scripture because it brings home forcefully the love and kindness of Christ and the faith in Himself that He expects from His children.

No matter what the circumstances, or how bitter the blow, or how grievous the sin, God holds out to all His strong, welcoming hand. When the soul fears that he is about to sink into the troubled waters of disappointment, sorrow, or even despair, let him raise up his heart to God, confident that He will not desert him. Peter wavered but Christ urged him on. He will do the same for every precious soul who cries out to Him. Everyone should memorize this beautiful story and put into practice the lesson Christ here gives to all. "How little faith you have . . . what made you doubt?"

"Faith is the beginning of man's salvation, the foundation and root of all justification, without which it is impossible to please God, and to be numbered among His children" (C. of Trent, Sess. 6).

"Man is born to labor, and the bird to fly"
(Job 5:7).

Occasionally, the summer tourist far from the path of usual travel will stumble upon a picturesque water wheel. A meandering forest stream will come to a waterfall, and there man, eager to put this energy to work, will place a paddle wheel. The rushing water agreeably splashes over the paddles, forcing them down and turning the wheel. The rotating disk turns the axle connected with it and the axle turns the stones that grind the grain into flour, the staff of life. Now, to the observant watcher, there is nothing more monotonous than a revolving water wheel, yet this simple instrument not only has produced the food that sustained the lives of the early settlers in this great land, but also has served as the basis for the country's prosperity.

God has been more than bountiful in giving to America the natural resources that have made it great and powerful. To utilize these gifts, man has employed the water wheel to transform them into the necessities of modern civilization.

Many people complain about the monotony of their work. They find the daily grind displeasing. Let them recall the work of the water wheel — for surely nothing could be less exciting. Yet this humble work has performed a "miracle." If each one does the work assigned to him in life, *he is doing God's will* — nothing is greater! The inanimate wheel acts thus because it is not free to do otherwise. Man freely does his work for love of God. "Hate not laborious works, nor husbandry ordained by the Most High" (Ecclus. 7:16).

> *"God appointed man to labor and formed his body with that object; therefore, the idle man falls . . . from his office"* (St. Chrysostom).

*"For whatever has been written beforehand has
been written for our instruction, that through
the patient endurance and consolation afforded
by the Scriptures we may have hope"*
(Rom. 15:4, 5).

The word "traitor," one of the most despised in the English
language, originated in the reign of the Roman Emperor
Diocletian. During the final persecution of the Christians,
Diocletian ordered all Christian churches to be leveled to the
ground, and the books of Holy Scripture to be turned over
to the Roman authorities for burning. Those unfortunate souls
who, under the stress of fear, handed over the Scriptures to be
destroyed were called *traditores;* whence, the word, "traitor."

Diocletian believed that if he could destroy the Scriptures,
he could destroy Christianity. Thus, the prominent position
held by the Bible even in the eyes of the pagan Romans in
the earliest days of the Church is evident. "By way of answer
Jesus said to them: 'You are wide of the mark, since you
understand neither the Scriptures nor the power of God'"
(Mt. 22:29, 30).

In those times, all books were written by hand and consequently were extremely costly and few in number. Today,
through the means of the high-speed printing press, everyone
can afford a copy of Scriptures. These books containing the
Word of God Himself, and preserved by the Church through
the ages at such a tremendous cost of sacrifice and love should
be read eagerly by those who glory in the name Christian —
follower of Christ. "The Lord is true in all his words, and
holy in all his deeds" (Ps. 144:13).

*"Let our chief effort, therefore, be to study
the life of Jesus Christ"* (Imit., Bk. 1, C. 1).

"Deep in my heart I shrine your utterance:
O may I give you no offence" (Ps. 118:11).

"Then Peter came up and said, 'Lord, how many times may my brother wrong me and still claim my pardon? As many as seven times?' 'No,' Jesus replied; 'I do not say, "as many as seven times," but "as many as seventy times seven"'"(Mt. 18:21, 22).

Forgiveness of one's enemy who has inflicted a grave injustice is most difficult. Yet, this act of forgiveness is one of the fundamental principles of Christianity and must be exercised at all times by those who recite the Our Father, "forgive us our debts, as we also forgive our debtors" (Mt. 6:12).

The human heart is so constructed that hatred of one's enemy takes its own toll. The bitterness engendered by meditating on past injuries, real or imagined, engulfs the soul with unhappiness and discontent. Rancor replaces righteousness. Soon, what was a small irritation festers and inflames the heart and consumes the energy and zeal that should be expended in working out one's salvation. Thus the penalty for uncharitableness is exacted even here. "You merciless man . . . I canceled that whole debt of yours because you pleaded with me. Was it not proper for you, too, to take pity on your fellow official just as I had taken pity on you?" (Mt. 18:32, 33.) For peace of soul and health of mind and also body, the faithful servant of Christ follows the example of Christ on the cross, "Father, forgive them; they do not know what they are doing" (Lk. 23:34).

> *"For with God nothing that is suffered for His sake, no matter how small, can pass without reward"* (Imit., Bk. 3, C. 19).

> *"Open my eyes: I wish to scan the wonders of your law"* (Ps. 118:18).

As the tourist casually walks past the beautiful cathedral, he admires its regal splendors, its mammoth size, its majestic lines, and its towering spires. Yet, he experiences no great warmth or sense of the Presence of God.

Once he enters this mighty edifice, however, he senses a complete change. The very atmosphere testifies to the fact that this is the House of God. The stained-glass windows that looked dull and lifeless from the outside are now alive with color and beauty. The brilliant sun shining through shows forth every detail and shading. The various figures in all their majesty come to life. The visitor is amazed that these beautiful windows could appear so cold and inanimate from the exterior and yet, when seen from inside the church, are so gorgeous and lifelike. "O well for those who dwell within your house, O Lord, unceasing is their praise of you" (Ps. 83:5).

All things in life are beautiful, but they must be seen in the proper light—in the light of God's Presence. "Then Jesus stopped, and called for them. 'What do you want me to do for you?' he asked. 'Lord,' they said to him, 'we wish our eyes were opened'" (Mt. 20:32, 34).

"O God, You Who are the truth make me one with You in love everlasting" (Imit., Bk. 1, C. 3).

*"To the Lord I cried in my distress, and he has
heard my prayer"* (Ps. 119:1).

The heavy bomber, just leaving the target, went into a
steep dive. The pilot grasped the controls and endeavored to
pull the rudder back to level off the plane. His efforts were
fruitless. The mighty ship was traveling for earth and destruction at terrific speed. The copilot took hold and both
exerted every effort to pull their "wheels" back. Near ex-
haustion, the captain of the ship cried out, "Let's give it one
more try before we give the signal to bail out!" The two
young airmen braced their feet and pulled with every ounce
of strength — and they prayed as hard as they pulled. Suddenly, the nose came up and the plane leveled off. Their
superhuman effort, and their supernatural petitions, had
saved themselves, the crew, and plane.

"Father," related the grateful pilot to the chaplain later,
"there was a third Man who gave us a hand in the cockpit
on that mission. I never prayed so hard in all my life as I
did on that final and successful try!"

The pilot's efforts and prayers should be an example to
all. God helps those who help themselves. When man does
his part, he may be sure that God will hear his plea, and be
right beside him to aid him in every need. "This is the
extent of confidence in him: no matter what we ask, provided it is in keeping with his will, he hears us" (1 Jn. 5:14).

> *"Take care not to fail in prayer; if He to whom
> you pray seems not to hear you, be vehement
> and carry violence even into heaven itself"*
> (St. Gregory).

"See with what large letters I write to you with my own hand!" (Gal. 6:11.)

The Pony Express rider is one of the most dramatic of the adventuresome figures of the old West. Hurling his pony across the open plain, over mountains, through angry rivers, he delivered the United States mail. Some lonely mother or wife or child along the Eastern seacoast was made to live again because of his battle with death.

Today the train, the bus, the plane, the boat speeds across the world the letter that some anxious person is waiting for, on which some important business transaction depends or perhaps some momentous decision of State may hang. Today, as always, mail is important and welcome.

St. Paul and the other Apostles, on their strenuous missionary journeys, realized the importance of the written word to encourage, to console, to instruct, to inspire; hence their letters or epistles to the faithful of their day. To those to whom they were instrumental in bringing the teachings of Christ, they sent back the admonitions, advice, and inspiration necessary for the neophytes' perseverance in the Word.

Today, the fourteen Epistles of St. Paul and the seven Epistles of the other Apostles in the New Testament, the inspired Word of God, are as fresh and living and instructive and inspiring as they were when penned by these devoted followers of the newly risen Christ. Every Christian should be familiar with these letters and strive to put into practice the teachings contained therein. "I adjure you by the authority of our Lord Jesus Christ to have this epistle read to all the brothers" (1 Thess. 5:27, 28).

"The word of God is the food of the soul"
(St. Augustine).

"I have come into the world as a light, so that no one who believes in me might remain in darkness" (Jn. 12:46, 47).

The New York subway system is one of the great engineering feats of the day. The visitor to Manhattan who takes his first train ride beneath the surface of the city is at first frightened, then amazed, and finally enthralled by this means of transportation.

While every means is taken to make the system as pleasant and comfortable as possible, the daily rider never quite becomes accustomed to traveling happily in such an artificial atmosphere. The engineers, the guards, the trackmen who have to spend eight hours a day in this subterranean environment realize their task is not an easy one.

Rider and worker alike await impatiently the hour when they may leave the sunless, gloomy, cavernous depths and ascend to the sunshine and fresh air above. The rapid change from the electric lamps and the damp air below to the glorious sunlight and invigorating breeze above brings about a complete transformation in all. "The heavens tell the glory of God" (Ps. 18:2).

All are workers and travelers here; working out their own destiny and traveling swiftly toward their ultimate destination. Even the brightest day or the happiest hour one enjoys here cannot be compared to the reward God holds out to all. St. Paul declares, "We see now by means of a mirror in a vague way, but then we shall see face to face" (1 Cor. 13:12).

> *"Man draws nearer to God in proportion as he withdraws himself farther from all earthly comfort"* (Imit., Bk. 3, C. 42).

*"Let us, therefore, confidently draw near to God's
throne, the source of grace, that we may obtain
mercy and find grace to aid us when we need it"*
(Hebr. 4:16).

The hospital emergency room was alive with activity. The
police had reported a serious automobile accident. When the
ambulance arrived, the doctor took one look at his patient
and ordered an immediate transfusion of blood plasma.
Almost at once a transformation took place in the victim's
features. His color returned, his body relaxed, his whole system
responded gratefully. Soon he was able to sit up and converse
with his family. The "blood bank" had saved the man's life.

Christ died on the cross in order that He might redeem
man from sin. He willingly shed His blood that His children might have life, and "have it in abundance" (Jn. 10:10).
By His supreme Sacrifice, He purchased for men sanctifying
grace — the life-giving plasma of the spirit.

When sinful man receives, in sorrow and repentance, the
Sacrament of Penance, he receives this "spiritual plasma,"
just as he does in the reception of every Sacrament. When
this grace enters the sinner's soul, it eradicates the cause of his
illness. The tenseness leaves the penitent's face, peace is restored to his soul, and his quiet countenance is external
evidence of the transformation within him. Christ holds out
the offer of this "blood bank" of grace to all sinners. The
spiritually sick should hasten to receive this life-giving Plasma.
"Renew yourselves constantly . . . and put on the new self
created after the image of God in the justice and holiness that
come from truth" (Eph. 4:23, 24).

"Come to Me when it is not well with you"
(*Imit.*, Bk. 3, C. 30).

*"The Lord loves those who hate the wrong; he
guards his dear devoted friends; from godless
hands he rescues them"* (Ps. 96:10).

"It's the third act that counts." The drama critic was simply
stating a fundamental principle of the theater.

The most difficult part of the writing of a successful play
is to demonstrate in the final scene, graphically and con-
vincingly, the victory or defeat of the hero. Ordinarily speaking, the playwright's success or failure depends upon his
ability to bring dramatic reality to the last act.

In this life each one plays a definite role in an exciting
and momentous drama that includes all the fundamentals
of histrionic art: love, laughter, sorrow, disappointment,
tragedy, comedy, failure, and success.

As man's life in this world advances rapidly toward completion, he must keep constantly before his mind the fact
that the final scene is the one that really counts, "In all
thy works, remember thy last end, and thou shalt never
sin" (Ecclus. 7:40).

By striving faithfully *each day* to prepare himself for that
last act of life — death — he assures himself, through God's
grace, of a glorious exit from this world's stage into the
presence of a just but merciful Judge. "To him then, who is
powerful enough to keep you from stumbling and to bring
you blameless and exultant to the presence of his glory, to
this only God, our Saviour through Jesus Christ our Lord,
belong glory, majesty, dominion, and authority before all
time and now and throughout all ages. Amen" (Jude 24, 25).

*"Take up your cross, therefore, and follow Jesus,
and you shall enter eternal life"*
(Imit., Bk. 2, C. 12).

"I loved the Lord because he heard my pleading voice" (Ps. 114:1).

The youngster playing on the lawn under the watchful eye of his father stumbled and struck his knee against a sharp rock. The little lad sent forth a howl of anguish that brought his father to him in an instant. The young man grasped the boy in his paternal arms and smothered the aching knee with kisses. The crying suddenly stopped and a smile of contentment spread over the youngster's face.

The sharp rock had caused much pain to the boy's knee, but the affection and love lavished upon him caused him to overlook his suffering in the certain knowledge that his father's affectionate kisses could cure all! " . . . that we may in turn be enabled to comfort those who are in any kind of affliction by imparting to them the comfort we receive from God" (2 Cor. 1:4, 5).

This confidence and faith and hope that the little boy placed in his father is the same faith and hope that God wants all His children to place in Him. "O come to me, all you who are weary and overburdened, and I will refresh you" (Mt. 11:28, 29). In all the sufferings that man endures in this life, he should remember that his heavenly Father is always close at hand, ready, willing, and able to alleviate his pain and to bring him contentment and peace. "I call on you, for you will hear me, God . . . O of your mercy give a wondrous proof: you rescue from their foes all those who fly to your right hand" (Ps. 16:6, 7).

"The devout man carries his Consoler, Jesus, everywhere with him, and he says to Him: 'Be with me, Lord Jesus, in every place and at all times'" (Imit., Bk. 3, C. 16).

"That saying is trustworthy and deserving of wholehearted acceptance, for we work and struggle to this end, because we hope in the living God, who is the Savior of all men, especially of believers" (1 Tim. 4:9, 10).

People are sometimes surprised to discover after the death of an acquaintance that the deceased possessed much worldly goods. "Why, I had no idea he was so wealthy!" or "Her will certainly shocked me — I didn't know she had a cent."

This conversation spreads among the departed's friends like wildfire. Immediately, unknown relatives appear like spring flowers on a warm day.

It might likewise come as a great surprise to many friends also if they were gifted to see the tremendous treasures some of their departed associates have stored up in heaven, where the results of their labors and good deeds are accepted "currency" in winning them eternal bliss. These quiet, unassuming souls have diligently labored for but one thing, not material wealth to leave behind them to be fought over by disappointed money grabbers, but for spiritual merits that *they can take with them* and which will prove an everlasting joy. These devoted souls, known only to their divine Friend, have gone about quietly and unostentatiously doing good for others, and striving at all times to conquer themselves for the love of Him. The day of final judgment will indeed prove to be a day of revelation. The faithful soul labors industriously to assure himself a place close to God on *that day*. "The Lord is near to the crushed of heart: and broken spirits he restores"

"God has placed it in our power to decide how we shall be judged" (St. Augustine).

*"God shall thunder wonderfully with his voice
he that doth great and unsearchable things"*
(Job 37:5).

According to a newspaper report five Torpedo planes took off from the Navy's Fort Lauderdale Air Station on December 5, 1945, on a navigation training flight. Hours passed. Darkness descended. Radio appeals to the aircraft went unanswered. Realizing the ships' fuel supply must be exhausted, the authorities sent out search planes. A PBM with a thirteen-man crew was among the searchers. The five Torpedo planes with fourteen crewmen were never found. The PBM rescue craft never returned. What happened to the unfortunate men and their planes is a mystery.

Just as there are mysteries in the natural order, so are there mysteries in the supernatural order.

It is not given to man to understand all the handiwork of God. These divine mysteries it must be noted, however, are not *contrary* to man's reason. They are *above* his reason.

Many people saw Christ perform His miracles. Yet, what these hardened souls saw with their eyes, they would not permit their hearts to believe. The humble soul accepts on the authority of God the works of God, realizing that in His own good time He will reveal His hidden mysteries. Every sincere Christian may cry out with St. Paul, "Oh, the depth of the riches and of the wisdom and of the knowledge of God! How incomprehensible are his judgments and how unsearchable his ways!" (Rom. 11:33.)

*"He reveals His secrets to the humble, and with
kind invitation bids them come to Him"*
(*Imit.*, Bk. 2, C. 2).

*"Shun what is bad, do what is good; seek after
peace in thought and deed"* (Ps. 33:15).

"What time is it?" The answer might well be: "It's later
than you think."

From Big Ben in London to the town clock in every village
and hamlet stretches a continuous line of clocks; time clocks,
alarm clocks, advertising clocks, every conceivable kind of
clock. In other words, most people are "time conscious."
They arise by the clock; they catch their bus or train by
the clock; they start and stop work; they rush home; they
go to the movies; and finally they retire at the command
of the clock.

It seems the difference between the joyful souls who built
the magnificent and timeless cathedrals of the Middle Ages,
and the tense and strained people of today who rush to
build bigger and better fighter planes, faster autos, and
streamlined trains, is this: those happy and contented children of God were "eternity conscious," while today's children are "time conscious."

The few brief years that even the oldest person spends here
are as nothing compared with endless eternity. Therefore,
it would be wise when one looks at a timepiece, to remind
himself that life is short, eternity long. "Why, what is your
life? You are but a puff of smoke that appears for a little
while, and then disappears" (James 4:15).

"Use temporal things but desire eternal things"
(Imit., Bk. 3, C. 16).

> *"Oh, what is man, that you should think of him? Oh, what is mortal man, that you should care for him!"* (Ps. 8:5.)

In his argument against astrologers who claimed that the position of the stars at the time of one's birth decided that individual's personality and future, St. Augustine pointed out that twins born under the same star have greatly diverse personalities and go widely separated ways. Augustine quotes the example of Esau and Jacob who were very unlike both in character and actions.

No two people are alike. Each has his own physical, mental, and moral characteristics which make him a distinct individual with a personality all his own.

It is evident, then, that each individual soul has his own particular gifts and shortcomings which make up his own personality. "Who among men knows the inner thoughts of a man save the man's spirit within him" (1 Cor. 2:11).

One thing, however, all men possess in common — their great dignity before God. Each soul is made in the image and likeness of his Creator, and that soul is created for eternal happiness. This great dignity which each one possesses demands the respect and reverence of all other men, regardless of his state of life. In a special manner, it demands that the individual soul respect himself. The Psalmist declares: "A little less than angels you created him: you created him with dignity and glory, him you crowned!" (Ps. 8:6.)

> *"May You be blessed, my God, for although I am unworthy of any benefits, yet Your nobility and infinite goodness . . . do good even for those who are ungrateful . . ."* (Imit., Bk. 3, C. 8.)

"Or, what price can a man pay down to purchase life forever?" (Mt. 16:26, 27.)

The newsboys, while waiting for the papers to be handed out, spent some of their time and most of their pennies in a nearby ice-cream parlor. In those days, before the so-called "one-arm bandits," the store boasted a penny contraption. When dropped in a slot, the copper drifted down through a series of pegs and sometimes landed in the twenty-five-cent pocket. The "jack pot" entitled the winner to six ice-cream cones. This day, a very cheerful lad had the rare good luck to land his penny in the quarter compartment. So grateful was the recipient of this good fortune that he wanted to share it with those present, so he invited all his chums in the store to have a treat on him. When the prize winner reached the head of the line, he discovered to his dismay and grief that his generosity had overstepped his judgment — there was no cone left for him, all six had been given away!

There's an old saying that "charity begins at home," and this maxim applies particularly in spiritual matters. Man must never neglect his own immortal soul. He has but one soul and if he loses that, he loses all. Therefore, while he should be solicitous for the welfare of others, he should always remember that his own salvation comes first. "He that shall find me, shall find life, and shall have salvation from the Lord" (Prov. 8:35).

> *"Take heed to yourself, O man! Take heed to yourself, that is, to your soul, which you know is your nobler part, which you know is your whole self, which you know is your better part"*
> (St. Ambrose).

"Whoever are led by the Spirit of God, they are the sons of God" (Rom. 8:14).

Christ told His Apostles at the Last Supper, "If you love me you will treasure my commandments. And I will ask the Father, and he will grant you another Advocate to be with you for all time to come, the Spirit of Truth! The world is incapable of receiving him, because it neither sees him nor knows him. You will know him, because he will make his permanent stay with you and in you" (Jn. 14:15–17).

Christ promises to send the Holy Spirit, the Third Person of the Blessed Trinity, "the Spirit of truth" to His faithful. In order that the Holy Spirit may dwell in the heart of the true Christian, he should recite this prayer to Him frequently:

Come, O Holy Spirit, fill the hearts of Thy faithful, and kindle in them the fire of thy love.

V. Send forth Thy Spirit and they shall be created.

R. And Thou shalt renew the face of the earth.

LET US PRAY. O God, who hast taught the hearts of the faithful by the light of the Holy Spirit, grant that, by the gift of the same Spirit, we may be always truly wise, and ever rejoice in His consolation, through Christ our Lord. Amen.

The Seven Gifts of the Holy Spirit are: Wisdom, Understanding, Counsel, Fortitude, Knowledge, Piety, Fear of the Lord.

"The Holy Spirit is sent to complete by His power what our Saviour began, to guard what He acquired, to sanctify what He redeemed"
(St. Augustine).

*"Besides, we have received this commandment
from God: He who loves God must love his
brother also"* (1 Jn. 4:21).

The young mother was frantic. Her little girl had wandered
off into the woods. Now darkness was coming on and there
was no trace of the lost child. Hundreds of friends and
neighbors were searching the surrounding resort area but no
word of hope had come back from the searchers.

In a cloud of dust, a car screeched to a stop. Out of the
machine came two determined-looking men followed by two
bloodhounds. Taking a quick whiff of the baby's clothing,
the dogs with their sensitive noses to the ground were soon
tugging at their leashes as they followed the invisible trail
left by the child. The well-trained dogs, following the scent
left by the baby, wherever she moved in her meanderings
through the forest, quickly found the child asleep beneath
an overhanging bush.

Not unlike this child, everyone as he goes through life
leaves his impression for good or evil upon those with whom
he comes into contact. This "scent" is the influence he has
on others. No one can escape the fact that his actions, his
character, his personality have an effect upon those about him.
"But the path of the just, as a shining light, goeth forwards
and increaseth even to perfect day" (Prov. 4:18).

Since one man's life has such an effect on his neighbors,
each of us must be circumspect at all times in setting a
good example to those about us. He who follows in the
footsteps of Christ will influence his neighbor only for good.

*"The countenance and image of Christ, by which
we are recognized as His, is engraved in us; it
is the glory of charity"* (St. Cyril).

*"What else is there in heaven for me but you?
And, if I am with you, the earth has no delights
for me"* (Ps. 72:25).

"*Ten* more shopping days before Christmas" is a frequent greeting to the reader as he peruses the newspaper as this beautiful holiday approaches. The merchants, anxious to avoid a last-minute rush, advertise the number of days, whether it be twenty-five or one, that the buyer has left in which to purchase presents for his relatives and friends.

Holy Mother Church, ever solicitous for the eternal welfare of her children, constantly warns them to prepare for the greatest event in their lives — death. The Church cannot say to her children, "You have only so many days left before you are called to give an account of your stewardship" — only God knows the day and the hour. But, the Church does keep before the minds of her members that they must constantly be on the alert lest death catch them unprepared.

In the Church the crucifix holds the next most important place after the Blessed Sacrament. This reminder of Christ's death and each one's own occupies a conspicuous place in every Catholic's home. The Church, in her preaching and teaching and writing, constantly reminds man that death is certain; the hour, uncertain.

Just as the feast of Christmas, the anniversary of Christ's coming, is awaited in great happiness, so, too, all the faithful children of God should look forward with joy to meeting their King face to face. " . . . Would I had wings as has a dove; then should I fly away and be at rest" (Ps. 54:7).

*"We should not dread that which frees us from
every cause of fear"* (Tertullian).

"If God is for us, who is against us?" (Rom. 8:32.)

"One man with God is a majority in any fight." This slogan has helped many an individual, beset on all sides by those who would overcome him, to go on to victory. If the cause is just the fighter may be sure that he has behind him the infinite grace and strength of God.

Too many people are too easily discouraged. They anticipate and worry about the unseen difficulties ahead. Their imagination builds up a formidable enemy out of whole cloth. They forget that "God helps those who help themselves."

In the struggle to save his soul, man is faced with a cunning, clever, insidious enemy who fights "with no holds barred." He uses all weapons of which he is the master. Deception is one of his greatest means of destruction, but the faithful soul need not fear him. "And should I cross a gloomy vale, no evil shall I fear, because you are with me" (Ps. 22:4).

With a human enemy to face, man can fight back with the weapons his adversary uses, but when he is engaged in battle with the Evil Spirit, he needs spiritual assistance of the highest order. In this hour, he must have the greatest faith in his Defender. He must plead with Him for the necessary strength, wisdom, and foresight to forestall his enemy. He can turn to Christ with the greatest confidence. If man does his share, he may be certain that he will not appeal to Christ in vain. With God's help, he is certain of victory, for, "If God is for us, who is against us?" (Rom. 8:32.)

> *"Grant me, O Lord, the grace to know what should be known . . . to esteem that which appears most precious to You, and to abhor what is unclean in Your sight"* (Imit., Bk. 3, C. 50).

*"None but a good gift, none but a perfect dona-
tion comes from above"* (James 1:17, 18).

Fire is a tremendous force for good or evil. Out of control, a conflagration can cause consternation. Under control,
fire does wonderful work for man. In most towns and cities,
fire produces the steam power that turns the turbines that
generate the electricity that lights the homes and the munici-
pality, that turns the wheels of industry, that pays the wages
of countless families.

The tremendous size of many of these steam boilers is
prodigious. The glowing flames, snapping and cracking, in
the firebox below the boilers, fills a visitor with awe. As
powerful and productive as these flames are, they would
cease to exist but for one very important element — oxygen —
and this life-giving ingredient is made possible by the
chimney.

The magnitude of the fire is dependent on the quantity
of oxygen it receives. When a traveler passes by a factory or
plant, he can tell to a great extent the productive power of
that mill by the height of the chimney. The closer the flue
is to the sky, the greater the heat-producing unit below.

Man, not unlike the energy-producing fire, draws his
strength and power and courage from above. The higher
his thoughts and ideals tower above the earth, the closer
is his contact with God, the Source of all his energy and
zeal for the things of God. The faithful soul should strive
each day to add "brick" upon "brick" of love to his spiritual
tower, to raise this funnel of grace nearer and nearer to
the Fountainhead of all graces.

*"No one will ever waver if he considers that
God is always present with him"* (St. Clement).

*"The word of the Lord rings true, and all his
works prove his fidelity"* (Ps. 32:4).

Frequently, the question is asked, "If you were cast adrift
alone on a deserted island what books would you prefer
as companions?"

Almost invariably, the one questioned answers, "First,
the Bible!"

Why the Bible in such distressing circumstances? Because
the Bible is the Word of God.

When one finds himself in a desperate situation and faced
with forces over which he has no control, he is not content
with the words of ordinary men like himself. He demands
something higher, something more inspiring, something more
powerful and consoling than mere ideas, true or false, expressed by the frail and limited minds of his fellow men.

His heart and his intellect cry out to his Creator and his
God for assistance and consolation, and for the assurance
that he is not alone but that Divine Providence is watching
over him. "To the Lord I cried with all my voice; He heard
me on his holy mount" (Ps. 3:5).

The faithful follower of Christ should not wait until he
finds himself in some extreme situation before turning to
the Word of God for encouragement and help but should
make it a practice to read a portion of the Bible each day.
Familiarity with God's written word will serve to make
the weakhearted strong, and the strong even more courageous,
in carrying out His will. "Take my yoke upon you and
master my lessons, for I am gentle and humble of heart.
You will find refreshment for your souls" (Mt. 11:29, 30).

*"Men pass away, but the truth of the Lord
remains forever"* (Imit., Bk. 1, C. 5).

"Do not, therefore, throw away your confidence,
since it has a great reward" (Hebr. 10:35).

The young pilot deep in the jungles of New Guinea fully realized the dangers that surrounded him.

His superiors considered the young lieutenant one of their most capable and bravest pilots. The airman's spiritual courage was perhaps even greater than his physical fearlessness. Each morning and evening he knelt beside his bed and read his prayers. At first, the other three members of his "suite" sneered at his piety, but after a few rough missions, the "sneerers" could be discovered surreptitiously reading their own particular prayer books.

On the toughest mission he endured, his B-24 was seventeen hours in the air. In the thick darkness of that humid jungle, he raised his ship aloft, loaded with his crew, his ammunition, his bombs, and nine tons of highly inflammable gasoline, and sped away into the night. The enemy was prepared for the attack, and the plane was blasted from land batteries and naval guns. At five o'clock in the afternoon, after fourteen hours in the air, the ship landed at an emergency field for gas, and immediately took off for the home port. Three hours later the exhausted pilot put his plane, riddled from end to end, safely down upon the ground.

Something stronger than racing engines and steel wings carried that bomber home. Who can doubt that the confident prayers of the faithful pilot held together that shattered plane until it deposited its precious cargo on the hidden runway of New Guinea? "Be watchful; be steadfast in your faith; act like men; be strong" (1 Cor. 16:13).

"Your care for me is greater than all the care
I can take of myself" (*Imit.*, Bk. 3, C. 17).

"But over all these virtues clothe yourselves with love; it is the bond that perfects and binds them together" (Col. 3:14, 15).

The Huskies who pull the heavy sleds in the Arctic region soon win the hearts of the missionaries. The courage, stout-heartedness, and endurance of these devoted animals is inspiring. Their uncanny ability to follow the trail in the face of the worst blizzard and impenetrable darkness lends a sense of security to the traveler in the Barren Land. In desperate circumstances, their endurance on the trail, even unto death, has often wrenched the heart of their owner.

One might think that these half-tame, half-wild Huskies possessed no such thing as affection. The opposite, however, is true. The surest way to sign the death warrant of one of the dogs is to show the slightest preference for him. The animals are quick to note the favoritism and at the first opportunity, the rest of the pack will "gang up" on the favored one and tear him to pieces. Each one is jealous of his master's affections.

If these self-sufficient, rebellious, ferocious creatures of God react thus to the slightest evidence of human kindness, how much more readily will man who is made to God's own image, respond to the love of his fellow man. The sincere soul who exercises the charity of Christ toward others is beloved by all. "If I should speak the languages of men and of angels, but have no love, I am no more than a noisy gong and a clanging cymbal" (1 Cor. 13:1, 2).

> *"We want them to be perfect, yet we do not correct our own faults"* (*Imit.,* Bk. 1, C. 16).

"When you give alms, your left hand should not know what your right is doing. Thus your alms is given in secrecy, and your Father, who sees what is secret, will reward you" (Mt. 6:3, 4).

"Come Christmas, I am going to outfit that whole family with new shoes," declared the gentleman pompously to the group of friends discussing an unfortunate and poverty-stricken family in the neighborhood.

This was October, so the speaker did not attempt to explain how the little ones were to endure the snow and ice in the meantime.

The next day the children appeared gloriously decked out in new clothes from head to foot. One of the members of the group, learning for the first time of the neighbor's need, quietly ordered the local store to outfit the family.

The first gentleman was really a good, kind, generous man, but his failing was that he could not give without announcing his generosity. The second gentleman preferred to perform his charity, not for applause, but because a need existed. He sincerely believed whatever wealth he had received was from God and was to be used in helping others. " . . . glory, honor, and peace will be the lot of every man intent on doing good" (Rom. 2:10).

It is surprising how many generous souls there are who quietly and nobly and humbly share their worldly goods with others, desiring only the approval of God. "God is not unjust, he will not forget what you have done, and the love that you have shown for his sake in the services you have rendered to the saints" (Hebr. 6:10, 11).

"Faith without works is dead, as are works without faith" (St. Gregory).

"The Lord has said to me: 'My Son you are:
this day have I begotten you'" (Ps. 2:7).

The author is proud of his creative work and sincerely hopes that the results of his labors and mental activity will redound to his credit. He takes just pride in his achievements and is happy when others praise and admire his work. The writer, the painter, the poet, indeed all artists, delight in the works that they have labored so long to produce.

Parents are extremely proud of their children. These little ones, who have cost them so much in suffering, sacrifice, and tears, bring great happiness and joy to their fathers and mothers. It is the fond hope and expectation of good parents that the children of their own flesh and blood will bring them honor and respect and distinction, and will acknowledge the debt of love they owe to those who have acted as God's agents in giving them life.

The catechism tells the faithful that God created man for His own honor and glory and for man's eternal happiness.

Every creature, therefore, has the obligation of adoring his Creator. He should strive daily to honor and glorify God, his Father in heaven. He should labor tirelessly to make his eternal Father proud of His child. In doing this, the creature is fulfilling his duty toward God, and assuring his own eternal salvation. "So marked, indeed, has been God's love for the world that he gave his only-begotten Son: everyone who believes in him is not to perish, but to have eternal life" (Jn. 3:16, 17).

> *"Speak to me for the comfort of my soul and for the amendment of my life for Your praise, Your glory, and Your everlasting honor"*
> *(Imit.,* Bk. 3, C. 2).

> " . . . but lay up treasures for yourselves in
> heaven" (Mt. 6:20).

Numismatology is a large word and, no doubt, many
people would not be able to define it. However, it has a very
simple meaning; it is the "science of coins and medals."

Many people have made a hobby of numismatology by
gathering together a collection of coins. The numismatist
derives his pleasure out of going over his coins and figuring
out their associations with historical events, for most coinage
commemorates some occasion in history.

The pastime is interesting, and sometimes remunerative;
but how much more profitable it would be if each Christian
soul would make a practice of gathering to himself "the coin"
that buys heaven. By good deeds and faithfulness to Christ,
he may gather an infinite amount of grace that will prove
consoling to him at all times and will be the "coin" that will
open to him the gates of eternity.

Christ has promised, "And whoever gives only a refreshing drink to one of these little ones, doing so because he is
a disciple, will not, I tell you truly, go without his reward"
(Mt. 10:42).

A mere cup of water given to the least of Christ's children
will win a bountiful reward for the giver. Such acts as these
in Christ's name are the "coins" that purchase eternal glory.
Be a collector of such good deeds. "Better for me the law
your lips proclaim — better than heaps of silver and of gold"
(Ps. 118:72).

*"He helps the unwilling man to will; He keeps
close to the willing man that he may not will in
vain"* (St. Augustine).

*"Blessed, rather, are those that hear the word
of God and observe it"* (Lk. 11:28).

"Gentlemen," said Professor Brown at the banquet given
to him by his graduate students, "I am deeply grateful to
you for this demonstration of appreciation for my humble
efforts in your behalf. Perhaps you students do not realize
what your generosity means to a teacher. I can best make
known my gratitude to you by relating this incident. As I
was leaving the university this evening to come to the hotel
for this very happy affair, Professor Smith happened to
ask me where I was going. Naturally, I was quite willing
to tell him. He seemed a bit startled that such an event
could take place, and congratulated me on having such
appreciative students. 'You know,' he spoke meditatively,
'I have taught philosophy for thirty-three years and in all
that time not one student has come back to thank me!'"

It seems to be taken for granted that teaching is its own
reward and that professors are immune to the niceties of
society. However, teachers are very human, and deeply appreciative of a word of thanks.

Christ was a teacher. He came into this world to be, as He
said, "the way, and the truth, and the life" (Jn. 14:6). He
has assured His children, "If you make my teaching your
rule of life, you are truly my disciples; then you will know
the truth . . . "(Jn. 8:31, 32). Man's gratitude to the divine
Teacher should be boundless. "O how I love your law, O
Lord! The livelong day I ponder it" (Ps. 118:97).

> *"Attend . . . to My words which enkindle the
> heart and enlighten the mind, which excite con-
> trition and abound in manifold consolations"*
> **(Imit., Bk. 3, C. 43).**

"O death, where is your victory?" (1 Cor. 15:55.)

Everybody wants to be on the winning side. This assertion is true in baseball and football, in the professional and business world, in the village and national elections. In all contests where men are involved, each one strives for victory. This determination to win in keen competition is a praiseworthy quality and admired by all.

If this condition prevails in worldly pursuits, how much more should men strive for victory in spiritual combat, where the stakes are infinitely higher: eternal suffering or eternal happiness?

St. Paul thoroughly understood this life-and-death battle when he declared, "Do you not know that whenever men run a race in a stadium, all run, but only one wins the prize? So run that you will surely win. Every contestant submits to all sorts of privations, and to receive a perishable crown, but we an imperishable one. Therefore, I run with a fixed goal in mind; I box not as one beating the air, but I buffet my body and make it my slave lest perhaps, after preaching to others I myself should be eliminated" (1 Cor. 9:24-27).

St. Paul understood clearly the strenuous struggle necessary to win the crown of eternal glory. Each Christian soul must emulate the faith, the courage, the inflexible will of the great Apostle in order to be able to say with him as death approaches, "I have fought the good fight, I have finished the course, I have kept the faith. What remains is the crown due to holiness which the Lord, the just Judge, will give to me on that day . . . " (2 Tim. 4:7, 8).

"No man is fit to enjoy heaven unless he has resigned himself to suffer hardship for Christ"
(*Imit.,* Bk. 2, C. 12).

*"And you will be the scorn of all because you pro-
fess my name. But he who holds out to the end
will be saved"* (Mt. 10:22, 23).

In the fall many movie houses show scenes from the most
important football games. These "shots" invariably show the
ball carrier doing some spectacular broken-field running.

It is a mystery to the audience how the player carrying
the ball manages to avoid being tackled. On his long run
toward the goal, the halfback is apparently cornered several
times; yet, he sidesteps the tackler; he worms his way through
a blockade of husky enemies; he slides; he sprints; he is almost
down; but he is up and away. Leaving the scattered opposition
far behind, he crosses the goal.

The noteworthy feature of the ball carrier's success is that
he never stops. He twists and turns, and retreats a few feet,
but he plows on again. Finally he calls up his reserve energy
and with a final burst of speed crosses the line. The victor
wins because he never stops trying. "I strain toward what
is ahead. With my eyes fixed on the goal I press on to the
prize in store for those who have received from above God's
call in Christ Jesus" (Phil. 3:14).

From the player's success all can learn a lesson. The faithful
should never let any difficulty, no matter how great, stand
in their way to final victory. It is well to remember that
nothing is impossible to God. "Whatever you do, work at it
heartily, as for the Lord and not for men, in the realization
that from the Lord you will receive the inheritance as your
reward" (Col. 3:23, 24).

> *"Without perseverance the fighter does not ob-
> tain the victory, nor does the victor obtain the
> palm"* (St. Bernard).

"We exercise mutual love because he first loved us" (1 Jn. 4:19).

"All the world loves a lover" is indeed true. The lovely bride in her immaculate wedding gown and the youthful bridegroom with eyes only for his sweetheart, standing at the altar of God, make a charming picture that touches the heartstrings of all. The sight of the young couple, confident and strong in their mutual affections, brings back to their elders happy memories and gives joy and encouragement to their juniors. If their love is sincere and pure and based on the noble principles of God, they will successfully weather every storm that may beset their pathway through life, and will enjoy with their family the greatest happiness.

Love is the greatest motive for good. A saint of God is nothing more or less than a great lover. The saint of God supernaturalizes his natural deeds by offering them to God. He strives to be perfect as His heavenly Father is perfect.

Christ is the greatest Lover of all. St. Paul writes: "He humbled himself, and became obedient to death: yes to death on a cross" (Phil. 2:8). And Christ Himself declares, "No one can give a greater proof of his love than by laying down his life for his friends" (Jn. 15:13). Christ made the supreme Sacrifice by His own death on the cross for His friends. "You are my friends, provided you do what I command you" (Jn. 15:14). The saints, seeking to demonstrate their love for Him who first loved them, gladly do what He commands in order to be numbered among his friends forever.

"When God loves, He wishes only to be loved;
indeed He loves nothing else than to be loved,
knowing by love itself the blessed who have
loved Him" (St. Bernard).

*"O guide me to obey your true demands; teach
me; you are my Savior God. In you I always
trust"* (Ps. 24:5).

"Lights!" "Camera!" "Action!" Another scene is being
enacted on the movie lot in Hollywood to be sent around the
world to entertain the waiting populace.

It is not the title nor the movie star nor the scenery that
is to decide whether or not the picture is "box office." As
important as all these elements are, the final appeal to the
public depends upon the ability of the director to persuade
the actors to interpret their parts correctly.

Millions of dollars have been spent on lavish costumes and
scenery and high-priced stars and advertising only to have
the picture rejected by the movie-goers because the characters
failed to "click." That spark of genius necessary was lacking
in the gentleman who guided the histrionic and artistic interpretation of the actors.

Life is frequently referred to as a play in which every
player has a most important role. There is some truth in
this metaphor. The men, women, and children who make up
the cast of this real-life theater are performers in a highly
important drama. The success of their efforts depends a
great deal upon themselves, but if they conform to the
guidance and direction and admonition of the "divine Director," each player's achievements will be richly rewarded, not
with a perishable "Oscar," but with a crown of eternal
glory.

*"Who is there that serves and obeys Me in all
things with as great care as that with which the
world and its masters are served?"*

(Imit., Bk. 3, C. 3.)

> *"Have courage, my son; your sins are now forgiven"* (Mt. 9:2).

Of all the blessings that man receives from God, the forgiveness of sin is the greatest. In Scripture, the blind man, cured by Christ, delighted in the knowledge that he could see all the beauties of the world again; the cripple, that he could take an equal place with his friends and companions; the leper, that he was restored to human society.

The sinner freed from the awful burden of his sins, rejoices that he is again restored to the company of Christ.

The first power that Christ gave to His Apostles and their successors after His resurrection is the power to forgive sins —"Receive the Holy Spirit. Whenever you remit anyone's sins, they are remitted; when you retain anyone's sins, they are retained" (Jn. 20:22, 23).

No joy can be compared with the happiness of the sinner released from sin; all the elect rejoice with him. "I tell you there is joy in heaven over one repentant sinner — more, in fact, than over ninety-nine saints that have no need of repentance" (Lk. 15:7).

On the roaring inferno of the burning deck of an airplane carrier during the war, a young sailor edged up to the Catholic chaplain and asked to go to confession. The priest gave him absolution amid the bursting bombs and the awesome flames. "Thanks, Father," yelled the lad above the tumult, as he rushed off to his place of duty, "now I ain't afraid of anything!" "For the wages that sin gives is death, but the gift that God bestows is life everlasting in Christ Jesus our Lord" (Rom. 6:23).

> *"Confession remits sins, restores merits; confession blunts the sting of the worm"* (St. Ambrose).

*"So, my beloved brothers, be steadfast, immov-
able. Devote yourselves fully at all times to the
Lord's work, realizing that your toil in the Lord
can never be in vain"* (1 Cor. 15:58).

During the recent war, American artillerymen used a
devastating system of fire control called T.O.T. (Time on
Target).

Slow guns and fast guns and heavy long-distance guns were
co-ordinated so that their shells all fell on a given spot at
the same time. This system was a cleverly devised method
of completely erasing a selected area. The secret lay in the
concentration of fire power.

Man has profited greatly in times of peace from the needs
of war. From noting the complete victory obtained from this
manner of concentration against the enemy, he can deduce
that the same system is effective against his spiritual enemy.
"Like a good soldier of Christ Jesus join the ranks of those
who bear hardship" (2 Tim. 2:3).

By concentrating all his faculties, with God's help, on
gaining the end for which he was created, he can win a
complete victory over Satan and his cohorts, and gain the
victorious crown of eternal life. "I raise my voice to God
Most High, to God, who is beneficent to me" (Ps. 56:3).

> *"Blessed are the simple of heart for they shall
> enjoy peace in abundance"* (Imit., Bk. 1, C. 11).

"Come, children, hear my voice, and I will lesson you in the fear of the Lord" (Ps. 33:12).

"Another meal! It seems as though all I do is cook and clean!" The good lady was a bit upset and tired, and she was taking advantage of her sister's presence to let off some steam. The sister was much older and her children were now grown, so she was in a position to give some good advice.

"Mary," the relative said, "I know you work hard taking care of your little brood, cooking, washing and ironing. It's no lark, to be sure. But," she added thoughtfully, "now is the happiest time of your whole life. Enjoy it while you may. You'll be surprised how quickly the little ones grow up. One day they are playing with dolls and toy guns, and the next, it seems that they are young men and women. You'll pass by the cooky jar, that now seems impossible to keep filled, many times in later life, and there will be plenty of cookies in it, but you would give a million dollars if there were little hands to lift the cover and remove the last one. Mary, you are the luckiest woman in the world. Enjoy these golden hours while you may!"

Every mother and father knows only too well the brief span of years that link babyhood with manhood. Yet it is this formative period, as short as it is, that molds the future character of the child. It is the job of parents to train their little ones well in the ways of God so that the future years of both will be years of happiness and peace. "He that feareth the Lord honoreth his parents and will serve them as his masters that brought him into the world" (Ecclus. 3:8).

"The more parents love their children, the more they should urge them to lead a good life"
(St. Augustine).

" . . . take up all the armor that God has forged,
that you may be able to resist in the evil day"
(Eph. 6:13, 14).

One of Aesop's fables tells about the cat and the fox in the forest discussing their ability to escape from enemies. The fox declares arrogantly that he has over a hundred tricks to fool those who would destroy him. The cat humbly admits she has only one such device, and if that adroitness fails her she is lost.

While the animals are talking, they suddenly hear the bay of the hunter's hounds. The cat quickly scampers up the nearest tree and hides herself in the thick foliage. The fox puts to work the methods in which he has placed his confidence. From her safe sanctuary the cat watches until finally reynard is cornered and killed.

There are many morals to be drawn from this fable but the one of interest here is that pride goes before a fall. This is particularly true in the moral order.

The self-sufficient have convinced themselves that they have no need of God's grace in the never ending war between the soul and its enemies. They scorn completely St. Paul's warning, "Our wrestling is not against weak human nature, but against the Principalities and the Powers, against those that rule the world of darkness, the wicked spirits that belong to an order higher than ours" (Eph. 6:12, 13). The humble soul, realizing thoroughly his own weakness, depends upon one thing only in his struggle against sin — the grace and strength of God. "Put on all the armor that God has forged, that you may be able to make a stand against the devil's cunning tricks" (Eph. 6:11, 12).

> *"In none can I fully trust to help me . . . but in*
> *You alone, my God"* (*Imit.*, Bk. 3, C. 59).

> *"Because he clings to me, I will deliver him, and shield him; for he knows my name"* (Ps. 90:14).

Christian hope is a supernatural virtue, by which we trust, with a firm confidence, that God will give us eternal life and the means necessary to obtain it, because He has promised to do so, and He is faithful to His promise.

Of the three theological virtues, Faith, Hope, and Charity, two of these, namely, Faith and Charity, are daily practiced by all the faithful. But for some unknown reason many people do not seem to realize that the virtue of hope is coequal with the other theological virtues; that there is the same necessity to exercise hope in God as there is to believe in and love Him.

Many people would avoid countless heartaches, long hours of useless worry, and untold sorrow, if they would only put into practice God's admonition to hope in Him; for this virtue induces the faithful to trust entirely in God in all their needs, spiritual and temporal. "My children, behold the generations of men: and know ye that no one hath hoped in the Lord and hath been confounded. For who hath continued in his commandment, and hath been forsaken? Or who hath called upon him, and he despised him?" (Ecclus. 2:11, 12.)

Man should always hope in God regardless of sin, fear, sickness, or any of the hundreds of things that he can worry over. Every faithful soul should repeat daily the words of St. Paul, "I can do all things in him who strengthens me" (Phil. 4:13).

> *"I consider three things in which all my hope consists; the love of adoption, the truth of the promise, and the power of the Giver"*
>
> (St. Bernard).

*"Humble yourselves, then, under the mighty hand
of God, that he may exalt you in due time"*
(1 Pet. 5:6).

"He also addressed the following parable to some of those
who confidently believed that they were observers of the
Law and, at the same time despised everybody else: 'Once
upon a time two men went up to the temple to pray, the one
a Pharisee, the other a tax collector. The Pharisee stood con-
spicuously apart and soliloquized this prayer: "O God, I
thank you that I am not like the rest of men — robbers,
rogues, adulterers — or like that tax collector over there. . . ."
The tax collector, on the contrary, kept in the background
and would not so much as raise his eyes to heaven, but struck
his breast and said: "O God, have mercy on me the sinner!" '
I assure you, this man went down to his home acquitted
of all guilt; not so the other. Everyone who exalts himself
shall be humbled, and he who humbles himself shall be
exalted" (Lk. 18:9–14).

The Pharisee was speaking the truth. He was a good man
in the sense that he did all he claimed he did; but he was
simply rejoicing in his own good deeds. He did not realize
that all his gifts came from God. While on the other hand,
the humble publican recognized his own weakness and his
complete dependence upon his Creator.

The most holy and devout servants of Christ fear pride
more than any other sin. They know that pride caused
Lucifer's fall and drove Adam from Paradise. Humility
appeals to all men, but is particularly acceptable to the Creator
of all men, God.

*"All men are frail, but you must admit that no
one is more frail than yourself"* (Imit., Bk. 1, C. 2).

> *"I have fought the good fight, I have finished the course, I have kept the faith. What remains is the crown due to holiness, which the Lord, the just Judge, will give me on that day, and not only to me but also to those who love his brilliant coming"* (2 Tim. 4:7, 8).

"You know, Father, I have to keep close to God. I can't take any chances on committing sin. I have a dangerous heart condition and may die any minute."

The priest congratulated the young man on his good judgment but wondered about his motives.

When a man knows he is near death, he is anxious to be in good standing with God. He wants to be God's friend, not his enemy.

But, has a young person in the bloom of health any guarantee that he will not die more suddenly than the heart patient? Christ warns, "Keep awake, therefore; you do not know on what day your Lord returns" (Mt. 24:42), and this admonition is addressed to all — the healthy, the old, the young, the sick.

The faithful soul lives each day as though it were to be his last. The prudent and devout person strives to avoid sin but if sin should overcome him, he quickly restores himself to the friendship of Christ.

The true Christian looks forward with great joy to his eternal union with God and, by prayer and sacrifice, endeavors to be ready at all times to greet his Creator and final Judge. "My eyes are ever straining toward the Lord; for he will draw my feet from out the snare" (Ps. 24:15).

"We should not fear that which frees us from every cause of fear" (Tertullian).

"The laborer is entitled to his support" (1 Tim. 5:18).

A $100,000 bill is the largest denomination printed by the United States Treasury. This bank note, however, is not for general circulation. It is reserved for credit between the government and Federal Reserve Banks.

If a lucky person could possess one of these bills, he might well consider himself wealthy. The ordinary individual, however, is quite content to have a few bills of one, five, and ten dollar value in his pocket.

It is surprising how much better one feels when his wallet holds a few greenbacks. Payday always cheers up the faithful worker, while the end of the week when his funds are low often finds his spirits in a similar lowly state. Money earned and held gives the owner a definite sense of security. It assures him of food, clothing, and housing for himself and his family, and occasionally, some of the luxuries of life. "A secure mind is like a continual feast" (Prov. 15:15). But the Book of Proverbs also quickly adds, "Better is a little with the fear of the Lord, than great treasures without content" (15:16).

Each one must remember that while it is necessary to labor for the necessities of life, it is absolutely essential that he work to obtain God's grace, the coin that will purchase for him eternal glory. If the worker feels secure in the possession of a few dollars, how much more secure will he feel in the knowledge that he possesses the eternal friendship of God? "The Lord is my salvation and my light: whom shall I fear?" (Ps. 26:1.)

> *"I am able to reward you beyond all means and measure"* (*Imit.*, Bk. 3, C. 47).

*"Obey your superiors and be subject to them,
since they keep watch over souls, mindful that
they will have to render a count"*

(Hebr. 13:17).

Sam received permission from the first National Bank to
set up a newspaper stand near the entrance. His business
prospered from the very beginning and word spread around
that Sam was making money. Before long, an old acquaintance, hearing of the news dealer's good fortune, approached
him and asked for a loan of twenty-five dollars.

"I certainly would like to help you out, Joe," Sam said,
"but I have an agreement with the bank. They promised not
to sell newspapers and I promised not to loan money."

In this bit of humor there is a lesson. When a person wishes
to obtain something, he should go to the proper source. If
he wants legal advice, he should go to a lawyer; if he wants
medical advice, he should visit his doctor; and if he wants
spiritual advice, he should go to his pastor. "For if he do
them, he shall be strong to all things: because the light of
God guideth his steps" (Ecclus. 50:31).

The Catholic has an obligation of presenting his spiritual
problems to those qualified to solve them. In seeking and
following the advice given him by his parish priest, he will
find peace of mind in the knowledge that he is following the
teaching of his Mother, the Church. The zealous priest is
always ready and willing to give any and every one, regardless of his beliefs, the benefit of his training and experience.
"Upon your precepts will I meditate, and study out your
ways" (Ps. 118:15).

"The road to the mercy of God is always open"

(St. Cyprian).

"Feed my lambs. . . . Feed my sheep"
(Jn. 21:16, 17).

The first principle laid down in the training of nurses is that a sick person is not a normal person. This does not mean that there is anything wrong with the patient mentally, but just that he is not his usual self.

This is quite understandable. An ordinary toothache is enough to bring the roughest character to bay. Every one of us knows from personal experience what great change is brought about in a person by the agony of pain.

Thus, those who are well ought to be considerate of those who are sick. No sensible person wants to be sick, but once ill, he wants and deserves consideration and kindness. Her charitable institutions throughout the world whether it be the leper camp, the incurable cancer sanitariums, or the ordinary hospital testify to the Church's love for the sick. In these health institutes, Holy Mother the Church, represented by her priests, her Brothers, and her Sisters, administers physically to God's ailing children.

As important as it is to assist those afflicted with bodily illness, it is still of greater importance to help the spiritually ill. To those suffering from a sick soul, the Church opens wide its arms and invites all to come in. Through her Sacraments and prayers, like a good mother, she will restore the sinner, the hopeless, the sorrowful to robust spiritual health. "And Jesus heard this, and said to them, 'The sick have need of a physician, not the healthy. It is my mission to call sinners, and not saints'" (Mk. 2:17).

"The noble lover does not rest in the gift, but in Me Who am above every gift"
(*Imit.*, Bk. 3, C. 6).

*"But they that are learned shall shine as the
brightness of the firmament; and they that instruct many to justice, as stars for all eternity"*
(Dan. 12:3).

St. Thomas Aquinas showed early indications of a religious nature, but did not, in his early years, demonstrate
any indication of outstanding intellect. He was so quiet and
retiring that his fellow students sometimes referred to him
as the "dumb ox." St. Albert, called the Great, on account
of his brilliance, was Thomas' teacher. Once he said to his
pupils, "You may call him the 'dumb ox' but one day he
will give forth a bellow of learning so that his voice will fill
the whole world." How truthfully Albert spoke is evident
by the fact that St. Thomas' teachings have influenced the
thinking of the world from the thirteenth century even down
to the present day.

Teachers of youth have a tremendous responsibility toward
their students. At all times, they should see in these children
souls made to the image and likeness of God. The God-loving
and sincere pedagogue wins the approval of God and the
undying gratitude of those who have profited from his kindly
instructions. "But the path of the just, as a shining light,
goeth forwards and increaseth even to the perfect day"
(Prov. 4:18).

All should remember that teaching is not reserved to
the classroom. Those who love God and do His will are
fitting examples of His teachings wherever they are and
whatever they do. "O Lord, make known your ways to me,
and teach me all your paths" (Ps. 24:4).

*"He who does God's will and renounces his
own is truly very learned"* (Imit., Bk. 1, C. 3).

*"Little children, let us not love merely in word
or with the tongue, but in action, in reality"*
(1 Jn. 3:18).

It was a beautiful ring. The inscription read: "To John,
with deepest love from Mother. On his eighteenth birthday."
The receiver of this heirloom sadly told its history.

The young boy who had received the present was dying
of tuberculosis. His mother, although very poor, had scraped
together whatever funds she could, and had denied herself
the real necessities of life, to buy this ring for her beloved
child. Her purpose was clear. The devoted mother had hoped
it would cheer her dying son by making him believe there
was no thought of death. Above all, it was a sacrificial offering that would help unite them forever in the inseparable
bond of love. "In God we gloried all the time: we never
ceased to praise your name" (Ps. 43:9).

What gift is a real gift without sacrifice on the part of the
giver? It is only those offerings that one cannot afford to
give that really count. Such gifts require sacrifice, and sacrifice
is the unspoken language of love. Christ died on the cross to
give His beloved children eternal life. His words speak
volumes, but His sacrifice on the cross needs no words!
Listen to St. Paul: "I am sure that neither death, nor life,
nor angels, nor principalities, nor things present, nor things
to come, nor powers, nor height, nor depth, nor any other
creature can separate us from God's love for us, which is in
Christ Jesus our Lord" (Rom. 8:38, 39).

> *"Blessed is he who appreciates what it is to love
> Jesus . . . Give up all other love for His, since
> He wishes to be loved alone above all things"*
> (*Imit.*, Bk. 2, C. 7).

*"Indeed, in your possession is the fount of life,
and in your light we see the light"* (Ps. 35:10).

The gentleman who conceived the appellation "The Iron Curtain" coined a most descriptive phrase. The very word "iron" has a hardness and coldness about it that is repellent to the warm, loving, joyous heart. The word "curtain" brings home quickly the thought of darkness and night. The combination of the two sets before the mind a black, impenetrable wall that hides all manner of things that hate the light.

Some countries have elected to lower such a curtain around themselves and to shut out from their brother nations all social, economic, and normal relationships — but, above all, they strive to keep out God.

Now, there are many people who, while decrying this national act, imitate in their personal lives the very evil they condemn. These lonely souls have dropped an iron curtain about their hearts, shutting out from themselves personal contact with God, while the patient Christ waits anxiously on the other side for an invitation to enter their hearts and bring with Him all His loveliness and beauty and brightness and grace. The cord that holds this curtain high is woven of either *pride* or *immorality* or *greed* and manipulated by the hand of Satan.

Let these people drive these evils forth from their hearts and this iron curtain will fall of its own weight, and the sunshine of God's love will flood their souls. St. Paul declares, "And then the wicked one will be brought to light, but the Lord Jesus will . . . reduce him to naught by the splendor of his coming" (2 Thess. 2:8).

*"No heart is so hard that it cannot be softened
by the mercy of God"* (St. Augustine).

*"Cast all your anxiety on him, because he takes
care of you"* (1 Pet. 5:7).

Occasionally in life "things begin to pile up," and the
heavy burden of past regrets and future fears seem to become
a superhuman burden.

Christ understands human nature thoroughly because He
is true God and true Man. St. Peter, from his own experience,
was aware of this understanding of God's mercy. He advises
in his First Epistle, "Humble yourselves, then, under the
mighty hand of God, that he may exalt you in due time.
Cast all your anxiety on him, because he takes care of you"
(5:6, 7).

The Evil Spirit selects such an unsettled time as this,
when man is worried and disturbed about many things, to
endeavor to confuse the soul all the more. The true Christian, however, will quickly and confidently seek out God
and wisely cast his doubts and fears and worries "upon him,"
because "he cares for you." The knowledge that God "cares"
is sufficient to carry man through any and all trials and
tribulations. "He that loves me will, in turn, be loved by
my Father; and I will love him, and will manifest myself
to him" (Jn. 14:21).

> *"Believe in Me and trust in My mercy. When
> you think you are far from Me, then often I
> am very near you"* (Imit., Bk. 3, C. 30).

"Give thanks whilst thou art living. Whilst thou art alive and in health thou shalt give thanks, and shall praise God, and shalt glory in his mercies" (Ecclus. 17:27).

Today much is written about the bumper crops that have been reaped in this country during the past few years. Most people take this bountiful harvest for granted and are interested only in whether it has brought about a reduction in the retail price. It is safe to say that few think to thank God for His generosity in giving to man such unlimited gifts.

Yet, Holy Mother Church is not unmindful of God's kindness. In the spring of the year she sets aside three days called Rogation Days in which she petitions the Infinite Giver of every gift to be considerate of his people and grant to them "their daily bread." On these days are recited the Litany of the Saints together with special prayers of thanks and supplication for the gift of bountiful crops. Everyone should join with the Church in reciting these prayers. "Have no anxiety, but in every concern by prayer and supplication with thanksgiving let your petitions be made known in your communing with God" (Phil. 4:6, 7).

In the Old Law, the first fruits of the crop and the first born of the flock were given as a thank-offering to God. "Honor the Lord with thy substance, and give him of the first of all thy fruits: and thy barns shall be filled and thy presses shall run over with wine" (Prov. 3:9, 10).

The receivers of God's bounty should be mindful of His gifts and daily thank Him for them. "I raise my voice to God Most High, to God who is beneficent to me" (Ps. 56:3).

"All things come from You; therefore, You are to be praised in all things" (*Imit.*, Bk. 3, C. 22).

"You are my friends, provided you do what I command you" (Jn. 15:14, 15).

God said to Adam, "It is not good for man to be alone" (Gen. 2:18), so He created Eve to be his helpmate.

If it is not good for man to be alone, it is far worse for him to be *lonely* — for there is a difference! Numbers in themselves do not decrease a man's loneliness. Times Square, with its teeming thousands, can be the loneliest place in the world for a stranger in New York.

He who truly loves God, however, is never alone for he knows he has his Father always with him. "Await the Lord, and act the man; be stout of heart; and await the Lord" (Ps. 26:14). Oftentimes through circumstances many people are forced to be alone, but if they have a true knowledge of the love of their Friend, Christ, they are never lonely. These people are not selfish, and it is only selfishness that creates loneliness.

The Psalmist sings, "I always keep the Lord before my eyes, and on my right is he; I shall stand firm!" (Ps. 15:8.)

Thomas à Kempis declares, "Where have I ever fared well but for You? Or how could things go badly when You were present?" (*Imit.*, Bk. 3, C. 59.) The sincere soul finds in Christ the sweetest of all company. " . . . in the shadow of your wings I jubilate! I cling to you with heart and soul; your right hand bears me up" (Ps. 62:8, 9).

> *"In the fight which you wage with the devil you have as witnesses the angels and the Lord of the angels"* (St. Ephraim).

"Because Christ, then, suffered in his body, you on your part should arm yourselves with the same ideal" (1 Pet. 4:1).

The canny Eskimo, who must use his wits to survive in the Barren Land of northern Canada, employs many subterfuges to lure game into his rifle's sights. He also uses a clever trick to get the most energy he can out of his Huskies when emergency demands.

The Eskimo keeps in reserve a certain word to urge the sled dogs on when they apparently have all but spent themselves. The secret word, which is rarely used and then only in great need, is Eskimo for "Caribou." The caribou or North American reindeer is the main source of meat for man and dog in the Arctic. When the dogs begin to drag and more miles *must* be traversed, the Eskimo driver shouts out this word. Immediately, the Huskies spring forward with amazing energy, sensing a full meal ahead.

The faithful soul at times is brought face to face with trials that test his faith. He should be prepared for these difficult times with some especially stimulating thought in the life of Christ.

The most energizing word at these times is the "Cross." Meditating on the scene of Christ's Crucifixion, His suffering and agony will serve to make the suffering soul realize that his own sorrow is small indeed compared with that of the dying Christ, his Redeemer. The cross is not the end but the beginning. Only three days after the Crucifixion Christ rose triumphant! Let the "cross" be the word that guides the soul through every trial to victory.

"This medicine given to man is so great that nothing greater can be thought of" (St. Augustine).

*"Make your ways and your doings good! and I
will dwell with you in this place"* (Jer. 7:3).

Even the heaviest smoker is surprised to learn that in one
year over 325 billion cigarettes and over 4 billion cigars were
sold.

The fact that people smoke so many cigarettes is an indication of these restless times, for ordinarily a person smokes
cigarettes in preference to cigars or a pipe because he has
just time enough for a "short smoke." The day when a man
could sit down and enjoy a lengthy pipeful or appreciate a
good cigar has given way to the rush and turmoil of
modern life.

Smoking, when not abused, is an indifferent act; it is
neither bad nor good in itself. However, it can be used as an
occasion for a high purpose. Since people are going to smoke
anyway, why not make it serve as an occasion to remind
one of God?

Every time a person lights up a cigarette or a cigar or
a pipe, let him make it occasion for offering up a prayer.
Each smoke could be just the reminder that the smoker needs
to say an Our Father or Hail Mary or some ejaculation
to his Creator. In this way, he would be doing much spiritual
good.

St. Paul advises: "Whether, then, you eat or drink, or
do anything else, do everything for God's glory" (1 Cor.
10:31).

> *"All works are virtuous when they are directed
> to that end, which is Christ"* (St. Augustine).

"Birds resort unto their like: so truth will return to them that practice her" (Ecclus. 27:10).

The baseball fan is always impressed by the catcher's ability to judge the position of a foul ball. At the crack of the bat, the catcher either rips off his mask and tears after the batted ball like a cat after a mouse, or he ignores it entirely. Years of *experience* have taught him to tell immediately from the sound of the impact where the ball is going.

The dictionary defines *experience* as "knowledge from one's own actions, practice, perception, enjoyment, or suffering." It would indeed be pleasant if one could have all the benefit of his years of experience without the suffering, sorrow, and bitterness that have taught him the wisdom and skill he now possesses. However, if he has profited from past mistakes, his own or others, these misfortunes have not been endured in vain. "Let our people also learn to excel in good works, so as to care for urgent cases. In this way they will not be destitute of good deeds" (Titus 3:14).

The humble, sincere man knows that sin is an offense against God's law and that this infraction brings about manifold bitter consequences, mental, moral, physical. Man's personal history, as well as the history of nations bears truth to this assertion. The unwise, proud, and wicked man must learn these sad facts from personal experience. The Christian soul, trained in the School of Christ, learns the lesson of sin from the Passion of Jesus. "For whatever has been written beforehand has been written for our instruction, and through the patient endurance and the consolation afforded by the Scriptures we may have hope" (Rom. 15:4).

"If you have spent the day profitably, you will always be happy at eventide" (Imit., Bk. 1, C. 25).

*"Therefore, welcome one another cordially, even
as Christ has cordially welcomed you to himself
for the glory of God"* (Rom. 15:7).

"Lord, make me an instrument of Thy Peace. Where there
is hatred, let me sow love. Where there is injury, let me sow
pardon. Where there is doubt, let me sow faith. Where there
is despair, let me sow hope. Where there is darkness, let me
sow light. Where there is sadness, let me sow joy. O Divine
Master, grant that I may not so much seek to be consoled
as to console; to be understood, as to understand; to be loved,
as to love; for it is in giving that we receive, it is in pardoning
that we are pardoned, and it is in dying that we are born to
Eternal Life" (St. Francis of Assisi).

*"Who is so strong as never to give way to temp-
tation if the Lord did not help him"*
(St. Augustine).

"But in all those things we are more than victorious through him who has loved us"
(Rom. 8:37).

There is an old poem which recounts the story of a spelling bee held in the country schoolroom. In those days this was quite an event. One of the young ladies present misspelled a word, and as was the custom, she was forced to withdraw from the contest. The next contestant, an admirer of the young lady who had failed, deliberately misspelled the same word; and the poem goes on something like this, "I could not go above her, because you see, I love her."

In a world where harshness and ungentlemanly conduct all too frequently have replaced consideration and courtesy, it is well occasionally to recall this bit of verse to mind.

Follow the admonition of Christ "A new commandment I give you! . . . as I love you, so I want you, too, to love one another" (Jn. 13:34). Christ's new commandment of love replaces the strict justice of the Old Law and the fiendish brutality of the pagans.

For one who really loves another, whether it be the boy who misspelled a word rather than humiliate his sweetheart, or one who lays down his life for his friend, no sacrifice is too great. Love bears no price tag — it is priceless. Christ, by dying on the cross for man, has taught him the true meaning of love. The faithful soul strives to follow Christ "for I have set you an example, so that what I have done to you, you, too, should do" (Jn. 13:15).

" . . . love is born of God and cannot rest except in God . . . " (Imit., Bk. 3, C. 5).

*"O hear, my people, what I teach; incline your
ears to the words I speak"* (Ps. 77:1).

"Who told you?" This question could be asked a thousand
times a day of those who claim to have the "dope" on everything from peanuts to atom bombs. The libraries of the world
are crammed with books which contain accurate information.
These citadels of learning, however, could not begin to furnish
the necessary room to hold all the *mis*information that is
spread throughout the world in a single day.

"They say" or "I heard" or "Someone told me" seems to
be sufficient authority for countless people to believe anything
and everything they hear. Doctors, lawyers, professors, policemen, priests know the amazing gullibility of most people. It
never dawns upon these naïve souls to ask upon *what authority* the speaker bases his statements. It is sufficient for the
"Know-it-all" to speak with a loud, convincing voice, mingled
with a dare to everyone to challenge his assertion, in order
to be believed. "Teach me your way, O Lord; your truth
shall guide my steps; direct my heart, that it may reverence
your name" (Ps. 85:11).

It is amazing what *mis*understanding and *mis*information
many non-Catholics have concerning the teaching of the
Catholic Church. Yet, St. Thomas Aquinas, over 700 years
ago in his *Summa Theologica,* proposed and accurately answered every conceivable serious objection that could be
raised against the Church and its doctrine. It is a wise man
who "goes to the source" when he wants the proper explanation of any doubtful statement.

*"Let Your truth teach me. Let it guard me, and
keep me safe to the end"* (Imit., Bk. 3, C. 4).

*"Ask, and you will receive; seek, and you will
find; knock, and you will gain admission"*
(Mt. 7:7).

Christ wants man to pray for the things he needs. He
not only wishes him to ask for help but He commands him
to do so. If the petitioner does what He commands, He
promises to answer his requests. Note, however, that action
is required on man's part, "ask," "seek," "knock." He must
petition before his desires are fulfilled. However, God does
not promise to give each one the very thing he seeks, but
the pleader may be sure that if his request is for his spiritual
welfare, it will be answered; but if not, God will bless him
with something just as good, or even better.

A young mother returns from shopping and brings home
a long-desired implement, a bright and gleaming bread knife.
Her baby cries out in delight at sight of this shiny object
and immediately pleads for its possession. The loving Mother
realizes the danger this object of her baby's pleading would
be to him. Naturally, she does not give her child anything
that would be harmful to him, but she does console her
offspring with some choice tidbit that satisfies the child
and brings joy to his heart. "Well, then, if you . . . choose to
give useful gifts to your children, how much more will your
Father in heaven give what is good to those that ask him!"
(Mt. 7:11.)

*"The prayer that is persevering and humble and
fervent will undoubtedly penetrate heaven, and
from there, it is certain, it cannot return unheard"*
(St. Bernard).

"For our present light affliction is producing for us an eternal weight of glory that is beyond all measure, while we direct our gaze not at what is seen but at what is not seen" (2 Cor. 4:17, 18).

Each person has within himself a tremendous capacity for good or evil. He is an individual with great powers of intellect and will.

He can dedicate this power to his own self-aggrandizement, as many evil men have done in the past, or he can concentrate his strength and determination to the glory of God.

Hitler was a genius but the object of his striving was the glorification of self. As in every case where man sets himself up as the end of his labor, he failed ignominiously. St. Paul, on the other hand, who sowed the seeds of the early Church so widely and so well, sought only the glory of God. In his Epistle to the Philippians, he writes in reference to sending Timothy to them, "I really have no one so like-minded, none so genuinely solicitous for your interests. They all seek their own interests, not those of Jesus Christ" (2:20). In Romans (2:7) he says "Life eternal he will give to those who by persevering in good deeds seek glory, honor, and immortality!"

Whatever state in life man enjoys, he can dedicate that position and his work therein to the honor and glory of God and to the salvation of his immortal soul. There is no greater ambition!

"There is this difference between eternity and time, that the one is lasting, whereas the other passes away" (St. Augustine).

> *"Go not after thy lusts, but turn away from thy own will. If thou give to thy soul her desires, she will make thee a joy to thy enemies"*
> (Ecclus. 18:30, 31).

All hearts beat faster when they behold the fire trucks dashing down the street. There is much glamor to fire fighting, at least on the surface.

A casual walk by the firehouse reveals nothing out of the ordinary. No tense expectancy is evident. Yet, as soon as the gong announces a fire in the precinct, the easygoing atmosphere changes to one of smooth, well-ordered motion. The speed with which the firemen, properly equipped for any emergency, depart is amazing. Their one objective is to be on the spot before the fire makes headway. On their promptness and ability hangs the difference between a burning stovepipe and a conflagration.

The efficiency of this department has been acquired only by strenuous preparation. Rigid training of personnel, fitness of apparatus, foresight of officers forestall many potentially disastrous fires. All may learn a lesson from these fire fighters.

Every man must be constantly on guard against a conflagration which may consume him. This danger comes from within himself, from the dangerous passions which lie dormant within him. By self-discipline, sacrifice, prayer, and the grace of God, the humble man prepares himself daily to meet and snuff out the smoldering fire of anger or envy or hatred or lust before it bursts into flame. "The patient man is better than the valiant: and he that ruleth his spirit, than he that taketh cities" (Prov. 16:32).

"There is no state so holy, no place so secret that temptations ... will not come" (*Imit.*, Bk. 1, C. 13).

"God resists the proud, but gives grace to the humble" (James 4:6).

The shrine of Our Lady of Guadalupe, the most beautiful church in Mexico, has an unique and supernatural history.

One day, an Indian boy, Juan Diego, was hurrying across the rugged countryside to attend Mass when he was amazed to behold a beautiful Lady standing in his path. He was frightened — speechless. The Lady spoke to him kindly and admonished him to be at the same spot the following day as she had a message for him. The native hurried off determined not to come that way again. On the following day, he took another route. To his consternation, the Lady again blocked his path. She told him to go to the Bishop and request him to erect a shrine to her honor on this spot.

But the Bishop, naturally enough, asked for a sign. When Juan reported this to the Lady at their next meeting, she directed him to a place where beautiful roses were mysteriously growing out of the rugged stone. She commanded the boy to give the flowers to the Bishop as a sign from her.

The Indian wrapped the roses in his rough shawl and obediently hurried off. Gaining access to the Bishop, he made known his mission, and to prove his authority in the matter, he unwrapped the shawl to display the roses.

There on the rough texture of his blanket was a magnificent picture of our Lady which today hangs over the main altar of the shrine. Artists from all parts of the world have admired it, but no one has ever discovered how the masterpiece could be placed on such a background. The secret lies in Mary's heart.

> *"Humility is the mother of wisdom. What then is the chief virtue? Humility certainly"* (St. Jerome).

*"If thou wilt keep the commandments . . . they
shall preserve thee"* (Ecclus. 15:16).

The day had been sultry, damp, and intensely hot for that
mountainous region in the small northern New York village.

Suddenly about five o'clock in the afternoon, the temperature dropped instantly and the windows were coated with
moisture so thick that it was impossible to see outside. Just
as suddenly, a tornado swept down without warning. For
five minutes the pressure of the wind seemed determined to
force the buildings flat to the ground. The crash of falling
trees, flying slate, and hurling debris was unbelievable. The
wind fortunately stopped as quickly as it started, but it
had turned the village into a shambles.

Just as uncontrolled nature wreaks havoc and destruction
wherever it strikes, so does man, once he steps outside the
bounds of God's law, bring death spiritually and physically
to himself — and unfortunately to countless others.

God gave to His children a free will in order that they
might exercise this will to prove themselves loyal and faithful
sons and daughters of an all-loving Father. Knowing human
nature, God set limits to men's activities in the form of the
Ten Commandments. Once the offender goes against these
laws of God, he breaks down the barriers that check his evil
nature. He becomes a whirlwind of destruction. The loving
and prudent soul follows God's laws; the sinner should hasten
to return to the protection of these heavenly safeguards.
"From your decrees I do not deviate, because you have instructed me" (Ps. 118:102).

*"He is very ungrateful who, being bound to re-
turn love for love, refuses to do so"*
(St. Augustine).

*" . . . I live by faith in the Son of God, who loved
me and sacrificed himself for me"* (Gal. 2:20).

The Oblate missionary, his Eskimo guide, and their sled
dogs were lost. In their attempt to take a "short cut" across
a frozen lake, an Arctic storm had swooped down and en-
gulfed them. All the bitter, cold, stinging sleet and piercing
gales of the Barren Land were concentrated in this black
whirlwind. So confounding was the maelstrom that the dogs
became confused and did not know which way to turn.

Suddenly, the Eskimo guide knelt down and, protected
from the wind by the loaded sled, carefully removed layers
of snow from ice. The missionary saw that the Eskimo had
drawn two intersecting lines — a perfect cross. Quickly rising,
the guide directed the dogs and soon the party was off the
dangerous lake and resting safely on firm ground.

What had happened? The Eskimo recalled that the wind
blew from the north all that day and from the west the day
before. Tracing the directions of the driven snow with his
delicate finger and his keen eye, he had managed to get a
cross section of his bearings — and quickly found safety.

In this terrible hour when every element of nature was
bent on destroying the lives of these men, what saved them?
— a simple cross traced in the drifting snow!

When one is faced with the complexities of life and it
seems that he has no direction in which to turn for safety,
let him *look up* to the cross of Christ. The most hapless, the
most confused soul will be directed to perfect security and
peace. "As for me, God forbid that I should glory except in
the cross of our Lord Jesus Christ" (Gal. 6:14).

> *"Indeed the life of a good religious man is a
> cross, but it leads to paradise"* (Imit., Bk. 3, C. 56).

> *"If you make my teaching your rule of life, you
> are truly my disciples; then you will know the
> truth, and the truth will make you free men"*
> (Jn. 8:31, 32).

Often we hear and see *part* of the above text offered by
speakers and writers as a so-called explanation of their arguments. These people will declare, "You shall know the truth
and the truth shall make you free." Out of their context,
however, these words mean nothing. Scientists frequently
lay claim to this oft-repeated scriptural quotation to prove
that the fundamental truths of science will make men free.
Free from what?

Science has taught many good things, but it has also made
known the truths concerning exploding bombs, yet this truth
has not freed man from the fear and horror and worry of war.

In reading this *whole* text of Scripture, the faithful follower
of Christ knows that by understanding His teaching and
by putting it into practice he learns the fundamental truths
of God and these truths make him free; free from fear, free
from doubt, free from sin, free from anything and everything that would force him into slavery and separate him
from the love of Christ. "If you abide in my word," you
will enjoy the freedom of the children of God. Then you
are truly free. "Consequently, if the Son should make you
free men, you will be free men in reality" (Jn. 8:36).

*" . . . he who is poor and humble of heart lives in
a world of peace" (Imit., Bk. 1, C. 6).*

"You shall draw waters with joy out of the saviour's fountains" (Isa. 12:3).

Cartoons often picture a frustrated bank teller trying to tell a lightheaded lady depositor that she has no more funds against which she may draw a check. It is quite apparent that the baffled depositor is at a loss to understand that in order to draw a check on the bank there must be sufficient money on deposit to cover the amount of the check.

Yet, there are many people who are far more inconsistent than the lady in question.

These people declare, "Oh, I do a lot of good; I help my fellow men, I assist the down and out, I feel as though I have accomplished a great deal of good." And these kind-hearted individuals are to be commended. But, they forget to put their "reward" for these good deeds into the bank. It never occurs to them to offer up their good works to Christ, to be deposited against their final drawing account.

" . . . when you are about to give alms, do not send a trumpeter ahead of you, as the hypocrites do . . . to win the applause of their fellow men. I tell you plainly, they have their reward already. When you give alms, your left hand should not know what your right hand is doing. Thus your alms is given in secrecy; and your Father, who sees what is secret, will reward you" (Mt. 6:2-4).

The prudent soul puts his earned dividend for good deeds done into the "Bank of Eternity" to be credited to him when he appears before God to account for his stewardship. "Mark my words: there is a great reward for you in heaven" (Lk. 6:23).

"I had rather be poor for your sake than rich without you" (*Imit.,* Bk. 3, C. 59).

> *"Consequently, brothers, strive even more to
> make your calling and election sure"* (2 Pet. 1:10).

The priest was invited to address a convention of insurance men. "I feel at home in this gathering," the Father declared, "because I also am in the insurance business — the life insurance profession; that is, eternal life, which, in fact, is the most important insurance of all."

Today, Underwriters issue policies against every conceivable loss. Man seeks to protect himself against the ravages of fire, wind, water, earthquake, and the hundred and one things that might war against him and those he loves. The good father and husband strives to leave sufficient insurance behind him to protect his family when he is gone. The prudent man protects himself at every turn lest he should suffer irreparable material loss from the unexpected.

Since man is so wise as to his worldly goods, it seems that he would be at least as circumspect concerning his eternal welfare. All material losses can be replaced. If one loses his soul, however, that loss is final. Thus, the thoughtful and sincere soul insures himself against such a catastrophe by faithfully performing his duties toward God each day. By prayer and sacrifice and devotion to his Redeemer and his final Judge, he strives to merit that greatest of all gifts, eternal life with God. "God, the source of all grace, who has called you to his eternal glory in Christ, will himself, after you have suffered a little while, perfect, steady, strengthen, and firmly establish you. To him belongs power for ever and ever" (1 Pet. 5:10, 11).

> *"In truth, the loss or gain of God's kingdom is
> no small matter"* (*Imit.*, Bk. 3, C. 47).

*"I therefore, the prisoner in the Lord, exhort you
to conduct yourselves in a manner worthy of the
calling to which you have been called"* (Eph. 4:1).

Vocation comes from the Latin word *vocare,* "to call."
The dictionary defines vocation as "a call to, or fitness for,
a certain career"; "a call to a given religious work."

Everyone has his vocation in life. A comparatively few are
called to the religious life. The most common vocation, however, is that to the married state.

Today, we hear much about "career girls." These young
ladies put off marriage, or after having entered the wedded
state, still wish to continue some occupation that interferes
with their carrying out their obligations as mother and
"Queen of the Home."

Because of selfish ambitions or the glamor of public life
the young bride sacrifices the most sacred privilege she possesses, that of bringing loved ones into the world; that of
co-operating with God in creating human beings made to
His image and likeness.

It is true that economic conditions sometimes demand that
both wife and husband be gainfully employed. In reality, such
conditions are comparatively rare, or at least temporary. The
young husband and wife who wish to avoid much unhappiness and desire to enjoy God's blessings on their home to
the fullest, will dispense with unessential luxuries and will
instead raise a family to the honor and glory of God. "His
will is in them that walk sincerely" (Prov. 11:20).

*"When concord, and peace, and the bond of love
exist between husband and wife, all other good
things come to them at the same time"*

(St. Gregory).

> " . . . *he who is the least among you all is the greatest"* (Lk. 9:48).

"One day the thought occurred to them as to which one of their group was the greatest. Knowing what was uppermost in their minds, Jesus took hold of a little child and placed it close beside him. 'Whoever,' he then said to them, 'befriends this little child for the sake of my name, befriends me; and he who befriends me, befriends him whose ambassador I am. You see, then, he who is the least among you all is the greatest'" (Lk. 9:46–48).

God selected a humble maiden, Mary, for His Mother; a poor carpenter, Joseph, for His foster father. He was born in a stable, among the poorest of the poor. The angels announced His birth to the shepherds who were looked upon as outcasts among the better classes. He passed over the mighty Romans and learned Pharisees to select His twelve Apostles from among humble, and for the most part, unlettered, men. Surely Christ means what He says when He speaks: " . . . he who is the least among you all is the greatest" (Lk. 9:49).

How ill it becomes a man to make little of his fellow man! "For God will not except any man's person, neither will he stand in awe of any man's greatness: for he made the little and the great, and he hath equally care for all" (Wisd. 6–8).

"Never set yourself above anyone because of the nobility of your descent; for our religion knows no distinction of persons, nor conditions of men, but considers souls" (St. Jerome).

"Love . . . is not envious" (1 Cor. 13:4).

There is a tendency in human nature to look across the street at the other fellow's "good luck"; to be envious of his possessions, position, or power. God understood this dangerous attitude on man's part, so He declares emphatically in the Tenth Commandment, "Thou shalt not covet thy neighbor's goods."

The happy man is not envious of his neighbor's achievements. He is quite content with what he has for he counts his own blessings. He thanks God for his good health, for his family, for his soul.

How often does one hear it said of a departed friend, one whom on occasion he has envied, "Why, I had no idea he was ill" or "I thought he had lots of money" or "I thought he and his wife were the ideal couple."

No one knows the inner thoughts of a person, "save the man's spirit within him" (1 Cor. 2:11).

Let each one be grateful to God for the great blessings that God gives *him* every day; yes, every minute of every day. "Let him count his own blessings," and he will have no time to be envious of others. "Recall the wonders he has done, his miracles, the judgments he pronounced" (Ps. 104:5).

> *"The envious man cannot but be proud, for envy is the daughter of pride. Great is the man who overcomes pride by humility"* (St. Augustine).

> *"Son, observe the time, and fly from evil"*
> (Ecclus. 4:23).

When one thinks about it, he is surprised how far back in history one's own knowledge goes. In the newspaper recently, a story was printed concerning a lady who had attended President Lincoln's inauguration as a young girl. That seems a great many years ago to today's children.

However, a man, let us say, of eighty years can recall stories told to him by his own grandmother concerning the early history of this country. This man would have been born in the 1870's. His grandmother of eighty years would have been born in the 1790's, a short time after the Colonies declared their independence from Great Britain.

To think of these facts brings home how brief life is. How few years we have "in this vale of tears" before going before God to account for our stewardship. Scripture warns us, "In all thy works remember thy last end, and thou shalt never sin" (Ecclus. 7:40). The last end is often sooner than one thinks. "Holy Mary, Mother of God . . . pray for us sinners now and at the hour of our death." One of these days — soon? — the "hour of our death" and "now" will coincide.

"The duration of all time is brief when compared with eternity" (St. Jerome).

"It is the real truth when I tell you that if you make any request of the Father, he will give it to you in my name" (Jn. 16:23).

During the Battle of the Bulge, the Allies were being forced back. The troops were discouraged; food was scarce; the weather was depressing; the rain was incessant; the fog, impenetrable. The American commander, General Patton, in that dreadful hour turned to God for assistance.

He himself prayed without ceasing. He had hundreds of thousands of prayers printed pleading with God to send clear weather so that the planes might get into the air. These printed prayers were given out to the soldiers.

A few days after these petitions stormed heaven, much to the amazement of the forecasters, the weather cleared. Bright skies gave ideal flying weather to the thousands of planes that were sent aloft. So long a spell of such good weather in that section during that time of the year was unheard of.

One often hears the saying, "God never seems to answer my prayers." Perhaps the reason is that many people never really pray. They gingerly petition God for some request. In their halfhearted way, they timidly expect failure. Our Lord Himself declares, " . . . from the day when John the Baptist appeared down to this day, the kingdom of heaven is to be taken by storm — and only by storm do men lay hold of it" (Mt. 11:12, 13). The sincere seeker after God's gifts puts energy, fervor, and zeal into his prayers.

"God wishes to be asked . . . to be overcome by a certain importunity; therefore it is said: The Kingdom of Heaven suffereth violence; and the violent bear it away" (St. Gregory).

> *"Guide me to do what you demand—to spite*
> *my enemies! Smooth out your path that lies*
> *ahead of me"* (Ps. 5:9).

"There's a difference between an idea and a *good* idea." The speaker was making a humorous observation concerning a fellow worker. The person referred to had the unhappy faculty of following almost any idea that popped into his head. His unwise application of these ideas had caused his associates much embarrassment and considerable expense.

The modern dictionary defines an idea as "a contemplated performance or procedure." The very fact that an idea is a "contemplated" action demands that the "idea" be given serious consideration before being executed. Good judgment, sufficient experience, sound advice, and, above all, sincere prayer should guide one in his important actions.

"I forgot to pray" is the lament of many unfortunate souls who have learned too late that their conduct was not only unwise, but ruinous. "The Lord is near to all who call on him, to all who call on him sincerely" (Ps. 144:18).

The faithful will plead with God each day for the knowledge, understanding, and wisdom that is so essential in leading a good Christian life. "He guides the humble by his just demands, and to the humble shows his ways" (Ps. 24:9).

> *"We frequently judge that things are as we wish*
> *them to be, for through personal feeling true per-*
> *spective is easily lost"* (*Imit.*, Bk. 1, C. 14).

"He who is conscientious in small things is conscientious in big things also; he who is unscrupulous in small things is unscrupulous in big things also" (Lk. 16:10, 11).

The lift bridge raised its towering sides contemptuous of the heavy midafternoon traffic rushing in both directions. Good-humoredly, drivers brought their vehicles to a stop and waited expectantly. The sight of a mighty lake freighter or even perhaps an ocean-going liner would be a welcome sight — a harbinger of the approaching spring season.

The autoists craned their necks in vain. No stately ship hovered into view. Suddenly, the interrupter of the smoothly running traffic appeared around the bend in the river. With a couple of cocky snorts from its steam whistle, a small, ungallant tug strutted up the stream. Almost as one, the drivers of the cars and trucks and buses clamped their hands hard on their respective horns — the raucous voices of angry people irritated at being halted by such an ignoble craft.

In life, it is the little things that annoy one the most. Big problems, for the greater part, are faced with courage and bravery and patience. The small and trivial obstacles are frequently the ones that gall and irritate. Therefore, it behooves each one to be on his guard lest he be overcome and conquered by an unworthy adversary. "Take care of the pennies, and the dollars will take care of themselves" can be applied to spiritual as well as material gain. "Afflicted in few things, in many they shall be well rewarded; because God hath . . . found them worthy of himself" (Wisd. 3:5).

"Habit already formed will resist you, but it shall be overcome by a better habit"
(Imit., Bk. 3, C. 12).

> *"Why are you so timid? How is it you are still
> without faith?"* (Mk. 4:40.)

All Christian souls know the Gospel account of Jesus and
His disciples crossing the Sea of Galilee. Suddenly, a great
squall arose and the huge waves threatened to engulf the
boat. The disciples were terrified at the prospect of being
thrown into the water and drowned. Christ calmly slept.

As the storm continued and the waves swept higher and
higher, the fear of the crew continued to mount. Every terrible moment must have seemed like a year.

Finally, "they awoke him with the cry, 'Rabbi! We are
going down! Is that nothing to you?' Then, rising to his
full height, he sternly said to the wind: 'Silence!' and commanded the sea: 'Be still!' The wind subsided . . . He also
said to them, 'Why are you so timid?' and 'How is it you
are still without faith?' " (Mk. 4:35-40.)

How many times in this life do souls cry to Christ with
fear, in pain, in sorrow, and Christ does not seem to hear
them? They are afraid that Christ has forgotten them; that
"He is asleep." But the Saviour of men, though asleep in
the storm-tossed boat, was cognizant of His disciples' needs.
He saw and heard and understood their fear but He wanted
their faith and trust in Himself. So with all faithful souls —
He wants their faith. He hears all prayers and petitions; He
is concerned with every soul, vitally concerned; but He wants
their faith — trust God! "He heals the broken hearts; he binds
their wounds" (Ps. 146:3).

*"Have firm trust in God, and place yourself en-
tirely in His hands. . . . He allows nothing to happen to you but what is for your good, though you
may not know it to be so"* (St. Augustine).

*"Abide not in the works of sinners: but trust in
God, and stay in thy place"* (Ecclus. 11:22).

"And the Lord rained upon Sodom and Gomorrha brimstone and fire from the Lord out of heaven. And he destroyed these cities, and all the country about: all the inhabitants of the cities, and all things that spring from the earth. And his wife looking behind her, was turned into a statue of salt" (Gen. 19:24–26).

God told Abraham that he was about to destroy the sinful cities of Sodom and Gomorrha because of their wickedness. He commanded Abraham to take his wife and daughters and flee. "Save thy life: look not back" (Gen. 19:17).

God fulfilled this promise and razed those vicious cities to the ground. Out of curiosity, and against God's explicit orders, Lot's wife looked back and "was turned into a statue of salt."

Countless sins are committed, many hearts are broken, and much strife caused by an unwise curiosity. Curiosity is defined as "habitual anxiety for knowledge of something, especially the private affairs of others." An inquisitive person prying into another's business can do great harm to himself and to his neighbor. St. Paul admonishes the Thessalonians, "And now we hear that some among you live in idleness and do no work but meddle in the work of others. Such people we command and exhort by the authority of the Lord Jesus Christ quietly to earn their own living" (2 Thess. 3:11, 12). "Strive not in a matter which does not concern thee: and sit not in judgment with sinners" (Eccles. 11:9). The lesson of Lot's wife should stay the curious.

> *"My child, do not be curious. Do not trouble
> yourself with idle cares"* (Imit., Bk. 3, C. 24).

"I have surveyed all things with my mind, to know, and consider, and seek out wisdom and reason: and to know the wickedness of the fool, and the error of the imprudent" (Eccles. 7:26).

The family was gathered around the television set absorbed in a cowboy serial. The villain was engaged in a nefarious plot to destroy the virtuous sheriff. Little Johnny, who had recently received an air rifle as a gift, stalked the rogue from behind a parlor chair. As the rascal was about to shoot the high-minded official from ambush, Johnny drew a bead on the knave and fired. To the consternation of the assembled gathering, the engrossing drama vanished before their eyes.

The expense to the father and the punishment to Johnny were directly traceable to an overactive imagination on the part of the youngster.

How many people there are, much older than Johnny, who make far more expensive mistakes than this because they let their imagination run away with them! These unhappy souls, disregarding solid reason, allow suspicions, doubts, mistrust, conjecture, envy, to take possession of their thoughts and before long their imagination has built out of whole cloth what to them is grim reality. This unfortunate condition brings much agony to themselves and great unhappiness to others. The wise and prudent and charitable person is keen and humble enough not to become a slave to an overactive imagination. "Better is wisdom, than weapons of war: and he that shall offend in one shall lose many good things" (Eccles. 9:18).

" . . . the more humble [a man] is and the more subject to God, the wiser and the more at peace will he be in all things" (Imit., Bk. 1, C. 4).

"God is faithful and will not let you be tempted beyond your strength. On the contrary he will, along with the temptation, supply you a way of escape . . . " (1 Cor. 10:13).

The so-called "law of the jungle" is nothing but the expression by the inhabitants of the forest of the natural law.

According to those familiar with wild animals, captivity does not greatly change their natural instincts. They never become tame in the sense that they can be trusted to abide by civilization's code. The caged animals are more or less contented when they have enough to eat and drink and are not annoyed. But the wild animal in the zoo or circus may be easily aroused and reverts to the "law of the jungle" in a twinkling of the eye.

From these followers of the natural law, man can learn a lesson — that he must constantly be on his guard against the natural instincts that lie dormant within him. Years of constant mortification and self-control are no guarantee that the terrific passions sleeping within his heart and body will not rise up and overcome him. He must constantly be on the alert lest he fall victim to these scourges. St. Matthew warns, "Keep awake and pray" (26:41), "for out of the heart proceed evil thoughts — murder, adultery, fornication, theft, false witness, and blasphemy" (15:19). Only supernatural grace can overcome natural passions. If you keep close to Christ you need not fear these evils, for God will "give you a way of escape."

"To mortify the motions of the flesh, and the passions, to weaken them each day, to restrain them, to crush them, is our work in this life"
(St. John Climacus).

"The fruit of humility is the fear of the Lord: riches and glory and life" (Prov. 22:4).

A great military leader has declared, "There is no substitute for victory." If this assertion be true in the battle of self-preservation among nations, it is doubly true in the spiritual conflict which man wages against his eternal enemies.

Job declared, "The life of man upon earth is a warfare" (7:1). The humble, sincere Christian soul working out his salvation here realizes only too well the truth of these words.

A defeated nation can somehow hope to rise again, but the man who loses his soul has been vanquished forever. "So, my beloved brothers, be steadfast and immovable. Devote yourselves fully at all times to the Lord's work, realizing that your toil in the Lord can never be in vain" (1 Cor. 15:58).

Just as there are military heroes whose courageous example leads the embattled soldier on to victory, so there are the saints of God who, through their victorious assault against sin, serve to encourage the weary soul to fight on to eternal victory. "Because this perishable nature of ours is destined to be clothed in imperishable glory, and this mortal nature of ours must be clothed in immortality. . . . Then will be realized the words of Scripture, 'Death is swallowed up in victory. O Death, where is your victory? O Death, where is your sting?'" (1 Cor. 15:53–55.)

"To lose or gain the kingdom of God is no small matter" (*Imit.*, Bk. 3, C. 47).

"O that they would be wise and would under-stand, and would provide for their last end!"
(Deut. 32:29.)

The storekeeper was wise in the ways of the world. He had faithfully served the public on the same spot for many years. He had seen human nature at its worst and at its best. One day as he stood in front of his store, a nicely dressed, young man came up to him. "Excuse me, sir," he said, "but can you tell me where there is a betting parlor near here?"

The older man surveyed the youth critically, then said: "Just stand here for a while and the first old man you see who needs a shave, is run down at the heels, and has a racing form sticking out of his pocket — follow him!"

It is a trite saying — the gambler cannot win. However, the knowledge that he is eventually bound to lose does not stop the gambler from taking a chance. The thought of making a "killing" warps his otherwise good judgment and he continues on his doubtful and hopeless way.

The man who gambles his money, however, is an intellectual giant compared with the man who gambles on saving his soul. This man is always going to change his ways; he is going to turn to God eventually; but he is also going to take a chance in "slipping under the wire" at the last moment.

Some have squeezed into heaven through the grace of God or the untiring prayers of loved ones. But, experience teaches that for the most part the gambler loses out. The Scripture is very explicit: "Keep awake therefore, you know neither the day nor the hour" (Mt. 25:13).

"The time of our death is hidden from us in order that we may be always ready to die"
(St. Augustine).

> *"Always be grateful. . . . Such sentiments God*
> *wills you to have in Christ Jesus"*
> (1 Thess. 5:16, 19).

The retired bank official was in a reminiscent mood. "One of the difficult things to understand in the banking business," he recalled, "is the ingratitude of some men. A customer wants a loan to start a business. The bank after consultation decides to finance his venture. A considerable sum of money is put into the undertaking. During the first few years, many risks and hazards must be endured, but the bank carries the businessman through these difficult times. Eventually the enterprise proves successful and the customer is now in sound financial condition. Then, for no apparent reason, the ungrateful borrower switches his business to a competing bank which reaps the reward without any risk."

Banks are not alone in having been hurt by the ingratitude of men.

Those who have benefited from the kindness of others should acknowledge their appreciation by their faithfulness and loyalty. "Always be grateful."

Especially should the children of God prove grateful to their Creator. "O come; let us exult in the Lord! Let us acclaim the rock, our savior!" (Ps. 94:1.) To God, man owes his existence, his life, all that he has or hopes to be. To Christ the Redeemer the faithful owe their hope of everlasting happiness. Truly man should prove grateful to God. "At all times I will bless the Lord, and ever be his praise upon my lips" (Ps. 33:2).

> *"Be grateful, therefore, for the least gift and you*
> *will be worthy to receive a greater"*
> (*Imit.,* Bk. 2, C. 10).

*"Keep in your grace your worshipers; and keep
your kindly disposition toward the true of heart"*
                                    (Ps. 35:11).

People are interested in places and persons they know.
The big-city family decides to take a vacation. They look
over the travel folders and plan to spend their holidays at
Big Bend. With keen anticipation and much luggage, the
vacation-bound family heads for this small, insignificant summer resort. All have a grand time. They like the little town;
they get acquainted with the natives. When their two weeks
are up, the happy and rested group head back home. They
had never heard of Big Bend before or Jim Hughes, the
boatman, or Jennie Smith, the postmistress, or Bill Green,
the milkman. But now that they know this town and these
people, all take a personal interest in them.

Once one person knows another, there is a personal link
forged between them, and each is anxious to know more and
more about the other. Their friendship ripens and pleasure
and joy are brought to both by this personal contact.

The same is true of man's relationship with God. Once a
soul really knows God, he learns to love Him, and since the
creature displays real affection for the Creator, the Creator
shows His love toward this faithful soul.

Those seeking to know God, or to know Him better, must
go to Him, visit Him, pray to Him, adore Him. In this new-
found relationship, in this new knowledge, man will find
great joy and happiness. "We know, moreover, that the Son
of God has come and has given us understanding that we
may know the True One" (1 Jn. 5:20).

> *"He who finds Jesus finds a rare treasure indeed,
> a good above every good"* (Imit., Bk. 2, C. 8).

"He declareth the things that are past and the things that are to come, and revealeth the traces of hidden things" (Ecclus. 42:19).

As winter approaches in the northern zones, the natives are anxious to know what kind of weather lies ahead. They are not content to sit back and wait for the north wind to blow and the snow to pile up. They seek out the "signs" that will foretell the elements for the coming months.

They look to Nature to furnish these prognostications. How thick is the wild animals' fur? What is the direction of the wind? How thick is the bark on the trees? Yet the weather, with utter disregard for all these so-called indications, follows its own erratic course.

The weather like everything else in the future is known only to God. Those foolish people who spend millions of dollars visiting fortunetellers are certainly wasting their money, and more than this, they may sin grievously by attributing to a poor creature the knowledge that alone belongs to God. "Who has known the mind of the Lord, or who has been his counselor?" (Rom. 11:34.)

Rather than waste time and money by trying to delve into the future, the faithful soul strives by present acts to prepare for whatever may lie ahead. By putting into practice in his own life each day the teachings of Christ, the true Christian prepares wisely for all eventualities. " . . . in every concern by prayer and supplication with thanksgiving let your petitions be made known in your communing with God" (Phil. 4:6).

"Oh, what great thanks I owe You, who have shown me and all the faithful the good and right way to Your everlasting kingdom"
                                        (*Imit.*, Bk. 3, C. 18).

"The precepts of the Lord are right — how they delight the heart! The Lord's command is clear — how it enlights the eye!" (Ps. 18:9.)

The studious-looking gentleman was reading a dusty tome as the airplane wended its rapid way toward New York City. By coincidence, the passenger seated next to him was engaged in a similar pursuit. From time to time, each traveler would put aside his spectacles to ease his eyes, while he meditated upon the profound matter he was reading.

Upon reaching La Guardia Field, each sought to hurry off to his respective destination. The first man felt most uneasy as he descended from the plane. For some unexplained reason, he almost fell. Suddenly it dawned upon him that his vision was failing. Panic-stricken, he hailed a cab and demanded to be taken to the nearest hospital. An emergency examination by an oculist quickly proved his eyes were all right — but he was wearing the wrong glasses. No doubt, his erstwhile traveling companion had undergone a similar ordeal.

The eyes are the windows of the soul. If the soul is to look out upon all things without distorted vision, it must use the proper means. To see in correct proportion the essential things in life, each one must look at them through the "spectacles" of God, " . . . and in your light we see the light" (Ps. 35:10). God, the Source of all truth, will quickly respond to the prayer of the sincere seeker after enlightenment. "Open my eyes: I wish to scan the wonders of your law" (Ps. 118:18).

> *"Nature . . . often errs, the other (grace) trusts in God and is not deceived" (Imit.,* Bk. 3, C. 31).

"Thou art all fair, O my love, and there is not a spot in thee" (Cant. 4:7).

In St. Peter's in Rome, there is a magnificent piece of statuary by Michelangelo called *The Pietà*. Carved in marble is the figure of the crucified Christ lying in the arms of His Sorrowful Mother. Only the taut hands of the Blessed Virgin portray the agony in her heart. Her lovely face is unlined and she appears extremely youthful. When one of the critics pointed out to the author of this masterpiece that Mary looked too young for such a setting, the great Michelangelo simply answered, "She was too beautiful to grow old!"

To the faithful child of Mary, she is indeed "too beautiful to grow old." The fullness of grace shining out from the framework of her immaculate body is glorious to behold. Through the eyes of faith, the devoted client of the Blessed Virgin looks upon the eternal beauty of her eternal youth, the ageless loveliness of sanctifying grace. Indeed, Mary, the Immaculate Mother of God, is too beautiful to grow old! A convert to Catholicism has said, "Every soul whom I know or ever heard of who has entered the Church has arrived there through devotion to Mary." The sincere seeker after Christ should plead with Mary, God's Mother and his own Mother, for help and guidance. Truly has the poet called her "our tainted nature's solitary boast" (Wordsworth).

" . . . whoever wishes to understand fully the words of Christ must try to pattern his whole life on that of Christ" (Imit., Bk. 1, C. 1).

" 'Blessed, rather,' he replied 'are those that hear
the word of God and observe it' " (Lk. 11:28).

Frequently, it is heard said, "I always go to him with all my troubles because he is so *understanding.*"

Everyone is always on the alert for some person who will understand him; someone who will listen to his problems and console him in his sorrows.

It is not easy to find an understanding person. So in their diligent seeking after consolation and help, the young, especially, will put their confidence in some who are unworthy of this sacred trust. Some will try to master materialistic philosophies; others will delve deep into incomprehensible poetry; still others will read avidly atheistic writings; all in the vain hope that they may be able thus to solve the problems that face them. They will cry out, "Oh, if I only had had the opportunity to talk with Plato, with Socrates, with Aristotle! These learned and brilliant men would have understood me and solved my every difficulty." "'Tis better far to fly to the Lord for help, than to trust in man" (Ps. 117:8).

How foolish these people are. There is only One who understands fully the creature and that is the Creator. God made man and only God understands man. Therefore, let the seeker after self-understanding turn to the Source of all knowledge. By seeking out Christ and His teachings, he will find the answer to every problem, and in the love of God, he will find perfect peace. "Take in what I tell you; the Lord will give you a ready-understanding in everything" (2 Tim. 2:7).

> *"If, however, you seek Jesus in all things you*
> *will find Jesus"* (*Imit.,* Bk. 2, C. 7).

" . . . acquit, and you shall be acquitted"
(Lk. 6:37).

One of the most difficult things for man is to forgive those who have grievously injured him. Yet, this act of forgiveness must be performed, if a man is to obtain forgiveness from God. This forgiveness is made a condition when the Our Father is recited, "forgive us our trespasses as we forgive those who trespass against us."

Yes, man must forgive his enemies, for love is the foundation stone of Christianity. St. Paul sums up this teaching definitely and clearly. "If I should speak the languages of men and of angels, but have no love, I am no more than a noisy gong and a clanging cymbal" (1 Cor. 13:1).

There is only one sure and complete example that will motivate man to forgive those who have brought great sorrow into his life — and that is the sight of the crucified Christ, true Man and true God, hanging on the cross, the object of man's hatred. Does Christ condemn His enemies? No! Through seared and feverish lips Christ pleads, "Father, forgive them; they do not know what they are doing" (Lk. 23:34). Has anyone ever suffered as much as Christ?

"If you wish to reign with Me, carry the cross with Me" (Imit., Bk. 3, C. 56).

*" . . . he was awaiting the city with foundations
whose architect and builder is God"*
                              (Hebr. 11:10).

" 'I am a Jew from Tarsus in Cilicia,' replied Paul, 'a
citizen of no mean city' " (Acts 21:39). St. Paul, the great
missionary, who had traveled over almost the entire known
world spreading the teachings of Christ, still loved and was
proud of his "home town."

Like most people, Paul gloried in his birthplace. Regardless
of the years or the distance that separates one from the scenes
of his childhood, there always lurks close to the surface of
his heart a longing and love for home.

Actually, however, the joys and delights and loves and
companionships of this much loved town are but a foretaste
of man's eternal home — heaven. For St. Paul emphatically
declares, "Here indeed we have no lasting city; but we are in
search of the city that is to come" (Hebr. 13:14).

The faithful soul looks forward to reunion with those loved
ones who have preceded him. In heaven in the company of
God, he will once again find the joys of his youth with
mother and father, sister and brother, friends and companions.
The difference will be, however, that this happy condition
will not be for a few years but forever. What a goal to be
striven for! The sincere seeker after this great reward sings
with the Psalmist, "How lovely is your dwelling place, O
Lord of hosts! My spirit pines — for the courts of the Lord
it faints with yearning" (Ps. 83:2, 3).

> *"What God prepares for those who love Him, is
> not understood by faith, nor tasted by hope, nor
> taken hold of by charity; it surpasses all desires"*
>   (St. Augustine).

> " . . . I count the sufferings of the present time
> as not worthy to be compared with the glory to
> come that will be revealed shining upon us"
> (Rom. 8:18).

Mink coats are looked upon as the quintessence of luxury.
There are few ladies who would not be pleased to own such
a luxurious garment. The vicious little animals who surrender
their skins so that milady may be dressed in fashion are of
two varieties: the domestic and the wild mink.

The most expensive fur is from the wild mink. Why?
Not only because these animals are free to run the forests and
streams, but especially because they endure the cold and
hardships of woodland life. The little creatures spend most
of their time in the ice-cold waters of the northern zones
in search of food. This bitter cold produces a more luxuriant
growth of shining fur than the domestic kind enjoys.

Faithful souls who endure hardships and sufferings and
sacrifices for Christ's sake are nearer and dearer to Him
than those who pamper themselves with luxury and ease.
St. Paul rejoices in the knowledge of his trials, "Not only
this, but we exult in tribulations also, aware that tribulation
produces endurance, and endurance proven virtue, and proven
virtue hope" (Rom. 5:3, 4).

Those who suffer for Christ should do so joyfully, realizing
their reward will be great in heaven. "The Lord lifts up
those that are bowed down; the Lord loves holy men"
(Ps. 145:8).

*"The strength of desires enables us to support
toil and sorrow; and no one willingly undertakes
to endure what gives him pain, unless it be for
that which gives him pleasure"* (St. Augustine).

" . . . rejoice to the extent that you share in the sufferings of Christ, so that you may also rejoice and exult when his glory will be revealed"
(1 Pet. 4:13, 14).

It is generally admitted that "a thing of beauty is a joy forever." There is some innate quality in beauty that attracts and holds attention; and over and above this quality, beautiful things grow in its possession.

One never tires of admiring a beautiful piece of jewelry. By close association with the gem something new and attractive can be discovered in it each day. The same holds true of great music and art. All beautiful things reveal more and more of themselves *to their possessor.*

God is all Beauty Itself. Thus it is that His saints, by meditating upon Him, discover more and more of the infinite joy that comes to those close to Him. "State and beauty herald his advance; might and splendor deck his holy shrine" (Ps. 95:6).

Many people find it difficult to meditate. Yet if they would make a real effort to know God, to strive in humility to come close to Him, to think upon Him, His limitless beauty would gradually be revealed to them, and in this revelation of Himself to His creatures, the faithful soul will find unending happiness. "At that time Jesus . . . said, 'I praise you, Father . . . for hiding these things from wise and prudent men and revealing them to little ones'" (Mt. 11:25, 26).

> *"But great — yes, very great, indeed — is the difference between delight in the Creator and in the creature, in eternity and in time, in Light uncreated and in the light that is reflected"*
> (Imit., Bk. 3, C. 34).

"You do not know what sort of spirit animates you; for the Son of Man did not come to destroy men's lives, but to save them" (Lk. 9:55, 56).

"These are expendable." This expression was frequently heard during the war. It meant that certain places and things, and even individuals, must be sacrificed so that a greater number of places and things and people might survive. War has an ethic all its own — the survival of nations being the only norm of action.

But man's way is not always the way of God. Listen to the words of Christ. " . . . to fulfill the statement he had made, namely; 'Of those you have entrusted to me, I have not lost a single one'" (Jn. 18:9).

Not infrequently, man looks with horror and disgust upon his fellow men who have sunk lower than beasts of prey, and even sometimes these righteous persons cry out that the world would be better off without these unfortunate souls.

But even in the lowest person there still lingers some nobility because that person was created to the image and likeness of God. In God's sight not one soul is "expendable."

Regardless of its present unsavory state, the soul of the sinner, no less than that of the saint, was purchased by Christ's agonizing death on the cross. Before God, every soul is priceless, created for eternal glory with his Creator. "The Lord does not delay fulfilling his promises, as some estimate delay, but he is long-suffering toward you, not wishing a single soul to perish, but that every last one should have a change of heart and mind" (2 Pet. 3:9, 10).

"Convert us to you, that we may be thankful, humble, and devout, for You are our salvation . . . and our strength" (Imit., Bk. 3, C. 8).

*" . . . through fire and water we have passed;
but now relief you granted us"* (Ps. 65:12).

In classical mythology, Charybdis was a ravenous woman, transformed into a whirlpool, on the Sicilian coast opposite the Italian rock, Scylla; hence the frequently heard expression "between Scylla and Charybdis," that is, between two grave dangers.

Not infrequently, as man goes through life, he finds himself beset on all sides by difficulties, trials, or temptations. He hardly knows which way to turn. He is, as it were, between Scylla and Charybdis. If he turns to the left, he flounders on the rock, Scylla; if he turns right, he is pulled down by the whirlpool of Charybdis. At such a time there is always one direction in which he can turn and find guidance and direction and consolation and hope. That direction is *upward* — Godward. Turning from the whirlpool of doubt and confusion and even despair, on the one hand, and evil, wickedness, harshness, and unkindness, on the other, he can address his cry for help to Him who always hears His children and who always renders them assistance. Following with confidence God's Commandments, secure in His love, and sure of His protection, the frightened and weary sailor will safely navigate the treacherous strait between Scylla and Charybdis. "And those who know your name will trust in you; you do not, Lord, abandon those who look to you" (Ps. 9:11).

> *"If we tried, however, as brave men in battle, the help of the Lord would surely sustain us. For He who gives us the opportunity of fighting for victory is ready to help those who carry on and trust in His grace"* (Imit., Bk. 1, C. 11).

"Look to yourselves, so that you do not lose what we have gained, but that you may receive a full reward" (2 Jn. 8).

Demosthenes, who lived in Athens 400 years before Christ, was perhaps Greece's greatest orator. He is remembered not only for his brilliant orations, but particularly also for his determination, industry, and constancy in overcoming a physical handicap. As a young man, Demosthenes was afflicted with a speech impediment — he stuttered. He realized that if he wished to fulfill his burning ambition to become a famous speaker, he would have to overcome this handicap. His biographers tell how he would place pebbles in his mouth and walk along the seashore, declaiming some favorite address. Day in and day out, year after year, the young Greek forced himself to practice this difficult and awkward exercise until finally he overcame his defect. Demosthenes' place in history testifies to his glorious victory over self. "The patient man is better than the valiant: and he that ruleth his spirit, than he that taketh cities" (Prov. 16:32).

The greatest obstacle to man's salvation is himself. His enemies from without can hurt him, but only his enemies from within can destroy him. The wise man daily seeks from God the determination, wisdom, and courage necessary to conquer self. "Thanks be to God, who gives us the victory through our Lord Jesus Christ" (1 Cor. 15:57).

"In the cross is salvation; in the cross is life; in the cross is protection from enemies"
                    (Imit., Bk. 2, C. 12).

*"Yes, to love God means to keep his command-
ments. They are not burdensome . . . "*
                              (1 Jn. 5:3, 4).

A hot July sun shone down upon the track as the section
gang labored to remove several rails from the right of way.
They worked rapidly since the ties would have to be repaired
and the track replaced for the express due in a couple of
hours. The new ties were clamped in place, the roadbed
tamped down, and the rails ready to be reset. The last section
of rail, however, refused to fit into position. Consternation
overcame the crew. They realized at once what had happened.
The terrific heat had expanded the rails and the space left
was too short for the remaining section.

The workmen had been caught napping. Ice water was
poured on the rails constantly, but the express had to be
rerouted with a consequent loss of time and much humiliation
to the workmen. A fundamental principle that all railroad
section gangs should observe had been overlooked. The workmen should have foreseen that this would happen. Their
lack of precaution was humiliating and expensive. "Get wisdom, because it is better than gold . . . " (Prov. 16:16.)

All laws and precepts, whether natural, civil, or ecclesiastical, are made for a purpose. The prudent man strives to
observe them. Those who choose to ignore the laws of
nature and nature's God are preparing themselves for chaos.
On the other hand, those who are faithful to the Commandments of God may look forward to material and spiritual
blessings. "Show me, O Lord, what your decrees demand;
and I will keep them perfectly" (Ps. 118:33).

> *"O sweet and joyful service of God which makes
> man truly free and holy"* (*Imit.*, Bk. 3, C. 10).

> *"The God who said, 'Let light shine from the midst of darkness,' has shone in our hearts, to give enlightenment through the knowledge of God's glory glowing in the face of Christ"*
> (2 Cor. 4:6).

When one is riding along a dark country road at night and the warm lights of a farmhouse suddenly appear around a bend, a delightful feeling of security and friendliness wells up in the traveler's heart. The glow of the lamps serves to lighten the dullest spirits.

These lights herald a home; a happy family; laughter of children; the quiet contentment of love. They beckon the weary traveler with a promise of rest and warmth and food.

Man is attracted by light; the darker the night, the more brilliant the lamp's radiance.

God's grace is the supernatural light that drives darkness from the soul. It is this grace shining forth from the hearts of the godly that attracts all good men to spiritual souls. "Let us therefore lay aside the works of darkness, and put on the armor of light" (Rom. 13:12).

It is the light of God's love in heaven that shines down upon the weary travelers in this life, brightening their hearts, guiding their footsteps, and lighting the way to their eternal home. Christ admonishes men, "As long as you have the light, believe in the light, so that you may become shining lights" (Jn. 12:36).

> *"Let us urgently beg for divine grace, because whatever else we ask for is nothing, not that it is absolutely nothing, but that in comparison with so great a treasure, whatever else we desire is nothing"* (St. Augustine).

*"Therefore fear the Lord, and serve him in truth
and with your whole heart; for you have seen the
great works which he hath done among you"*
(1 Kings 12:24).

The steward of the dining car was anxious to talk. He sat
down in the almost empty car beside the priest. After a few
inconsequential sentences, he came to the point. "Father,
I want to show you a picture of my baby." As though bringing forth the most precious jewel in the world, he tenderly
reached into his pocket and laid before his guest a snapshot
of a beautiful little girl. Pride and love filled his countenance.
"That's whom I am working for, Father," he declared. "Believe me, nothing seems difficult since Mary came."

What joy and consolation this picture brought to that
traveler in his hours away from those he loved best!

Those outside the Church frequently accuse Catholics of
paying adoration and worship to statues and holy pictures.
If these same people could have sat there and saw what this
picture of his offspring meant to this father whose duties
kept him from home, they would understand what holy
statues and pictures mean to the weary travelers in this
world longing for the eternal home.

The good Catholic does not adore or worship pictures or
statues. He does, however, honor them as being a pictorial
reminder and representation of those he loves: Christ, the
Blessed Virgin, and the saints. "Thy name, and thy remembrance are the desire of the soul" (Isa. 26:8).

> *"We honor the relics of the martyrs in order to
> adore Him whose martyrs they are. We honor
> the servants, that the honor given to them may
> redound to the honor of the Lord"* (St. Jerome).

*"The goodness of the Lord our God descend
on us"* (Ps. 89:17).

"I will establish my covenant with you: and all flesh shall
be no more destroyed with the waters of a flood: neither shall
there be from henceforth a flood to waste the earth. And God
said: This is the sign of the covenant which I give between
me and you, and to every living soul that is with you, for
perpetual generations.

"I will set my bow in the clouds, and it shall be the sign
of a covenant between me, and between the earth. And when
I shall cover the sky with clouds, my bow shall appear in
the clouds" (Gen. 9:11-15).

What is so beautiful as a rainbow? Its myriad colors defy
description. The work of the greatest artists pales when compared to this handiwork of God. Circling the ceiling of the
heavens after a terrifying storm, the resplendent rainbow en-
lightens the heart as nothing else could. The poet expressed
not only his own joy but the elation of all who see it when he
declares, "My heart leaps up when I behold a rainbow in the
sky" (Wordsworth).

The brilliance and the beauty of the rainbow, however,
are but symbols of the grandeur and magnificent presence of
God. It is, as it were, a beam of light which God lets slip
out from under the door of heaven. "Indeed in your possession is the fount of life, and in your light we see light" (Ps.
35:10). If all men love the sight of the rainbow, how much
more should they love its Source, God Himself?

*"O Light eternal, surpassing all created bright-
ness, flash forth the lightning from above and
enlighten the inmost recesses of my heart"*
                            (Imit., Bk. 3, C. 34).

"Humble yourselves, then, under the mighty hand of God, that he may exalt you in due time" (1 Pet. 5:6).

The diamond is the most precious of all jewels. Its purity, its sparkling brilliance, its loveliness have an attraction for all. How did the diamond acquire all these attractive qualities? Only by a long, arduous process of nature.

A diamond is pure carbon, the hardest substance known to man. Buried deep down in the dark earth, its constituent elements, after being subjected to tremendous pressure and burning heat for countless years, finally emerge as a rough and dirty jewel. The cutter's patience and skill finally turn this jewel into the most precious material possession that man can strive after.

Just as in the material life the most luxurious gems are produced only after the most laborious treatment of nature, so in the spiritual life man must undergo great trials and tribulations in order that he may perfect his soul. If he endures these hardships for Christ's sake, he is forming his soul into the most brilliant of all jewels, one that is worthy of beautifying the palace of the King of Kings. " . . . reassuring the disciples, and exhorting them to continue in their faith, and reminding them that through many tribulations we must enter the kingdom of God" (Acts 14:21, 22).

> *"Oh, what great thanks I owe you, who have shown me and all the faithful the good and right way to your everlasting kingdom"*
> *(Imit.,* Bk. 3, C. 18).

"He who is sprung from God gives ear to God's message" (Jn. 8:47).

Frequently, when one is daydreaming a friend will say, "A penny for your thoughts" — implying, of course, that at this particular time the individual is thoughtless.

However, for the most part thoughts are priceless. Thoughts are wellsprings of action. Out of the ponderings of the great philosophers, Socrates, Plato, and Aristotle, have come the principles that guide the *natural life* of modern man. From the profound meditations of St. Augustine and St. Thomas Aquinas have come the enlightening knowledge that helps to guide their supernatural lives. Yes, and from the dark recesses of the human heart have come many false philosophies that have led men and nations to material and spiritual ruin. Before he expresses himself, the individual ordinarily thinks out his ideas. "After all, a man's speech is but the overflow of his heart" (Lk. 6:45).

Good and holy thoughts should be the constant companion of the faithful soul. Bad actions have their basis in bad thoughts. Good deeds come from the sincere heart. "Have confidence in the Lord with all thy heart, and lean not on thy own prudence" (Prov. 3:5).

By meditating on the life of Christ and the lives of His saints, there will be stirred up in the heart the noblest of thoughts, and from these holy thoughts will come forth actions that can conquer the world. "In your commandments will I take delight; I love them from my heart" (Ps. 118:47).

" . . . a certain man, by loving me intimately learned divine truths and spoke wonders"
(Imit., Bk. 3, C. 43).

Tenderness [357]

"I will remember the tender mercies of the Lord"
(Isa. 63:7).

A profitable slogan for all people would be "Try a little tenderness!" It is indeed a rare creature, man or beast, who does not react to kindness.

The divorce courts are crowded with men and women who once pledged their undying love for each other. The years, or sometimes the weeks, have wrought havoc with their good intentions and now their only objective is to be rid of each other.

These unfortunate people, for the most part, have reached their present stage because they forgot the word "tenderness." They have concentrated their hearts and minds on some real or imagined injury, forgetting the goodness and kindness that existed before.

For the most part, their hatred for each other started with some small insult or injury. Forgetting all past good shown toward each other, they multiply and aggravate the present condition until it becomes a pleasure to dwell on their anger — and then it becomes almost impossible to think about the good deeds done. "In case one member is in pain, all the members share it. In case one member is honored, all the members share its satisfaction" (1 Cor. 12:26).

Yet, down deep in their hearts, if they will but give it a chance to rise, is a mutual love and affection. If they would give these happy thoughts an opportunity to come to the surface, their injuries would be assuaged and their pride, the real basis of their anger, would be driven from their hearts. "Try a little 'tenderness!'" "Beloved, let us love one another, for love takes its origin in God" (1 Jn. 4:7).

"Our love is proved by our deeds" (St. Gregory).

"Let us not become desirous of vainglory, provoking one another, envying one another"
(Gal. 5:26).

Most people, at one time or another in their lives, lament their inability to accomplish some deed or to acquire some possession. If they only could do so and so, or if they only could have such and such a thing, they would be quite happy. Perhaps the acquisition of these desired objects might bring a measure of contentment, but ordinarily possession is not accompanied by the anticipated pleasure. Quite often the attainment brings with it an added responsibility that was not foreseen. "Those who seek to become rich fall into temptation and a snare and many senseless and harmful desires, which plunge men into ruin and destruction" (1 Tim. 6:9).

A poor man walking by a beautifully lighted house and gazing through the plate-glass windows at the magnificent furnishings becomes envious of the possessors of such grandeur. But, he soon discovers that his own little home, housing his loved ones, is far superior to the garish mansion when he reads in the "Society Column" that the owners of all this wealth have entered into marital conflict. Material possessions may be desirable, but they will never fill a spiritual soul which was created for spiritual ends. "For the wages that sin gives is death, but the gift that God bestows is life everlasting in Christ Jesus our Lord" (Rom. 6:23).

"Blessed is he who goes not after those things which, when possessed, are burdensome; when loved, corrupt; when lost, cause torture"
(St. Bernard).

"And the Word became man, and lived among us" (Jn. 1:14).

CHRISTMAS

Heaven's splendor lights the sky,
   Angels' voices sound on high,
Shepherds' awe, a lullaby;
   And Christ is born.
Palace Royal, oxen shed,
   Crumpled straw, His Kingly bed.
He has come as He had said
   On Christmas morn.
Down the years a sweet refrain
   Echoes back, His Childhood reign,
And a Babe He comes again
   Each Christmas morn.
Gather children, young and old,
   Kneel beside His manger cold.
He wants love and not your gold,
   On Christmas morn.
Come to Him with hearts of joy!
   Bring your soul, His cherished toy!
Welcome Mary and her Boy
   This Christmas morn!

"Who for us men, and for our salvation descended from heaven" (Nicene Creed).

"For she is the brightness of eternal light, and the unspotted mirror of God's majesty, and the image of his goodness" (Wisd. 7:26).

The mighty aircraft carrier dropped anchor in the harbor of a large Eastern seaport. When the chaplain came ashore, a delegation of young ladies was waiting for him.

"Father, we want to do something for your crew," the leader explained, "so we have collected several hundred dollars. Will you use this money for the sailors?"

The priest thanked the girls for their kindness. Then he went on, "Frankly we do not need money. The government takes good care of all the men's material requirements. What we do ask for, however, is your prayers." As a result of this request, most of the young ladies agreed to say one Rosary every day to the Blessed Virgin petitioning her protection for the ship and crew. Each member of the group received a beautifully designed certificate with the name of the carrier and a statement of their agreement.

Throughout the years that followed, this mighty ship saw service in the Pacific. The carrier was engaged in many battles and endured the nerve-racking attacks of the Kamikaze. Despite the terrible onslaughts of the enemy during this time, the carrier was never hit by a shell from land or sea or air. "Of all the aircraft carriers in the Pacific," related the chaplain, "our ship was only one of two carriers that escaped all damage from the enemy. And," he added, "I feel certain it was the prayers of these good ladies to our Blessed Lady that won for us her special protection."

"Hail! Most excellent mediatrix of God and man; hail, most efficacious conciliator of the whole world" (St. Ephraim).

*"O guide me to obey your true demands; teach
me; you are my Savior God. In you I always
trust"* (Ps. 24:5).

A compass has a very necessary and important duty to
perform. Travelers the world over depend upon this magnetic
device to bring them quickly and safely and directly to their
destination, whether they proceed by land or sea or air.

If the compass is to be of any value to its user, it must be
absolutely accurate. A slight deviation of the all-important
needle from true north would mislead the traveler and direct
him far from his intended destination. Thus, it is evident that
the compass must be regularly adjusted and corrected.

God has given to His children the necessary means of
gaining their eternal destination — heaven. Jesus Himself
has declared, "I am the way, and the truth, and the life"
(Jn. 14:6). And again, "I am the light of the world. He who
follows me will not walk in the dark, but have the light
of life" (Jn. 8:12, 13).

Man, however, of his own nature, is gradually led away
from the things of God. Therefore, it is necessary for him
to turn frequently to the Source of all truth and light and
knowledge, and to request guidance and direction, for unless
God is the focal point of all his actions, his life becomes
as useless as a compass whose needle does not bear true.
Man's destination is eternity, with God. Thus, he should
always keep his mind and his heart and his soul centered
upon God and the things of God. "And now, Lord, what
do I expect? My trust is all in you!" (Ps. 38:8.)

> *"My Child, I must be your supreme and last
> end, if you truly desire to be blessed"*
> *(Imit.,* Bk. 3, C. 9).

*"Yea, I have loved thee with an everlasting love;
therefore have I drawn thee ... "* (Jer. 31:3).

The mother was distraught. Her only little girl had died.
Her pastor, in seeking to console the distressed mother in the
saddest of hours, said, "God has been kind to this little one.
He has taken her to Himself in order that she might be
saved from much sorrow."

As the years advanced and the separation became less
severe, the good mother realized more and more the truth of
the priest's words. As old age crept upon her it was a consolation to the mother to realize that she had a lovely saint
of her very own waiting for her in Paradise.

To those left behind, the consoling words spoken to the
saddened mother may serve to soothe their aching hearts
and gradually bring home to them the truth of Christ's
teaching, "Yes, I tell you frankly, he who heeds my message ... is in possession of eternal life, and is not liable to
judgment. On the contrary, he has once for all passed out of
the realm of death into that of life" (Jn. 5:24).

To those sorrowful hearts who have suffered the separation
from a dear one, St. Paul addresses these words, "We do not
want you to be ignorant, brothers, concerning those who are
asleep, lest you should grieve, as the rest who have no hope.
Since we believe that Jesus died and rose again, so God will
bring with Jesus those who have fallen asleep in his faith"
(1 Thess. 4:13, 14). Then Paul adds, "Therefore, encourage
one another with these words" (1 Thess. 4:18).

*"Precious is the death of the saints; clearly
precious as the end of their labors, as the crown-
ing of victory, as the gate of eternal life, and the
entrance to perfect security"* (St. Bernard).

"And in that day the deaf shall hear the words of the book; and out of darkness and obscurity the eyes of the blind shall see" (Isa. 29:18).

The accomplishments of blind persons, are remarkable. These people who have been deprived of their sight now take their rightful position in all walks of life.

Through the generosity and labor of their more fortunate brothers, many receive the training that fits them to earn their own livelihood and to continue in the pursuit of happiness. Today through the Braille system of reading, the blind are no longer helpless members of society.

Far more to be pitied is that unfortunate individual who is suffering from blindness of the soul. He who through pride or stubbornness, or for whatever reason, has shut out from himself the brightness of the understanding and love of God. He is indeed deserving of compassion who goes his darksome way unguided by the law of God, that law which he has cast aside with reckless abandon or holds in contempt or never took the necessary time to understand. Indeed, his is a sad case. The spiritually blind should hasten to ask the Giver of every gift to erase the cataracts from their souls so that they may understand the things of God. Let them experience in a spiritual manner the joy of the blind man cured by Christ, "And I went and washed, and got my sight" (Jn. 9:11).

> *"I think it is clear to all that it is simply impossible to spend our time and pass through this life virtuously without the help of prayer"*
> (St. Chrysostom).

"And (Peter) went out and wept bitterly!"
(Lk. 22:62.)

"Under a strong escort they marched him off and took him to the palace of the high priest. Peter, meanwhile, followed at a distance. When the men had lit an open fire in the courtyard and seated themselves, Peter was sitting among them. As he sat . . . a slave girl . . . said: 'This man was with him.' But he denied it. 'Woman,' he said, 'I have nothing to do with him.' After a little while another person saw him and said: 'You are one of them.' 'No sir,' Peter sair, 'I am not.' After . . . about one hour, another stoutly affirmed: 'This man was certainly with him. Why he is a Galilean.' 'Sir,' Peter rejoined, 'I do not know what you are talking about.' And immediately . . . a cock crowed. Then the Lord turned round and looked full upon Peter, and Peter remembered the Lord's prediction — . . . 'Today, before a cock crows, you will disown me three times!' And he went out and wept bitterly" (Lk. 22:54–62).

The intenseness of Peter's sorrow and humiliation when Christ looked upon him can be judged somewhat by the legend which declares that Peter's tears were so constant that deep furrows were formed by them in his cheeks.

Judas, too, denied Christ, but his greater sin was in denying Christ's mercy. Christ's mercy is so infinite and limitless that it cannot be understood but only be experienced by the greatest sinner. Regardless of the greatness of the sin, His mercy is still greater. Christ died for all men — sinners and saints.

"Show forth, I beg, Your wonderful works and let Your right hand be glorified, because for me there is no other hope or refuge except in You, O Lord, my God" (Imit., Bk. 3, C. 34).

"Out of love he predestined us for himself to become through Jesus Christ his adopted children . . . " (Eph. 1:5).

It sometimes happens that one runs across a reference in the newspaper about some individual with the added explanatory clause, "his present whereabouts is unknown."

For some reason known only to the person concerned, he has chosen to separate himself from his dear ones and pursue happiness elsewhere.

This wanderer may visit the outposts of the world or lose himself in the crowded metropolis. He may feel that he has cut off everything that bound him to his former associates, and perhaps he has.

There is One, however, from whom he cannot hide. That One is the most concerned, for that One is *God*. Many souls have sought to separate themselves from God completely by denying Him, by sinning against Him, by ridiculing Him, by ignoring Him, by a thousand different means; but if these unfortunate souls hesitate a moment in their precipitous scramble to get away from Him, and cast only a fleeting glance over their shoulders, they behold the anxious, long-suffering, gentle Christ gazing pleadingly upon them. The Psalmist sings, "Where can I go to escape your spirit? And whither can I fly to flee your face?" (Ps. 138:7.) And St. Paul declares, "I am sure that neither death, nor life, nor angels, nor principalities, nor things present, nor things to come, nor powers, nor height, nor depth, nor any other creature can separate us from God's love for us, which is in Christ Jesus our Lord" (Rom. 8:38, 39).

> *"My God, my life, who didst pursue me when I was forgetful of Thee"* (St. Augustine).